T0220940

Brain-Computer Interface

Scrivener Publishing
100 Cummings Center, Suite 541J
Beverly, MA 01915-6106

Publishers at Scrivener
Martin Scrivener (martin@scrivenerpublishing.com)
Phillip Carmical (pcarmical@scrivenerpublishing.com)

Brain-Computer Interface

Using Deep Learning Applications

Edited by

M.G. Sumithra
Rajesh Kumar Dhanaraj
Mariofanna Milanova
Balamurugan Balusamy
and
Chandran Venkatesan

Scrivener
Publishing

WILEY

This edition first published 2023 by John Wiley & Sons, Inc., 111 River Street, Hoboken, NJ 07030, USA and Scrivener Publishing LLC, 100 Cummings Center, Suite 541J, Beverly, MA 01915, USA
© 2023 Scrivener Publishing LLC
For more information about Scrivener publications please visit www.scrivenerpublishing.com.

Wiley Global Headquarters
111 River Street, Hoboken, NJ 07030, USA

For details of our global editorial offices, customer services, and more information about Wiley products visit us at www.wiley.com.

Limit of Liability/Disclaimer of Warranty
While the publisher and authors have used their best efforts in preparing this work, they make no representations or warranties with respect to the accuracy or completeness of the contents of this work and specifically disclaim all warranties, including without limitation any implied warranties of merchantability or fitness for a particular purpose. No warranty may be created or extended by sales representatives, written sales materials, or promotional statements for this work. The fact that an organization, website, or product is referred to in this work as a citation and/or potential source of further information does not mean that the publisher and authors endorse the information or services the organization, website, or product may provide or recommendations it may make. This work is sold with the understanding that the publisher is not engaged in rendering professional services. The advice and strategies contained herein may not be suitable for your situation. You should consult with a specialist where appropriate. Neither the publisher nor authors shall be liable for any loss of profit or any other commercial damages, including but not limited to special, incidental, consequential, or other damages. Further, readers should be aware that websites listed in this work may have changed or disappeared between when this work was written and when it is read.

Library of Congress Cataloging-in-Publication Data

ISBN 978-1-119-85720-4

Cover image: Pixabay.Com
Cover design by Russell Richardson

Set in size of 11pt and Minion Pro by Manila Typesetting Company, Makati, Philippines

Printed in the USA

10 9 8 7 6 5 4 3 2 1

Contents

Preface

The Brain-Computer Interface (BCI) is an emerging technology that is developing to be more functional in practice. The aim is to establish, through experiences with electronic devices, a communication channel bridging the human neural networks within the brain to the external world. For example, creating communication or control applications for locked-in patients who have no control over their bodies will be one such use. Recently, from communication to marketing, recovery, care, mental state monitoring, and entertainment, the possible application areas have been expanding. Machine learning algorithms have advanced BCI technology in the last few decades, and in the sense of classification accuracy, performance standards have been greatly improved. For BCI to be effective in the real-world, however some problems remain to be solved.

The book provides the reader with the fundamental theories, concepts, and methods in neuroscience, brain recording and stimulation technologies, signal processing, and machine learning. Readers have the chance to review their knowledge and assess their comprehension of the subjects presented in each chapter with exercises and questions at the end of each chapter. Some assignments provide the student the option to explore topics outside of those covered in the textbook by looking for new information online and following leads in research articles. Highlighting most of the research directions in the digital world, this book is more suitable for researchers from biomedical background, data analysts, AI researchers, machine and deep learning engineers, students and academicians.

The book is organized as follows: In chapters 1 and 2 provides an introduction to Brain–Computer Interface: Applications and Challenges. Chapter 3 discusses the statistical learning of brain compute interface was discussed. Chapter 4 begins with the impact of brain computer interface on the lifestyle of elderly people. Chapter 5 reviews the innovation to human augmentation in brain computer interface and its potential limitations in artificial intelligence. Chapter 6 details the Resting-State fMRI: large data analysis in neuro imaging. Chapter 7 describes early detection of epileptic seizure using deep learning algorithms. Chapter 8 describes the application of brain computer interface based on the real time upper limb protheses to improve the quality of the elderly. Chapter 9 describes another application of brain computer interface to assisted automated wheelchair control management. Chapter 10 shows the application of convolutional neural network to identify Bengali vowels from EEG signal using activation map. Chapter 11 discusses the optimized feature selection techniques for classifying electrocorticography signals. Chapter 12 reviews some of the challenges, application and advancements in brain computer interface.

The editors thank all contributors for their time and effort and have collectively delivered high quality work.

The Editors
December 2022

1

Introduction to Brain–Computer Interface: Applications and Challenges

Jyoti R. Munavalli[1]*, Priya R. Sankpal[1], Sumathi A.[1] and Jayashree M. Oli[2]

[1]ECE, BNM Institute of Technology, Bangalore, India
[2]Amrita School of Engineering, ECE, Bengaluru, Amrita Vishwa Vidyapeetham, India

Abstract

Brain–Computer Interface (BCI) is a technology that facilitates the communication between the brain and the machine. It is a promising field that has lot of potential to be tapped for various applications. To begin with, this chapter explains the basics of the brain and its function. It describes the BCI technology and the steps: from signal acquisition to applications. The signal capturing is done through invasive and non-invasive methods. The features from the brain signals are extracted and classified using various advanced machine learning classification algorithms. BCI is extensively helpful for health-related problems but it also has applications in education, smart homes, security and many more. BCI has its own share of challenges that it has to overcome so that it could be beneficial in the future use. We discuss about all the issues like ethical, technical and legal. This chapter provides an overview on BCI through basics, applications, and challenges.

Keywords: Brain-Computer Interface, BCI technology, BCI applications, BCI challenges

1.1 Introduction

"A man sitting in a garden enjoying his regular walk. There are three devices that are in use in the garden; a drone, a wheelchair, and a laptop. Each of them is controlled by the man without using any remote

*Corresponding author: jyothimunavalli@gmail.com

M.G. Sumithra, Rajesh Kumar Dhanaraj, Mariofanna Milanova, Balamurugan Balusamy and Chandran Venkatesan (eds.) Brain-Computer Interface: Using Deep Learning Applications, (1–24) © 2023 Scrivener Publishing LLC

controller. Yes, he is controlling them with his mind. This is one of the
examples of brain-machine interface and we will be having numerous of
them in the near future."

In the past 20 years, the world has seen tremendous changes in the technology. Many technologies were invented that really affected the society for/in their well-being. We are witnessing new arenas like Artificial Intelligence, Virtual Reality, electronic health records, robotics, Data Science, and many more. All these have revolutionized the healthcare delivery system. Artificial Intelligence has paved its way in diagnosis, prediction of diseases through its advanced algorithms like machine learning and deep learning [1]. Virtual reality assists in treatment plans like phobias and neurological disorders [2]. EMR-based real time optimization has improved the efficiency of hospital systems and aid in decision making, again through technological intervention [3–7]. It has been observed that robotic assisted surgeries and the extent to which data science was utilized during pandemic are the big marking of technology in healthcare (Healthcare 4.0). With these technological interventions, Brain Computing Interface (BCI) is one among them.

In 1920, the first record to measure brain activity of human was by means of EEG but the device was very elementary. Later in 1970, research on BCI that was particularly for neuro-prosthetic, began at the University of California, Los Angeles, but it was in 1990s that these devices were actually implemented in humans.

A Brain–Computer Interface is also referred as Brain Machine Interface or Mind-Machine Interface. BCI is a computer-based system that acquires the signals based on the activities in the brain and analyzes and translates the neuronal information into commands that can control external environment (either hardware or software). It is an Artificial Intelligence system that identifies the patterns from the collected brain signals. The electrical signals that are generated during brain activities are used in interaction or change with the surroundings. It allows individuals that are not capable to talk and/or make use of their limbs for operating the assistive devices that help them in walking and handling and controlling the objects [8]. BCI is extensively used in Medicine and Healthcare [9].

This chapter presents the overview of BCI: its history and basics, the process details with hardware components, its applications and then finally the challenges faced while dealing with BCI. We begin with the description of functional areas of brain.

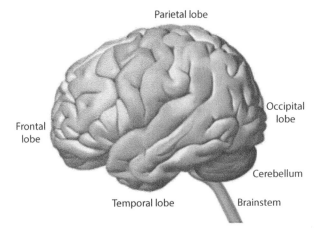

Figure 1.1 Brain parts.

1.2 The Brain – Its Functions

The brain is a soft mass made up of the nerves and tissues that are connected to the spinal cord. The main parts of the brain are Cerebrum, Cerebellum and Brain stem (see Figure 1.1). Frontal lobe, temporal lobe, parietal lobe and occipital lobe, are the four lobes of cerebrum. They are responsible for reading, learning, thinking, emotions, walking, vision, and hearing (regarding senses). Cerebellum is responsible for balancing and coordination. Brain stem is responsible for heartbeat, breathing, blood pressure, swallowing, and eye movements [10, 11].

Brain generates many signals and the electrical signals generated are used in BCI system. These signals are measured using invasive or non-invasive techniques.

1.3 BCI Technology

BCI as mentioned earlier is a communication channel between the brain and the external processing device. The goal of BCI technology is to give a communication model to those people who are severely paralyzed and do not have control over their muscles [12]. It takes the bio-signals measured from a person and predicts some abstract facet of cognitive state.

Most commonly, the BCI focuses on patients that have problems with motor state and cognitive state. In normal humans, there is an intersection of brain activity, eye movement, and body movements. If any one of them is missed, it results in constrained state. Figure 1.2 shows this intersection. It is observed that BCI is applicable to the areas where patients have normal to major cognition levels working along with no motor state response to minor motor state response. So under this umbrella, we get patients that experience completely locked-in syndrome (CLIS) or Locked-in Syndrome (LiS) [13].

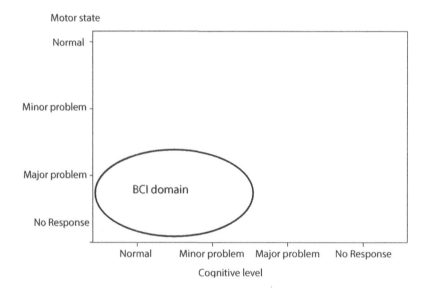

Figure 1.2 BCI domain.

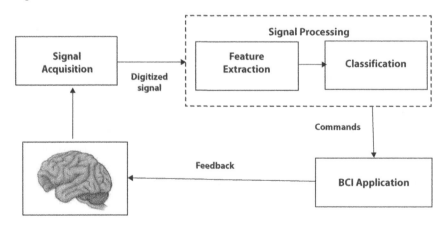

Figure 1.3 Block diagram of BCI.

Locked-in syndrome is a neurological disorder also known as pseudo coma where patient is completely paralyzed that is losing control of voluntary muscles, except the eye movements. Therefore, such people can think and analyze but not speak and move. In recent past, it is seen that chronic LIS can be unlocked with the aid of BCI [14].

The block diagram of BCI is as in Figure 1.3. It begins with recording of signals from brain, then processing of these recorded signals. Here various features from the signals are extracted and classified as per their properties or characteristics. Based on these signals' commands are generated and the BCI device works accordingly.

1.3.1   Signal Acquisition

In BCI, signal acquisitor plays an important role. There are different recording techniques in BCI and are broadly classified as invasive and non-invasive methods as shown in the Figure 1.4. These methods aid to bring out/pull out electric and magnetic signals of brain activity.

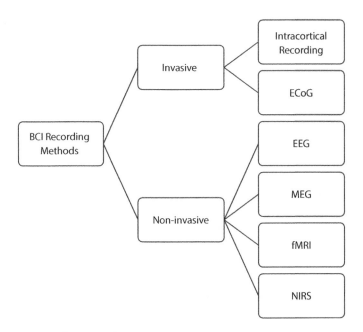

Figure 1.4 Types of BCI signal acquisitor.

1.3.1.1   Invasive Methods

Electrodes are implanted in the scalp to extract the required parameters and in non-invasive method, external sensors are used to measure the parameters.

a. Intra-Cortical Recording:
A single electrode or sometimes array of electrodes are in the cortex of the brain. These interfaces are been used for the past 70 years and some of the popular kinds of hardware for intracortical recording are as follows:

  i.   Wire-based arrays
  ii. Micro-machined micro-electrodes
  iii. Polymer microelectrodes

i. Wire-Based Arrays
They are also called Microwire arrays, Wire arrays are made up of insulated metal wires with an uninsulated tip that is used to observe the bipotential form of neurons in a bipolar environment [15]. The diameter of those wires is in the range of 10–200 micrometers the limitations of microwire-based arrays are as follows:

- They are limited because of recording failures and FBR effects.
- Microwire arrays are highly prone to variation, disappearance, or disappearance of recorded signal in the timeframe spanning from weeks to months post-implantation [16].
- The wires are tedious to place and route to microelectronic packages.
- Isolation cracks, corrosion – analysis of tungsten microwaves extracted from rats after 9 months of use, revealed material deterioration in the form of isolation fractures and defamation.
- Extensive use of electrodes leads to electric leakages which result in errors when recording.

ii. Micro-Machined Micro-Electrodes
The introduction of photolithography and subsequent advancements in micromachining technology prompted the development of a new generation of silicon-based brain probes. (micromachined microelectrodes) [17]. Ex: Michigan Planar electrode arrays, Utah Electrode arrays [18].

The limitations are as follows:

- They degrade with time.
- Recording loss due to vascular mutilation.
- Failures in interconnection.
- Size and rigidity of the probes.
- Expensive (GoldPlatinum, Iridium are widely used in planar recording areas).
- They are prone to fracture.
- Failure in persistent recordings is mainly because of the 2D. geometry of MMEA-based reading electrodes.
- The size and mechanical mismatch of silicon-based and wire microelectrode arrays with the brain are two of the most important problems limiting the quality of neural recordings.

iii. Polymer Microelectrodes
The disadvantages of stiff materials can be potentially deviated using Polymers [19]. But they have certain limitations:

- The accuracy and depth of implantation of soft and flexible implants into the brain is hampered, making them difficult to implant [20].
- Complicated structural design.
- Expensive methods of fabrication.
- As these are internally placed, they pose challenge for using in long term cases [21]. Fabrication methods and the characteristics of the materials used also impact on its durability.

b. Electrocorticography (ECoG)
Intracranial electroencephalography is a technique for recording brain signals by putting electrode grids on the cortex's surface. ECoG is an invasive BCI recording method that records with electrodes put directly on the brain's exposed surface [22]. These are used when performing an internal brain surgery.

- They are expensive.
- They are bulky.
- They are prone to the formation of scar tissue, which obstructs the signal when the body reacts to the foreign item.

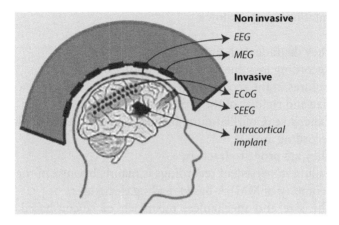

Figure 1.5 Recording places in/on brain.

- Limited sampling time – Seizures may not be recorded with EcoG [23, 24].
- The region of the exposed cortex and operation duration restrict the number of electrodes that may be placed. Errors in sampling are possible.

ECoG is a minimal invasive method. Stereotactic electroencephalography (sEEG) also used electrodes to measure brain activity. sEEG provides measurements from much deeper brain structures than ECoG, yet it has received very less attention in BCI applications [25, 26]. All, the intracortical, ECoG and sEEG are invasive methods and their placing in cortex is as shown in the Figure 1.5. ECoG is sometimes referred as semi-invasive method.

1.3.1.2   Non-Invasive Methods

a. EEG (Electroencephalogram)
EEG is a method of signal acquisition that records the electrical signals of the brain by the help of metal discs(electrodes) that are attached to the scalp [27]. There are four types of electrodes:

1) Traditional wet electrodes
2) Dry electordes
3) Active electrodes
4) Passive electrodes

Hardware concerns with EEG-based BCI equipment with wet electrodes:

- Maintenance and use of wet electrodes is cumbersome.
- Electrical impedance of the skin has its impact the signal acquisition, that is the quality of recording the brain signals. The water content in association with the electrodes reduces electrical impedance whereas the air in association with the electrodes increases the electrical impedance.
- The interface betweeen the skin and electrode causes noises which considerably affect the signal.
- The setup of wet electrode is not well tolerated by subjects over longer periods of recording a) because of the electrolytic gel used which causes irritation to the subjects b) because of the discomfort caused by the elastic straps to hold the eeg cap in place [28].
- The electrical impedance also depends on various factors like surface area of the electrode, room temperature, and the interface layer. The people who were taking the EEG readings must keep all these factors in check.

Hardware concerns with EEG-based BCI equipment with dry electrodes:

- The Quality of the signal obtained using dry electrodes is low when compared to wet electrodes [29].
- For dry electrodes the electrical impedance deteriorate rapidly with use and generally should be replaced after 30 days of usage.
- The electrode caps are prone to movement since there will be no gel to hold the caps in place.
- Highquality electrode caps are generally made of gold and titanium, for prolonged hours of usage change of electrode caps is recommended so it will be costly to buy and maintain the electrodes [30].
- Elastic straps are used to maintain the electric caps in place which causes discomfort to the subject over longer periods of time.

b. MEG (Magnetoencephalography)

It is an imaging test which reflects the activity of the brain by recording the magnetic fields produced by electric currents occuring naturally in the brain [31].

Hardware concerns with MEG-based BCI equipment:

- The MEG equipment is very expensive.
- MEG equipment requires liquid helium to maintain its superconducting equipment.
- The equipment must be used in a magnetic shielded room and the food used by the subjects and the examiner must also be administered ad managed.
- The patients need to remain relatively still during a MEG examination and the patients with a vagus nerve simulator, pacemaker, or similar device may not be able to undergo an MEG study [32].

c. Functional Magnetic Resonance Imaging (fMRI)

This method acquires the brain activity parameters based on blood flow changes. So, this method depends on cerebral blood flow coupled with neuronal activation. When brain is in use, the blood flow varies depending to the task being performed. Hence, the parameters also vary. fMRI is used to detect and evaluate the brain abnormalities that could not be captured in other imaging techniques like x-ray or MRI.

d. Near-Infrared Spectroscopy (NIRS)

This method measures brain activity in frontal cortex. Here light absorption is used to calculate oxygen and hemoglobin levels.

Before extracting the features from the measured parameters, pre-processing is required. Pre-processing generally consists of Referencing, temporal filtering, and signal enhancement. Referencing is comparing the measured brain signal to a standard or reference signal in the form of voltage. It can be common reference, average reference, or current source density. Temporal filtering removes unwanted noise signals that are present in the measured brain signals. Signal enhancement techniques like Principal component Analysis (PCA), Surface Laplacian, automatic enhancement methods are used to enhance the parameters measured.

1.3.2   Feature Extraction

Based on the signal processing, the commands are generated. So, identification of correct features is an essential step. Feature extraction in BCI is recognizing the events or useful properties that are captured by various neuroimage methods. This will reduce the complexity and help in classification. Generally used method is EEG and in feature extraction, frequency information of each electrode and between electrodes is extracted.

The noise and the outliers are important features of brain signals. Along with them, we also have to consider that brain signals are highly dimensional, timely information, non-stationary and non-linear. Particularly for EEG, the data collected is time series. There are EEG bands based on frequency range. These bands are Delta for frontal lobe, theta for temporal and parietal lobe, Alpha for occipital lobe, Beta for frontal central lobe, and Gamma for parietal lobe [33]. These bands are used in feature extraction.

A cross correlation is analyzed between different frequency bands and it helps to extracts few important properties. It is observed that Fourier transforms are not efficient when the signals are non-linear and non-stationary, so time-frequency methods are used in feature extraction, like wavelet algorithm (based on the physiological activity knowledge) and empirical mode decomposition.

Any EEG signal has features that are measured in time domain. These parameters are referred as Hjorth parameters that basically are activity, mobility, and complexity. In addition to this, parametric models are used to model time series. Autoregressive parameters, Multivariate autoregressive parameters, adaptive autoregressive parameters and these parameters with exogenous input are considered [34].

There is another set of models called Inverse models. These models represent the brain as a set of volume elements called as voxels. Specific patterns are identified in the regions associated with cognitive component. These are the peak picking methods. Another method is the slow cortical potentials calculation in which amplitudes are extracted, corrected, and used as feedback.

Poor feature detection and extraction would reduce the accuracy and efficiency of the BCI model. The feature extraction of brain signals directly depends on the signal types being measured and recorded. Along with the above mentioned feature extraction, commonly used features include mean, slope, peak, signal minimum, skewness, and kurtosis, number of occurrence of peaks, variance, root mean square, standard deviation, median, power spectrum density (PSD), logarithmic band power and common spatial patterns [13].

1.3.3   Classification

The signal patterns in the brain are dynamic stochastic processes because of the biological factors and technical issues like amplifier noise and electrode impedance changes. The identified signals before being translated into commands have to be classified. That is grouping of the signals based on their appropriate features. There are many categories of classification algorithms used in BCI systems. With the advancements in Artificial Intelligence, Machine Learning (ML) and Deep Learning (DL), more advanced algorithms for feature extraction and classification are in use.

There are four classifier taxonomies in contrast to each other.

- Generative/Informative and Discriminative classifiers
- Static and Dynamic classifiers
- Stable and Unstable classifiers
- Regularized classifier

1.3.3.1   Types of Classifiers

1. Linear Classifiers
These classifiers use linear algorithms to differentiate between two or more classes. A hyper plane is used to distinguish the considered data falls in first or second class. The classic examples of linear classifiers are Linear Discriminant Analysis (LDA) and Support Vector Machine (SVM).

Linear Discriminant Analysis is a popular classification algorithm used in BCI applications. It is a dimensionality reduction technique. LDA uses single hyperplane to separate the data representing the two classes and several hyperplanes if multiclass problems are used. The discrimination rules used in LDA are "maximum likelihood", "Bayes Discriminant Rule", and "Fisher's linear discriminant rule". This method is used because of its very low computational requirement and as well provides good results.
Support Vector Machine was originally designed for binary classification and to maximize the margin compared to LDA. SVM uses statistical learning theory. It searches the maximum margin hyperplane between two classes. Maximization of the margins extends the generalization capabilities of the algorithm. The accuracy is improved by adjusting the parameters. A variant in SVM is the Gaussian SVM that provides excellent accuracy in classification.

2. Neural Networks Classifiers
A neural network is an arrangement of processing units in layers that convert the input to output using weights associated with the nodes. These are commonly used classifiers for BCI along with linear classifiers. Multi-Layer Perceptron (MLP), Learning Vector Quantization, Adaptive Logic Networks, Time Delayed Neural Network, Recurrent Neural Network are

few neural network classifiers. An MLP contains multiple layers of neurons in the form of an input layer, either one or more hidden layers, and an output layer. The neurons of the output layer determine which class the input feature vector belongs to (that is classifying which class). MLP classifies to any number of classes which makes neural network more flexible. It is also called as universal classifier and can be applied to most of the BCI problems that have either two (binary) or multiple classes to discriminate [35].

3. Non-Linear Bayesian Classifiers
Bayes quadratic, Bayesian Graphical network (BGN) and Hidden Markov Model (HMM) are the Bayesian classifiers used for BCI: Although Bayesian Graphical Network (When compared BGN is slow compared to other two. Hidden Markov Models are very efficient nonlinear techniques used for the time series data or signal classification. HMMs are the dynamic classifiers that are used for speech recognition. HMMs work on a probabilistic automaton for a given sequence of feature vectors.

4. k-Nearest Neighbor Classifiers
k-NN classification is a non-parametric model in which a new feature is assigned to a class depending on nearest neighbors. It is described as instance-based learning where the model memorizes the training datasets. It provides better accuracy in classification with less training and testing datasets. Features of EEG signals can be extracted by Hjorth's parameters like activity, mobility and complexity are extracted and, on that k-NN classification would result in improved accuracy. First the number of nearest neighbors is found and then data points are classified based on that. Euclidean distance is used to find the neighbors. It selects k samples from training set. This classifier is based on giving new samples to the class with majority of votes [36, 37].

1.4   Applications of BCI

BCI has taken a big leap in its applications with the growth in modern computing and cognitive levels of humans in understanding the brain. BCI applications are making the unconquered world into reality. With BCI, it is possible to manipulate the thoughts with computers. BCI, in its nascent days involved recording brain signals, in contrast to designing implants in today's world. These implants act as a communication tool between the brain and outside world. Implants are designed for some important brain functions such as feeling, hearing and vision to name a few.

Earlier BCI was used for decoding the thoughts of the handicapped people with speaking and mobility issues. These applications used methods such as speech communications and spelling applications that aided as an alternative means of communication. With modern computing, BCI is even used for healthy people. Now days, BCI is used as measuring tool to assess an individual's physiological quotient involving emotions, cognitive level and effectiveness.

Just as the brain functions in diverse areas, BCI applications span over a diverse area such as Healthcare, Education, Smart environment, Security and authentication, Marketing and advertising, Gaming and entertainment. Since BCI acts as a medium between the brain and the outside world, its application domains are infinite and very promising i.e., BCI applications are to be considered that are pertinent to specific business.

a) Healthcare
Healthcare applications of BCI have transformed to various clinical products used in daily life. BCIs can be classified under the clinical uses as the direct assistive control technologies and neuro rehabilitation. These assistive control BCI applications encircle areas of communication, locomotion and movement control, environment control, prevention, detection and diagnosis [38].

b) Communication
BCI is mainly used for communicating with people with locked-in syndrome. Three types of BCI systems based on EEG, that measure electrophysiological features tested on humans for commination purpose are: Slow Cortical potentials (SCPs), P300 event-related potentials and sensorimotor rhythms (SMRs) [38].

c) Movement Control and Locomotion
Paralyzed patients can restore their motor control with BCI. This scanty clinical application is solely based on SMRs. These applications support the controlled movement of motor neuro prosthesis in multidimensions such as robotic arm. Also, for paralyzed patients with intact lower motor neuron and peripheral nerve function, restoration of motor functions is done with Functional electrical stimulation (FES). BCI driven wheelchairs are used for restoring mobility for paralyzed patients. These wheelchairs control mental activities of the patient with a shared control system which use intelligent software for assisting the patient in navigating the wheelchair [38].

d) Prevention

BCI are used in various consciousness level detection system. These appli-cations prevent loss of function and decrease in alertness level which are the side effects of smoking of due to consumption of alcohol. BCI is also used in detecting motion sickness, which arise due to confliction of sensory generated between eyes, ear and brain during motion of the individual [39].

e) Detection and Diagnosis

BCIs are used in monitoring mental state for detecting and forecasting of abnormal variations in the brain structure such as brain tumor, brain sell-ing, seizure, and sleep disorders. BCI uses EEG in contrast to MRI and CT Scan for discovering tumors, which develop basically because of self-dividing of cells. Plantar pressure measuring systems exploit the relation-ship between the human gait cycle and EEG signals for diagnosing dyslexia, peripheral neuropathy and musculoskeletal diseases [39].

f) Rehabilitation

Patients with mobility issues are given physical rehabilitation for restoring the lost functions and regain their previous mobility levels, so that they can adapt to the disabilities. With these physical rehabilitations, patients suf-fering from strokes can also recover fully. BCI uses mobile robots for eases the daily life activities of such patients. BCI based neuro-prosthetic devices are used for patients wherein their previous levels of communication or mobility cannot be recovered. Nowadays BCI is diving into the arena of virtual reality for monitoring and controlling the avatar movements gen-erated from the brain waves. Augmented reality-based BCI system such as augmented mirror box uses brain signals that are generated by incor-porating both the injured as well as healthy limb. BCI driven therapeutic tools have the potential to the aide patients with impaired neuro muscular functions because of trauma, to re-learn the motor functions. These BCI systems enable patient's functional recovery and thus enhance their quality of life [39].

g) Education

In BCI enabled education systems, brain signals are used to understand the level of clarity in processing the information. Non-invasive BCI techniques are used for self-regulating the learning experience and improve the cog-nitive therapeutic methods. fMRI-based EEG BCI trainings are used for emotional regulation, fight depressions and other neuropsychiatric disor-ders [39].

h) Smart Environment
Severely disabled patient's quality of life can be improved significantly with BCI-based environment control system. These control systems effectively manage their daily life environment around them such as lighting systems in the house, room temperature, TV units and power beds. Smart environment systems enhance the patient's well-being and relieve them from being dependent on others. Smart environments based on BCI enhance well-being, safety, and independence of patients in daily life. Modern computing has tied up BCI technologies and Internet of Things (IoT) that create smart houses, workplaces, and transportations for monitoring the patient's mental state and adapt the surrounding environment appropriately. These functionalities are extended to use of universal plug and play home networking. Working conditions can be greatly improved by assessing the user's cognitive state. BCI systems are used for studying the impact of mental fatigue and stress levels because of workload. Various BCI techniques are used in assessing the user's cognitive state. Even virtual audio-visual set-ups are used for analyzing and evaluating the brain signals associated with the user's response [39].

i) Security and Authentication
Authentication in security systems is based on algorithms, objects, and biometrics. Such systems are vulnerable to attacks because of the use of insecure passwords, surfing, spoofing and data theft. Cognitive biometrics is making space in the field of security and authentication, as they possess least vulnerabilities. Cognitive biometrics, also termed electrophysiology, is the only modality that uses brain signals for identifying the data in secured manner. Security is greatly enhanced in cognitive biometrics, as brain signals cannot be acquired by the hackers. Cognitive biometrics are difficult to synthesize and in turn enhance the biometric systems resistance to spoofing attacks [39].

j) Marketing and Advertising
BCI technologies have also conquered the marketing and advertising domain. BCI systems enable to measure a user's attention when watching a TV commercial or any other channels. These measures try to assess the impact of user's cognitive function in the neuromarketing and advertising field. BCI systems are also used to estimate the user's inclination for TV commercials and use the same for advertising [39].

k) Gaming and Entertainment
Non-medical BCI has invaded the entertainment and gaming arena. The brain controlling capabilities combined with the gaming features provide experience of involving multiple brains. A game called Brain ball was developed for reducing stress levels in individuals. This game involves a user moving the ball only in relaxed mode. In this game, only a calm player can win the game, as they need to control stress and play [39].

1.5   Challenges Faced During Implementation of BCI

In the recent years substantial research is seen to develop BCI assistive technologies. In BCI invasive and non-invasive research is growing fast and a number of challenges are to be resolved to have lower impact on the patients. A number of neurosurgeons, neurologists, neuroscientists and engineers are investigating in this field for a significant breakthrough. There exist many challenges and issues in different areas such as technical, ethical, etc.

Even in recent times people are not deploying BCI in an effective way due to various obstacles faced such as ethical, legal, usability, and technical challenges. Challenges are also caused due to the signals received from brain activity are liable for intrusion, can also cause harm to patients controlling the device or an issue of protecting the data of the patient. In this section let's discuss the challenges that affect the advancement in this technology.

A. Usability Challenges
It talks about the issue of acceptance by patients to use BCI technology. These usability challenges can be either issues related to training process or ITR (Information Transfer Rate) [1]. The user has to be trained to deal and control with the system and is a time-consuming process. This training is either in the preliminary phase or in the calibration phase. The most common available solution to this is to adopt single trial instead of multiple trials. One of the solutions is to use zero training classifier.

Information Transfer Rate is the method used widely for evaluating BCI systems. This parameter depends on the accuracy of detection, the number of trials and the average detection time taken. Increase of accuracy of detection can be achieved by increasing signal to noise ratio and should be considered in pre-processing phase. An approach called dynamic stopping is use to reduce average detection time is certain applications. Another method to reduce average detection time is to use single trail classifier which uses machine learning. Healthier individuals' groups have higher data rates as compared to disabled.

B. Technical Challenges

These are related to recording of the electrophysiological properties of brain signals. The technical challenges include the issues related to non-linearity, noise, non-stationary, quality of the dataset, limited number of training sets, data fusion, inability of data interpretation

i. *Non linearity:* The function of the brain cannot be thought as a serial machine which reads the input from sensors and gives a corresponding output. Brain is a complex machine which can be termed as a memory-based predictive machine which by experience builds results depending on the relation between the inputs. Hence the signals from the brain are an ensemble of neural behavior which can be characterized as non-linear dynamic signals. Hence the machine representing a brain has to be dynamic and non-linear which remains as a challenge.

ii. *Noise:* It is another unwanted signal which causes random variation of the brain signals due to improper placement of electrodes, movement artifacts of skeletal muscles, blinking of eyes. This leads to improper analysis of the pattern. Removal of noise is carried out by using frequency band filters which will also remove the signal of interest lying in the same band.

iii. *Nonstationary signals:* The electrophysiological signals of the brain change continuously make it from minute to minute. During the recording session the emotional and mental state differ with different trials. Hence the EEG signals obtained can have varied signal levels over different sessions. Other nonstationary factors such as fatigue, concentration and stress produce varied EEG signals.

iv. *Quality of the data set:* In BCI application the quality of the EEG signals depends on the quality of the headsets or electrodes used for the measurements. The electrodes used for measurement usually requires gel or liquid which cause discomfort to users. Practically when user's comfort is to be considered dry electrodes are preferred. Some investigations reports that the data acquired from dry electrodes consists of more noise when compared with wet electrodes whereas another set of studies reports that the quality of data are almost same for both electrodes. There is a need for further investigations on the usage and efficiency of electrodes for the validation of the data. Another investigation infers that the performance of water-based electrodes and dry electrodes are better than gel-based electrodes in case of short hairs. Hence the challenge is to determine the type of electrodes to be used by further investigations and validation [40].

There are numerous EEG head-sets available in the markets with different number of electrodes. The number of electrodes used for BCI applications varies with different companies and are not compatible with each other. Hence there is a need for standardization for number of electrodes. The cost of these electrodes is very high, hence requiring cheaper electrodes for BCI applications.

v. *Limited number of training sets:* The efficiency of the BCI system depends on the number of training sets used in a model. Small data sets can be used for training the model which has less complexity. Overfitting occurs when limited number of training set are used which in turn reduces the efficiency of the predicting models.

vi. *Data analysis methods:* There are numerous algorithms which are used for removal of artifacts in data pre-processing. Different algorithms have different limitations when used in analyzing the EEG data. Some algorithms focus on the removal of certain artifacts some focus on increasing the accuracy in the removal of artifacts. Different applications use different algorithms like ICA algorithms are used for artifacts removal in EEG recordings, CCA, and its combination for removal of muscle artifacts. When artifacts overlap with the spectral components then Wavelet transform fails completely. Hence the challenge arises for a single algorithm which can be efficient and accurate to satisfy different conditions satisfactorily. Thus, the goal for future researchers would be to develop algorithms which are application specific and has good accuracy and time efficiency and standardize the methods for a particular application [40].

In context to feature extraction techniques CSP and its combination algorithm gives encouraging results for EEG data. Based on the investigations done by researchers SVM is considered as the most powerful classifier powerful classifier for classification of high dimensionality feature vectors. Another study shows that the deep learning methods, CNN and RNN are better when compared with other methods and the accuracy of CNN is high for time-series values.

vii. *Inability to interpret data:* Another major challenge is to interpret data that is extracted from brain activity. There are numerous methods to extract information from the brain either through invasive or non-invasive methods. Usually in most of the cases the obtained data is partial or noisy. This may be due to unstable recording or due to built-in flexible nature of brain. Hence learning of neural signal processing is essential to understand the adaptive nature of the brain [41].

All BCI experiments are conducted in a controlled environment (lab) where realistic target users are not considered. Studies show that heart rate and cortisol influences characteristics of EEG data. EEG data varies with sensory stimulus such as smell, sound, and movements which affect the quality of EEG data. Hence in order to make BCI the system robust the engineers should consider the environment where the BCI system is applied along with the target set of users. For example, the design criteria change for a user who stays at home most of the times and controls household articles and for a person who is taxi driver who drives in a heavy traffic, the level of attention and concentration are different. Hence during design phase, it is important to consider the environmental aspects and the target user for a more efficient BCI system.

C. Psychophysiological and Neurological Challenges

The BCI performance depends on Psychological and neurological to a greater extent. The neurological factors such as anatomy and functional behavior vary from individual to individual. Similarly, the psychological factors such as memory, attention span, fatigue and stress also vary from individual to individual. Apart from these other characteristics such as gender, lifestyle, age also influences the brain signals. Hence a generalized approach to develop BCI without considering these aspects will decreases the efficiency [42].

D. Ethical and Socioeconomic Challenges

The factors such as safety, data confidentiality, and social and economic factors are to be considered to maximize the benefits to the users. The BCI user's physical and mental safety should be considered as the most important aspect. One of the invasive procedures such as deep brain stimulation should not cause physiological and neurological effects. Bleeding and infections are caused when electrodes are implanted which in turn leads to behavioral changes. These invasive methods are sometimes potential threats to memory and emotions.

The target application of most of the BCIs is the disabled people. Hence the user's expectation of attaining their freedom sometime may not be satisfied. Even a small risk can rule out the usage BCI system. Creating awareness in the users with advantages and disadvantages is an important social responsibility. During the implementation of BCI there can be alteration in human cognitive level is a serious ethical issue. During commercialization of BCI ethical and legal policy has to be maintained between the user and the service provider.

BCI has a lot of potential and growth opportunities. Its global market size is huge and it is projected to be close to $4 billion by 2027. Many start-ups and SMEs can pitch in this market with their innovative devices. The advanced technological developments have paved a way for BCI extensively in healthcare sector and other fields like entertainment, gaming and communication. As with any technology, there are certain issues with this BCI technology also, particularly ethical issues and we need to wait and watch how this technology would be utilized for the betterment of human-kind.

References

1. Vaidya, R.R., Nagendra, A., Shreyas, B., Munavalli, J.R., Predictive and comparative analysis for diabetes using machine learning algorithms. *Int. J. Adv. Sci. Technol.*, 29, 3, 14407–14416, 2020.

2. Nalluri, S.P., Reshma, L., Munavalli, J.R., Evaluation of virtual reality opportunities during pandemic. *2021 6th International Conference for Convergence in Technology (I2CT)*, 2021.

3. Munavalli, J.R., Rao, S.V., Srinivasan, A., Manjunath, U., van Merode, G.G., A robust predictive resource planning under demand uncertainty to improve waiting times in outpatient clinics. *J. Health Manage.*, 19, 4, 563–583, 2017.

4. Munavalli, J.R., Rao, S.V., Srinivasan, A., van Merode, G.G., An intelligent real-time scheduler for out-patient clinics: A multi-agent system model. *Health Inform. J.*, 26, 4, 2383–2406, 2020.

5. Munavalli, J.R., Rao, S.V., Srinivasan, A., van Merode, G.G., Integral patient scheduling in outpatient clinics under demand uncertainty to minimize patient waiting times. *J. Health Inform.*, 26, 1, 435–448, 2020.

6. Munavalli, J.R., Rao, S.V., Srinivasan, A., van Merode, G.G., Workflow-based adaptive layout design to improve the patient flow in the outpatient clinics. *Ann. Romanian Soc. Cell Biol.*, 25, 3, 8249–8257, 2021.

7. Munavalli, J.R., Rao, S.V., Srinivasan, A., van Merode, F., Dynamic layout design optimization to improve patient flow in outpatient clinics using genetic algorithms. *Algorithms*, 15, 3, 85, 2022.

8. Shih, J.J., Krusienski, D.J., Wolpaw, J.R., Brain–computer interfaces in medicine. *Mayo Clinic Proceedings*, vol. 87, pp. 268–279, 2012.

9. Kummar, R.G., Suhas., S.J., Vismith, U.P.J., Munavalli, J.R., Brain computing interface-applications and challenges. *IOSR J. Comput. Eng.*, 23, 2, 29–40, 2021.

10. Abdulrahman, S., Roushdy, M., Salem, A.B.M., Overview of acquisition techniques brain signals in human identification and disease diagnosis:

Applications and challenges. *TEST Engineering & Management*, 83, 10564–10575, 2020.

11. Batista-Garcia-Ramo, K. and Fernández-Verdecia, C., II, What we know about the brain structure-function relationship. *Behav. Sci. (Basel, Switzerland)*, 8, 4, 39, 2018.

12. Cho, J., Jeong, J., Kim, D., Lee, S., A novel approach to classify natural grasp actions by estimating muscle activity patterns from EEG signals. *2020 8th International Winter Conference on Brain–Computer Interface (BCI)*, 2020.

13. Hong, K.S., Khan, M.J., Hong, M.J., Feature extraction and classification methods for hybrid fNIRS-EEG brain–computer interfaces. *Front. Hum. Neurosci.*, 12, 246, 1–25, 2018.

14. Khanna, K., Verma, A., Richard, B., The locked-in syndrome: Can it be unlocked? *J. Clin. Gerontol. Geriatr.*, 2, 4, 96–99, 2011.

15. Baek, C., Jang, J., Park, S., Song, Y., Seo, K., Seo, J., 3D printed wire electrode carrier for a pilot study of the functional brain mapping. *39th Annual International Conference of the IEEE Engineering in Medicine and Biology Society (EMBC)*, 2017.

16. Chuan, Z., Jingquan, L., Hongchang, T., Xiaoyang, K., Yuefeng, R., Bin, Y., Hongying, Z., Chunsheng, Y., Control of swimming in crucian carp: Stimulation of the brain using an implantable wire electrode. *8th Annual IEEE International Conference on Nano/Micro Engineered and Molecular Systems*, 2013.

17. Gardner, A.T., Strathman, H.J., Warren, D.J., Walker, R.M., Impedance and noise characterizations of Utah and microwire electrode arrays. *IEEE J. Electromagnet. RF Microwaves Med. Biol.*, 2, 4, 234–241, 2018.

18. Sharma, M., Gardner, A.T., Silver, J., Walker, R.M., Noise and impedance of the SIROF utah electrode array. *2016 IEEE Sensors*, 1–3, 2016.

19. Kim, M., Park, S., Chung, W.K., Flexible polymer-based micro needle array sEMG sensor. *10th International Conference on Ubiquitous Robots and Ambient Intelligence (URAI)*, 2013.

20. Al-Othman, A., Alatoom, A., Farooq, A., Al-Sayah, M., Al-Nashash, H., Novel flexible implantable electrodes based on conductive polymers and Titanium dioxide. *IEEE 4th Middle East Conference on Biomedical Engineering (MECBME)*, 2018.

21. Szostak, K.M., Grand, L., Constandinou, T.G., Neural interfaces for intracortical recording: Requirements, fabrication methods, and characteristics. *Front. Neurosci.*, 11, 665, 1–27, 2017.

22. Krishnan, J., Rethnagireeshwar, R., Benjamin, B., Panicker, N.V., Ramu, A.R.B., High precision resistance spot welding with subdural electrodes for acute electrocorticography applications. *IEEE International Conference on Power, Control, Signals and Instrumentation Engineering (ICPCSI)*, 2017.

23. Hill, N.J., Gupta, D., Brunner, P., Gunduz, A., Adamo, M.A., Ritaccio, A., Schalk, G., Recording human electrocorticographic (ECoG) signals for

neuroscientific research and real-time functional cortical mapping. *J. Vis. Exp.*, 64, 3993, 2012.

24. Yang, T., Hakimian, S., Schwartz, T.H., Intraoperative Electrocorticography (ECoG): Indications, techniques, and utility in epilepsy surgery. *Epileptic Disord.*, 16, 3, 271–9, 2014.

25. Herff, C., Krusienski, D.J., Kubben, P., The potential of stereotactic-EEG for brain–computer interfaces: Current progress and future directions. *Front. Neurosci.*, 14, 123, 1–8, 2020.

26. Young, J.J., Friedman, J.S., Panov, F., Camara, D., Yoo, J.Y., Fields, M.C., Marcuse, L.V., Jette, N., Ghatan, S., Quantitative signal characteristics of electrocorticography and stereoelectroencephalography: The effect of contact depth. *J. Clin. Neurophysiol.*, 36, 3, 195–203, 2019.

27. Min, B., Eeg/sonication-based brain-brain interfacing. *2013 International Winter Workshop on Brain–Computer Interface (BCI)*, 2013.

28. Lee, S., Shin, Y., Woo, S., Kim, K., Lee, H., Dry electrode design and performance evaluation for EEG based BCI systems. *2013 International Winter Workshop on Brain–Computer Interface (BCI)*, 2013.

29. Yang, S.Y. and Lin, Y.P., Validating a LEGO-Like EEG headset for a simultaneous recording of wet- and dry-electrode systems during treadmill walking. *42nd Annual International Conference of the IEEE Engineering in Medicine & Biology Society (EMBC)*, 2020.

30. Kim, D., Yeon, C., Chung, E., Kim, K., A non-invasive flexible multi-channel electrode for *in vivo* mouse EEG recording. *IEEE Sensors*, 17, 326, 1–14, 2014.

31. Waldert, S., Braun, C., Preissl, H., Birbaumer, N., Aertsen, A., Mehring, C., Decoding performance for hand movements: EEG vs. MEG. *2007 29th Annual International Conference of the IEEE Engineering in Medicine and Biology Society*, 2007.

32. Lefevre, J. and Baillet, S., Mapping and tracking the flow of brain activations using MEG/EEG: Hypothesis and methods. *2007 Joint Meeting of the 6th International Symposium on Noninvasive Functional Source Imaging of the Brain and Heart and the International Conference on Functional Biomedical Imaging*, 2007.

33. Manjula, K. and Anandaraju, M.B., A comparative study on feature extraction and classification of mind waves for brain computer interface (BCI). *Int. J. Eng. Technol.*, 7, 19, 132–136, 2018.

34. Resalat, S.N. and Saba, V., A study of various feature extraction methods on a motor imagery based brain computer interface system. *Basic Clin. Neurosci.*, 7, 1, 13–19, 2016.

35. Sridhar, G.V. and Mallikarjuna Rao, P., A neural network approach for EEG classification in BCI. *Int. J. Comput. Sci. Telecommun.*, 3, 10, 44–48, 2012.

36. Anupama, H.S., Cauvery, N.K., Lingaraju, G.M., k-NN based object recognition system using brain computer interface. *Int. J. Comput. Appl.*, 120, 2, 35–38, June 2015.

37. Bablania, A., Edla, D.R., Dodia, S., Classification of EEG data using k-nearest neighbor approach for concealed information test. *8th International Conference on Advances in Computing and Communication (ICACC-2018)*, 2018.
38. Mak, J.N. and Wolpaw, J.R., Clinical Applications of brain–computer interfaces: Current state and future prospects. *IEEE Rev. Biomed. Eng.*, 2, 187–199, 2009.
39. Abdulkader, S.N., Atia, A., Mostafa, M.-S.M., Brain computer interfacing: Applications and challenges. *Egypt. Inform. J.*, 16, 213–230, 2015.
40. Rashid, M., Sulaiman, N., Abdul Majeed, A.P.P., Musa, R.M., Ab. Nasir, A.F., Bari, B.S., Khatun, S., Current status, challenges, and possible solutions of EEG-based brain–computer interface: A comprehensive review. *Front. Neurorobot.*, 14, 1–35, 2020.
41. Vaadia, E. and Birbaumer, N., Grand challenges of brain computer interfaces in the years to come. *Front. Neurosci.*, 3, 2, 151–154, 2009.
42. Saha, S., Mamun, K.A., Ahmed, K., Mostafa, R., Naik, G.R., Darvishi, S., Khandoker, A.H., Baumert, M., Progress in brain computer interface: Challenges and opportunities. *Front. Syst. Neurosci.*, 15, 578875–578875, 2021.

Introduction: Brain–Computer Interface and Deep Learning

Muskan Jindal[1], Eshan Bajal[1]* and Areeba Kazim[2]

[1]*Amity School of Engineering and Technology, Amity University, Noida,*
Uttar Pradesh, India
[2]*Noida Institute of Engineering and Technology, Greater Noida, Uttar Pradesh, India*

Abstract

Brain signals or radiations are a relatively new concept that works with information collected via human brain and cognitive activity. These signals like human brain are influenced by all the physical, geographical, emotional, and cognitive activities around it, are individualistic in nature, and follow numerous patterns. Complying with the same Brain–computer interface (BCI), is the area of science where these signals are contemplated to advance the human-computer interaction applications. This area of research ties the cord between human cognitive to computer's processing and speed, aiming to create a unique field in biomedical sciences to introduce infinite applications like, neural rehabilitation, biometric authentication, educational programs, and entertainment applications. Although nascent, Brain–computer interface (BCI) has four major grades of processing steps – signal acquisition, signal pre-processing, feature extraction, and classification. This study firstly, thoroughly elaborates upon its various processing steps while exploring the origin, need, and current stage of development of Brain–computer interface (BCI) with respect to brain signals. Post complete understanding of basic concepts and terminologies of brain signals, Brain–computer interface (BCI) and their interconnection along in the field of bio-medicine; this study elucidates upon primordial methodologies of Brain–computer interface (BCI) along with respective merits and demerits with intensive classification. A differential based analysis is provided to insight into new age deep learning-based method in the field of Brain–computer interface (BCI) while comparing them with primordial techniques. A complete data intensive review is

*Corresponding author: eshanbajal@gmail.com

M.G. Sumithra, Rajesh Kumar Dhanaraj, Mariofanna Milanova, Balamurugan Balusamy and Chandran Venkatesan (eds.) Brain-Computer Interface: Using Deep Learning Applications, (25–62) © 2023 Scrivener Publishing LLC

performed for new era deep learning techniques while properly classifying the same into multiple gradations based on deep learning framework and their various versions implemented namely, neural networks (CNN) and recurrent neural networks (RNN), long short-term memory (LSTM) architecture, U-net among other. This chapter also aims to provide real world application, challenges, scope of future growths, avenues of expansion and complete industry specific guide for implementing insights gathered from brain signals in the nascent area of Brain–computer interface (BCI). Lastly, to fathom the performance of Brain–computer interface (BCI) this study also provides its application in multiple case studies with desperate health hazards like brain tumor, Dementias, Epilepsy and Other Seizure Disorders, Stroke and Transient Ischemic Attack (TIA), Alzheimer's Disease, Parkinson's and Other Movement Disorders. This chapter aims to not only provide background, current status, future challenges and case studies but also an application specific perspective in Brain–computer interface (BCI) in the field of bio-medical.

Keywords: Brain–computer interface (BCI), brain signals, convolutional neural networks (CNN), recurrent neural networks (RNN), long short-term memory (LSTM) architecture, functional magnetic resonance imaging (fMRI), electroencephalogram (EEG), electrocardiogram (ECG or EKG)

2.1   Introduction

Brain–Computer interface primarily thrives on brain signals, which is biometric information that is compiled or processed by human brain. These brain signals can be result of any kind of thoughts or activity that is result of active and passive mental state. A normal human brain always emits brain signals due to the constant state of activity that occurs even when the physical body is at complete rest, i.e., brain emits signals when humans are sleeping as well. Thus, there is no paucity of brain signals [1]. Psychologists have often used the emotions or thoughts a human think to understand or interpret the real meaning of these brain signals but often human mind does not let complete visibility into these brain signals [2]. Thus, by the implementation of precise brain signal decoding one can comprehend or interpret the actual meaning of these brain signals without disturbing the current mental and physical state of prospect's psychology. These brain signals when interpreted correctly can improve the prospect's quality of life or provide insight into their inner mind-set or psychology [3]. Based on the research done by various experts and psychologists, brain signals collation had two kinds of signals-invasive signals and non-invasive signals [4].

Invasive signals require deeper penetration and can be collected via deploying electrodes on human scalp. While non-invasive signals are acquired rather easily without any penetration or use of electrode as they are collected over the scalp [5].

Brain–computer interface (BCI) systems uses certain mechanism to use these brain signals to create a constant mode of communication between human brain and computer, such that the messages, communication, commands, and emotions of human brain are conveyed to computer without any physical moment of either the human brain or the computer interface [6]. This is done by the Brain–Computer Interface (BCI) systems via monitoring the conscious electric brain activities by the application of electroencephalogram (EEG) signals that can detect any impulse of thoughts or activity that occurs in human brain [7]. These EEG signals have been actively use by neurologists in the healthcare industry to diagnose multiple diseases, help identify any incumbent brain activity, medical procedures like surgeries, provide insights into real anatomy and implications of human brain and other medical and psychological applications [8, 9]. For Brain–Computer Interface (BCI) systems, EEG signals use captured and then digitalized or processed by the use of various processing algorithms, so that these EEG signals or brain signals are converted to real time control signals [10]. This establishes a link between the prospect or the human brain and the computer, such that all the active or passive activities in the human brain can be detected by the computer system. This connection enables the computer to comprehend all the activities, emotions, or demands that human brain exhibits, enabling many revolutionary tasks. Like, help physically disabled people or people with temporary limb or people with any kind of disability perform almost all the tasks [11]. This makes them independent, self-sufficient, confident and improve their quality of life that medical science cannot even imagine to do [12–14]. Different Brain–Computer Interface (BCI) systems control different types of brain activity, considering there are diverse activities that the human brain performs – classifying Brain–Computer Interface (BCI) systems into different kinds based on the activities they perform or the organ replacement they are responsible for [15]. Another way to classify Brain–Computer Interface (BCI) systems is the kind of brain signals they use considering there are multiple kinds namely, electroencephalogram (EEG), electrocardiogram (ECG or EKG), functional magnetic resonance imaging (fMRI), or hybrid input of any two or more brain signal [16]. A very established EEG based Brain–Computer Interface (BCI) system is P-300, Steady State Visual

Evoked Potential (SSVEP), Event Related Desynchronization (ERD) and other include slow cortical potential based Brain–Computer Interface (BCI) System [17–20]. This research study based book chapter will evaluate classical Brain–Computer Interface (BCI) Systems like P300 and its various hybrids due to its splendid user adaptability as compared to others, plethora of applications and economic viability [20].

2.1.1   Current Stance of P300 BCI

This study has surveyed all the journey of P300 Brain–Computer Interface (BCI). This was founded in the year 1988 [21], but the subsequent two years saw no research publications in terms of recognized journals on the topic. The next couple of years precisely from 2000 to 2005 saw some minor increment on the published research publications, most of which were focused around processing the data in different formats or from disparate sources of data [22, 23]. However, the next decade witnessed some path breaking work on P300 Brain–Computer Interface (BCI) with plethora of studies continuously improving the previously released models in multiple peer reviewed research publications. With each passing year, the new models that were proposed were more efficient, robust, easy to implement, economically viable and required less time or space complexity-running on limited computation processing framework [24–26].

To provide a more factual and bigger picture, this has shown graphically how many research publications were released on Google scholar that were indexed by Scopus or any other reputed indexing criteria like SCI from the year 2000 to 2020 in the graph attached below:

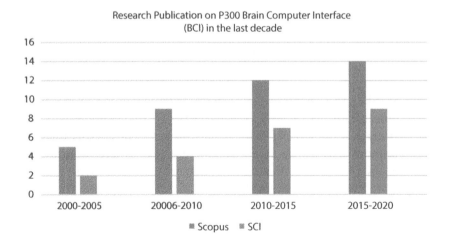

Research Publication on P300 Brain Computer Interface (BCI) in the last decade

This study, firstly, thoroughly elaborates upon its various processing steps while exploring the origin, need, and current stage of development of Brain–computer interface (BCI) with respect to brain signals. Post complete understanding of basic concepts and terminologies of brain signals, Brain–computer interface (BCI), and their interconnection along in the field of bio-medicine; this study elucidates upon primordial methodologies of Brain–computer interface (BCI) along with respective merits and demerits with intensive classification. A differential based analysis is provided to insight into new age deep learning based method in the field of Brain–computer interface (BCI) while comparing them with primordial techniques. A complete data intensive review is performed for new era deep learning techniques while properly classifying the same into multiple gradations based on deep learning framework and their various versions implemented namely, neural networks (CNN) and recurrent neural networks (RNN), long short-term memory (LSTM) architecture, U-net, among others. This chapter also aims to provide real world application, challenges, scope of future growths, avenues of expansion, and complete industry-specific guide for implementing insights gathered from brain signals in the nascent area of Brain–computer interface (BCI). To further edify the application understanding, this study also aims to provide an extended gradation based on the representation of technique used for gathering brain signals namely, electroencephalogram (EEG), electrocardiogram (ECG or EKG), functional magnetic resonance imaging (fMRI) or hybrid input of any two or more brain signal capturing techniques, this information aids the further classification of application to create industry specific inputs.

2.2   Brain–Computer Interface Cycle

This section of the research study evaluates various steps with their respective details that are involved in the processing of a classical Brain–Computer Interface (BCI) System as summarized in Figure 2.1. The significance of this section increases as the rudimentary knowledge of various processes are cardinal before getting into various approaches of Brain–Computer Interface (BCI) Systems and their respective applications [27, 28].

Step 1: Task and Stimuli
If one considers an ideal Brain–Computer Interface system then theoretically user just needs to send strong and active brain stimuli, a task that requires limited effort and the user does not fatigues his/her

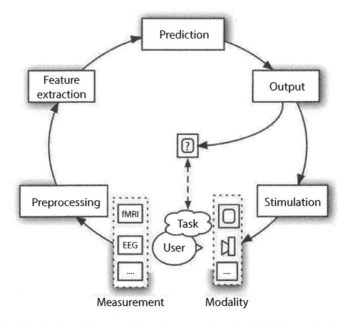

Figure 2.1 The ideal cycle for any Brain–Computer Interface (BCI) System begins with a stimulus in the user's brain – i.e., the activity in active brain that is created in precedence of an action. This stimulus creates brain signals that can be detected by the sensory devices of the computer's processor. The outcome of these brain signals are predicted by the processors and computation abilities of the computer, i.e., the action that brain intended.

physical system. Theoretically, a Brain–Computer Interface system is very easy to control and use, in fact the measure of brain signals can determine the strength of the activity performed, the user has to be conscious enough to intend a particular activity and the computer can process the respective task. But, most of Brain–Computer Interface systems are very far from ideal, and there exists no system that can actually execute all the above mentioned features, i.e., become ideal [29]. Most of users are also not ideal; they are trained to use a BCI system, but often not many users tend to send brain signals without any intention to produce action or manually proceed to do the action when the brain–computer interface fails to do [30]. The environment in which the user's brain signals are transmitted also pose an issue as when the media of communication is not clean or is scattered, the signals are either interpreted wrong or are lost in the environment noise. Thus, voluntarily generated active brain signals and noise free environment are required a perfect Brain–Computer Interface to work. The first such Brain–computer Interface was developed as a spelling device that enabled users with paralysis to write, after huge amount of training [31]. Another way of training any BCI system is via neurofeedback training, which includes validating the intentions of the user by feeding him/her the features of brain signals extracted, providing users full control of the activity [32].

As mentioned above and the various publication that discuss challenges of Brain–computer Interface, training such a detailed computer system is a huge task as it requires huge amount of time, attention along with plethora of data to feed on [33]. Thus, more recent models of the BCI systems are looking for effective alternatives instructive cognitive tasks that require comparatively less training [34]. Another approach is tagging a particular stimuli to be important by watermarking it or providing it a neuronal signature. For instance, when our brain is aware of a particular sight or entity it can identify that entity in very noisy environment as well like a fast moving car, plethora of signs, or any such diverse situation as our brain has already registered that particular symbol via a neuronal signature [35]. Similar neuronal signatures can be in different forms like ranging from visual signatures to musical signatures or metal navigation. Higher cognitive tasks can also be done by signatures that are then converted to stimuli which are cue based or synchronous in nature either by active signals or by passive signals. For cue based or Synchronous signals the BCI systems have a particular response time on the other hand for non-cue based or Asynchronous based BCI systems the response time is not defined – this further delays the process creating other issues or problems [36]. Coming of age tech makers and minds like various researchers in the field are expanding to beyond brain signals like use of internal speech as that's the most direct, easy and effective way of communication one's direct thoughts to the Brain–Computer Interface, as this would be as effective or robust as detecting the thoughts but this approach comes with its own set of challenges like understanding different dialects, languages and their actual meanings since human use sarcasm, metaphor among other figure of speech [37].

Step 2: Brain signal detection and measurement
The classification of various brain signals capturing and measuring devices are categorized based on the type of the signals these devices capture – Invasive and Non-Invasive methods. Electroencephalography (EEG) and Magnetoencephalography (MEG) are graded into the category of Non-Invasive signals, these can aid in capturing and detecting average brain activity via detecting the activities of neural cells and their dendritic currents. While their capability to capture the sense of activities and respective

brain signals is cogent but the exact location of origin of this brain signal cannot be determined by the Non-Invasive signals. This happens due to the spatial noise in the medium of traversal, like bones, tissues, skin, organs or different cortical areas in the brain tissue that are not responsible for producing the brain signals. Also, Non-Invasive signals are very sensitive to the noise created by very minute body moments like muscle moment or slight eye moments [38]. Apart from Electroencephalography (EEG) and Magnetoencephalography (MEG) signals, recent developments in Brain–Computer Interface (BCI) systems also use Functional magnetic resonance imaging or functional MRI (fMRI) [39, 40]. Since fMRI measures the changes in magnetic properties of hemoglobin levels in the blood that is directly related to neural activities in the brain, its spatial resolution is very advanced and refined as compared to EEG and MEG but again lacks in temporal resolution [41].

An approach to obtain much better performance with both spatial and temporal resolution is using non-invasive brain signals capturing techniques and use electrode implantation [42]. These electrodes are capable of recoding both minor and major spikes in brain signals, like spikes in multiple regions and multiple spikes in the same region. Their abilities can identify the increased or decreased intensity in brain signals and also determine their exact epicenter of origin. After seeing the theoretical results of this technique, it was implemented on monkeys [43, 44] but when it was approved for human trials some risks were identified, later these risks turned out to be very severe for all most all the BCI systems. Other risks and challenges associated with this technique are operational challenges – due to the complicated and delicate nature of electrodes, a continuous monitoring team of experts and heavy hardware is needed on daily basis. The recent advances in brain signals capturing or detecting devices is deriving innovation for optimized techniques in brain–computer interface systems. But some issues remain open challenges to solve – tissue scaring, operational challenges, economic viability, use of complicated hardware and risk to human life. Moreover, less noisy environment, spatial and temporal visibility and light weight scanners are also few loop holes to improve in future under the Brain–computer Interface domain [45].

Step 3: Signatures
The next step in the Brain–Computer Interface cycle is feature or characteristic detection or feature extraction that includes extracting features from the brain signals received from the user. This feature extraction is the first insight gathered from the brain signals received by user, which if gathered incorrectly can create issues in detecting intend to action of user.

These features or characteristics are called neural signatures or signatures. This signature is contingent to a particular task or an activity, such that the presence of a signature is a direct indication of occurrence of that task. For instance, when a person is asleep the brain induces or sends a particular signal know as sleep spindle. Thus, when sensors detect this signature, it is clear that prospect is at sleep [46] – refer to Figure 2.2.

The current stance in medical science are still trying to find various signatures for any period or frequently occurring activity via their respective brain signal signature. The signatures in Brain–computer Interface can be classified into two categories namely – Evoked and Induced. While Induced signatures are power locked, the former (Evoked) signatures are time or phase fixation. The responses received are calculated via an event-related potential (ERP) or event-related field (ERF) [47]. But both these techniques have their own set of drawbacks and merits, most of the issues and challenges are due to the internal and external noise-like similar signatures or signals that occur in various parts of the brain or brain tissues, continuous and unpredicted moment of the prospect, any sudden emotion or secretion of any hormone on prospect's body.

With a more in-depth understanding of how various parts of brain communicate with each other, how and when a particular neural activity takes place, what triggers these sudden activities, how visual, sensory or temporal stimuli are triggered in the human brain and knowledge other intricacies is required [48]. More anatomy intensive research is required to aid the Brain–computer interface systems breakthrough.

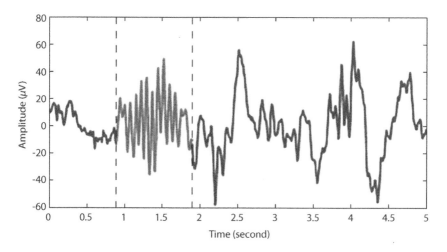

Figure 2.2 A typical sleep spindle – between dashed lines.

Step 4: Feature Processing or Pre-Processing

After successfully extracting the feature or characteristics, it is cardinal to process them in order to obtain the intention of action from the respective brain signals by maximizing the signals to noise ratio. This step is most important and intensive task in terms of time or computation capabilities. Apart from knowledge of various incoming signals and their signatures, use of optimal image capturing technology is also a requisite. This study elaborates upon feature processing of electromagnetic signals out of the available technology for other types of brain signals. This process mainly deals with denoising or filtering out the unwanted artifacts from the captured features. The unwanted entities are known as noise – that can corrode the captured signals and create disruption in identification of intend of action of user. These disruptions include unwanted signals of brain captured to other activities like blinking of the eye, involuntary action of the user, signals corroded by brain tissues or any other type of activity. The two main categories discuss in this section of the research chapter – spatial filtering and spectral filtering. Spectral filtering deals with the denoising part, i.e., eradicating noise or other signals from the required brain signal to clear out way for feature recognition. Spatial filtering is ideally done after spectral filtering or denoising, it combines the linearly loose or weak signals

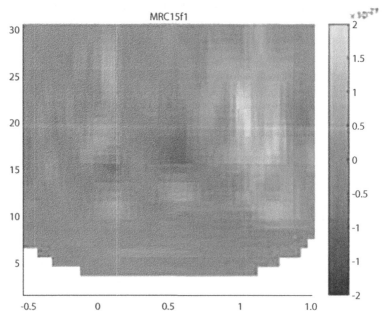

Figure 2.3 A general representation of time-frequency representations (TFRs).

to provide a concentrated signal. During feature extraction we pre-process the received signals by robust identification of spectral and temporal characteristics. Spectral features are derived directly from the signals captured or the signals averaged over time, while temporal signals are derived from the straight or intensity of the captured signals. An alternate approach here is Time-frequency representations (TFRs) that are obtained by combining spectral and temporal features as represented in Figure 2.3.

Thus, feature extraction and feature recognition are two most intensive and equally important steps in the Brain–computer interface cycle as they are vital for identification of user's intent.

Step 5: Prediction

The subsequent step or the penultimate step includes predicting or determining the outcome from the processed and extracted features. This is generally done via the application of machine learning theorems. So, the application of machine learning theorem produces the final output is either discrete or continuous depending on the algorithm implemented. Like, if the algorithm implemented is regression based then output is continuous or if the algorithm used is classification based then result is discrete as shown in Figure 2.4.

In the past decade, a lot of machine learning algorithms have been applied in the prediction process of Brain–computer Interface Systems – popular algorithms being linear discriminant analysis and Support Vector machine [49, 50]. But the performance of the output received does not completely depend on machine learning algorithm selected but the quality of extracted features, training data availability, technique implemented for validation.

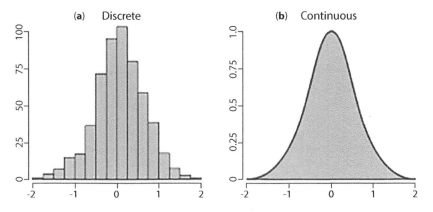

Figure 2.4 Graphical representation of discrete and continuous distribution.

The nature of neural signal data is very eccentric – it has many features, each with individual characteristics and since the amount of data is limited model over fitting becomes a problem [51]. Solutions to this issue include – implementing a simpler or linear fitting algorithm or using feature selection to remove unwanted features in order to prevent over fitting. Another concept that has got attention of Brain–computer interface researcher in machine learning is transfer learning (Figure 2.5) or multi-task learning. Here, the performance is improved by avoiding over fitting the model on signal data but it also avoids inclusion or processing of new data or any kind of outlier data [52]. Researchers in the field are looking for alternatives and diving into hybrid algorithms that combine classification and regression, but human brain is a complex system that contain endless number of internal processes, signals and concepts that medical science is still trying to unveil. Thus, with more in-depth knowledge of anatomy of human mind, Brain–Computer Interface Community will able to innovate further. Alternate algorithm based solutions that attempted to address issues in BCI are – hybrid classification algorithms namely, hidden Markov and optimized Bayesian networks [53, 54] as they enable time to time monitoring or mapping and are flexible enough to adjust to the continuously changing human brain signals [55].

Conclusively, selecting an optimal algorithm is not an issue as over fitting can be easily avoided by using a linear or simple algorithm, it's the

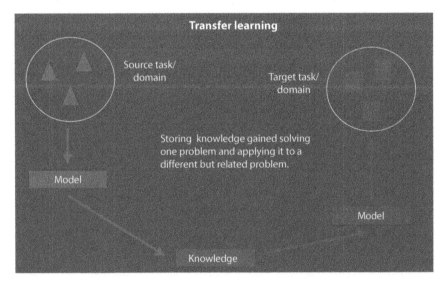

Figure 2.5 A regular transfer learning set up for any machine learning environment.

inclusion of all the features, continuous mapping and adjusting to changing brain signals that creates an issue with almost all the classification algorithms in Brain–Computer Interface community.

Step 6. Results and Action Performed

The result and final stage of a Brain–Computer Interface system is when user's intended action is predicted correctly after feature extraction, pre-processing and predicted using machine learning algorithm, this action is then performed via any computer or physical device like prosthetic arm or wheelchair or any computer system as seen in Figure 2.6. After predicted action is performed by the external output device, feedback is given by the user to further improve the Brain–Computer Interface system. There are

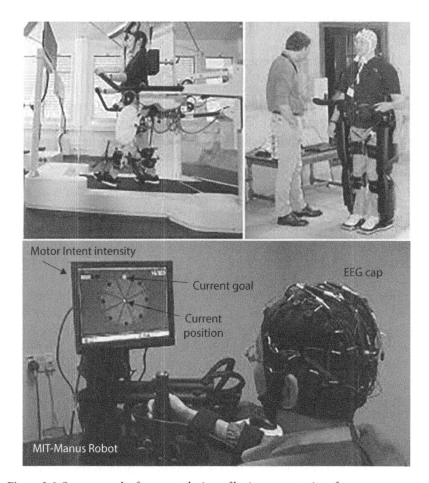

Figure 2.6 Some examples for output devices of brain–computer interface.

multiple types of output devices out here to use depending on the type of activity performed or the need of user like audio [56], text [57], graphical [58], motor commands [59] and vibrotactile [60] is among others.

2.3   Classification of Techniques Used for Brain–Computer Interface

In this section the various techniques and research documentation available pertaining to use of different techniques for brain machine interface has been discussed. The entire collection is organized and based on the four core domains, namely, predicators and diagnostics in mental and neurological disorders, observation and analysis of sleep pattern, brain activity associated with mood and lastly some miscellaneous topics.

2.3.1   Application in Mental Health

Epileptic seizures are the most common aspect which is of great interest to the researchers. Many methods have been used for this implementing CNN to various degrees [61]. Johansen et al. implemented AUC to depict the 1 Hz high pas of epileptic episode in an EEG graph using a custom CNN setup. Morabito, et al. [62] devised the use of CNN in the detection Alzheimer's and associated motor decline. This set used the rapid eye movement data for providing with results at 82% accuracy. Chu et al. [63] combined the traditional and stacking models to detect schizophrenia [64]. In the domain of psychological disorders, Acharya et al. [65] devised a multi layered CNN to detect depression consisting of more than 10 layers. Ruffini et al. [66] described an Echo State Networks (ESNs) model, a particular class of RNN, to distinguish RBD from healthy individuals.

Hosseini et al. [67] modeled a sparse bi-layered D-AE for studying the EEG during an epileptic seizure. Similarly, Lin [68] created a model with three hidden layers to parse EEG data. Page et al. [69] designed a system to use DBN representative model to analyses seizure EEG signals. The system combined said method with a regression-based model to detect onset of seizures. A depression detection system consisting of DBN-RBM was used by Al et al. [70] which used two streams of EEG which was later merged with PCA.

2.3.2   Application in Motor-Imagery

In the field of motor imagining, that is, scans pertaining to the motor cortex of the brain different techniques are used as the techniques of normal

EEG have certain shortcomings. In this field also we see the most number of implementations of CNN, as follows. MI-EEG for mapping of neural connection was done by Wang et al. [71] using CNN. General performance enhancements in the CNN structure have been done by Zhang et al. [72] and Lee et al. [73]. MI-EEG images and their spectral features have been documented by Hartmann et al. [74], showing gradient features proportional to the strength of the EEG signal.

For the representative class, DBN based systems have shown the most impressive results [75]. Following this direction, Li et al. [76] applied DBN-AE to the EEG of wavelet transform and followed it up with denoising techniques. Similarly, Ren et al. [77] showed the feature representation of the EEG signals by means of CDBN. Other notable works include implementation of LSTM and reinforced learning [78], XGBoost augmentation [79], Genetic algorithm use [80] and KNN classifiers [81] for the analysis of signals.

2.3.3   Application in Sleep Analysis

The EEG data generated during sleep is the most well researched domain among all fields using BCI. EEG data from sleep can provide information about the persons sleep patterns, mental and physical wellbeing and act as predictor for onset of disorders [82–84].

In this field most of the work involves EEG scans of a phase of sleep at constant frequency [85]. Time-frequency based features were analyzed by Viamala [86] with a generous score of 82% accuracy in prediction. Tan et al. [87] achieved a 92% accurate F-1 score in sleep spectral pattern by Power Spectral Density analysis. A multi-step sleep feature extraction with the combination of DBN and CNN was performed by Zang et al. [88]. Further work has been done in the form of implementing KNN [89] and LSTM [90].

2.3.4   Application in Emotion Analysis

Emotions are a core aspect of humans and other higher mammals. Although research into the exact mechanism of development of emotions is still ongoing, the presence of an emotional state can be easily understood with the help of EEG scans. As such many deep learning techniques have been proposed and many studies conducted to research into the emotional changes of the brain.

RNN and CNN are gaining popularity in the domain of emotion development [91, 92] while the classic MLP techniques have a long standing history of use for the same [93]. Zhang *et al.* [94] proposed a spatial-temporal recurrent neural network, which employs a multi-directional RNN layer to discover long-range contextual cues and a bi-directional RNN layer to capture sequential features produced by the previous spatial RNN. Talathi [95] proposed a deep learning model for the GRU cell type model. The study spatial configuration of the EEG matrix by transformation into two-dimensional matrix was done by Li *et al.* [96].

A novel model called Bimodal Deep AutoEncoder (BDAE) was created by Yan *et al.* [97] in which a gender based research into the EEG patterns of males and females were fused with the eye movement data via a SVM to discover emotional response variations. Chai *et al.* [98] put forth a solution to the problem of training dependency by designing a Subspace Alignment AutoEncoder (SAAE) that used unsupervised domain adaptation. The technique had a mean accuracy of 77.8%. Zheng [99] combined DBN with a Hidden Markovian Model while Zhao *et al.* [100] combined it with SVM to address the state of emotion in the unsupervised learning subspace.

2.3.5   Hybrid Methodologies

It has been observed that a hybrid technique, that is the amalgamation of two or more techniques can synergies with each other and provide better results. Also, this synergy opens up new avenues for evaluation and processing of EEG data. In this domain, the majority of improvements have been made in the last 7 years due to advances in sensor technology, improved neural network codes and development of innovative hardware.

Popular models involve the combination of two of the most widely used techniques: CNN and RNN. This was done by Shah *et al.* [101] for a multi-channel seizure detection system with 33% sensitivity. A combination of the temporal and spatial features of EEG was done by Golmohammadi *et al.* [102] where CNN and LSTM were combined to interpret EEG of the THU seizure corpus with a specificity of 96.85%. Morabito *et al.* [103] implemented a combination of MLP and D-AE for early stage detection of Creutzfeldt-Jakob Disease. This system passed the EEG was processed via the D-AE with additional hidden layers for feature representation and MLP classified the results after training with a mean of 82% accuracy. In unsupervised learning models CNN has been used instead of generic AE layers with favorable results [104].

Tan *et al.* [105] implemented a combination of CNN and RNN with a DBN-AE for dimensional reduction to discover buried details in spatial domain with an average accuracy of 73%. Tabar *et al.* [106] combined

CNN and a seven layered DBN-AE to extract representation of frequency domain and location information for high precision.

Dong *et al.* [107] trained a hybrid LSTM-MLP model for deducing hierarchical features of temporal sleep stages. Manzano *et al.* [108] devised a CNN-MLP algorithm to predict the states of sleep. This algorithm used the CNN to process the EEG waveform while the MLP was fed a pre-processed signal of <32 Hz. A similar model pertaining to neonatal sleep was designed by Fraiwan *et al.* [109]. An automated scoring system to qualify sleep efficacy was proposed by Supratak *et al.* [110] which used a bi-directional LSTM to parse the sleep features.

2.3.6   Recent Notable Advancements

The relation of EEG with change in auditory and visual stimuli is of great interest to researchers. Stimuli have been presented in many ways varying from repeated sounds of a frequency or a flickering light. They are also used to distinguish between the different moods of a subject [111]. Many studies have been conducted at different institutes around the world, of which the most prominent ones are mentioned here.

Stober *et al.* [112] focused on the effect of repeated stimuli and its relation with changes in EEG. In the study performed, used CNN along with AE in 12 and 24 category classification with 24.4% to 27% accuracy. Sternin *et al.* [113] tried to map a CNN to the EEG changes when a subject hears music. Sarkar *et al.* [114] designed a CNN and three-stage DBN-RBM to classify audiovisual stimuli with 91.70% accuracy. EEG changes during intense cognitive activity and straining physical workload has also been studied [115, 116]. In this regard, Bashivan *et al.* published two studies [117, 118]. The former extracted the spatial features via wavelet entropy which was fed to a MLP, and the latter analyzed general changes in wave pattern formation during a dynamic workload. Li *et al.* [119] mapped variations at different mental states of fatigue and alertness, while Yin *et al.* [120] imposed a binary classifier on the data of EEG during varied mental workloads, combined with D-AE refining. These researches have practical indications, like the detection of response time of drunken drivers based on their EEG as done by Huang *et al.* [121]. Similarly, the work of Hajinoroozi *et al.* [122] involves the processing of EEG by an ICA followed by evaluation by the DBN-RBM net which gives satisfactory results of 85% accuracy. Another DBN-RBM method for the same case of alcohol influence on brain function was structured by San *et al.* [123] with 73.29% result accuracy. Almogbel *et al.* [124] proposed a method that directly associates the mental condition of a subject based on the raw EEG signals parsed by a CNN.

Event-related desynchronization refers to the change of EEG signals, specifically in the power of the waveforms during different brain states [125]. In this context, there are two important factors: ERD and ERS. The former denotes the decrease in power while the later measures the increment in power of the EEG scan. Research based on these factors are limiting owing to the low accuracy across subjects [125]. However, there are promising avenues with great potential. For example, Baltatzis et al. [126] trained a CNN to detect if the subject is a victim of school bullying by analyzing the EEG patterns. Similar work by Volker et al. [127] has performed or par and beyond the other existing frameworks. Furthering this stream of work, Zhang et al. [128] discovered latent information by including graph theory into the CNN.

Mood Detection

Similar to previous examples the most common technique involve a combination of CNN with RNN to predict mood and correspond mood changes based on external stimuli. As an example, a CNN-RNN combined cascading framework was built by Miranda-Correa et al. [129] to predict the personalistic characteristics. Attempts have been made to study the efficacy of such systems to identify genders based on EEG signals [130]. The study reached an accuracy of 81% using unaugment CNN on public data libraries. Hernandez et al. [131] proposed a framework that deduced the state of a driver, time taken for intention to brake after getting a visual cue, using CNN algorithms. The resultant accuracy was 71.8%.Lawhern et al. [132] introduced a EEGNet based on CNN to evaluate the various robust aspects of brain signals in response to perceived changes. Teo et al. [133] created a recommendation system that learned from the like to dislike ratio when a subject was shown an image of a product.

ERP

In the last section the strategies were based on the analysis of EEG signals. In this section the studies reviewed pertain to ERP (Evoked Potential). ERP studies are mostly done using the P300 phenomena, hence most studies here are related to publication of P300 scenarios. ERP has two subcategories VEP and AEP which will be discussed in the next section.

Ma et al. [134] combined genetic algorithm with multi-level sensory system for the compression of raw data which was send to DBN-RBM for analysis of higher level features. Maddula et al. [135] analyzed the low frequency P300 signals using a 2D CNN to extract the spatial features in combination with a LSTM layer. A high accuracy of 97.3% was observed using a DBN-RMB model with SVM classifier by Liu *et al.* [136]. The experiment by Gao *et al.* [137] used a combination of SVM classifiers followed by AE for filtration. This experiment had an accuracy of 88.1% when executed for a sample of 150 points per data segment. Cecotti *et al.* [138] modified P300 with low pass CNN in an attempt to increase the alphabet detection of the P300. A batch normalized method, which was a variant of the CNN method was proposed by Liu *et al.* [139]. The framework comprised of six independent batch layers. Kawasaki *et al.* [140] achieved an accuracy of 90.8% using MLP to differentiate between P300 and other models.

Works focused on AEP include Carabez *et al.* [141] who proposed an experiment to test AEP and CNN models. An auditory response to the oddball paradigm was the basis of this experiment. 18 different models were tested which showed accuracy comparable to other competing models. Better results were obtained when the signal to the AEP was downsampled to 25 Hz.

RSVP

This model has also garnered much attention due to its recent success [142, 143]. The most used models consist of pass bands with frequency filtered between 0.1Hz and 50Hz. Cecotti *et al.* [144] performed an experiment with a scenario where cars and faces were labeled as target and non-target. The images were presented in each session with a frequency of 2Hz. A specialized CNN model was used for the detection of targets in the RSVP. The experiment gave promising results with an AUC score of 86.1%. Mao *et al.* [145] created a trio consisting of MLP, CNN, DBN to differentiate between the subject's perceptions of a target. This had accuracy of 81.7%, 79.6%, and 81.6% respectively. Another work from Mao *et al.* [146] involves person identification in RSVP model. Vareka *et al.* [147] verified the performance of P300 system in different scenarios, where target identification was the main goal. The model was a DBN-AE comprising of five hidden AE layers and two sofmax layers following it, which gave it an accuracy of 69%. A representative deep neural network for RSVP after a low pass by Manor *et al.* [148] achieved an accuracy of 85.06%.

SSEP

This system focuses on the SSVEP which refers to brain oscillation observed when a flickering visual stimuli are introduced. This phenomenon is mainly concerned with the activities of the occipital lobe which is responsible for processing our vision. Notable examples in this field include, the CNN-RNN hybrid method by Attia *et al.* [149] to capture and process information from this region of the brain. Waytowich *et al.* [150] used a CNN to process SSVEP signals and study the accuracy across subjects. Thomas *et al.* [151] processed the raw data from a low pass SSVEP using a CNN and LSTM to get 69.03% and 66.89% accuracy respectively. Aznan *et al.* [152] applied a discriminatory CNN over the standard SSVEP signals to reach a high accuracy of 96%. This study used signals from dry electrodes which were more challenging to process than standard EEG signals. Hachem *et al.* [153] studied the use of automation of wheelchairs based on the fatigue levels of the user. This study used a SSVEP and MLP to detect the fatigue of the patient. Kulasingham *et al.* [154] applied DBN-AE and DBN-RBM to study results of guilty knowledge test. This study generated results of accuracy 86.02% and 86.89% respectively. Prez *et al.* [155] achieved an accuracy of 97.78% using sofmax function layers to process SSVEP signals from multi-sourced stimuli.

fNIRS

In [156] Naseer *et al.* extracted the fNIRS data of a brain during rest and workload(mathematical tasks). The six features extracted from the prefrontal cortex were fed into the fNIRS and analyzed by a number of different models. Of the models tested, the MLP model gave the best result of 96.3% accuracy outperforming all the other systems such as KNN, SVM, Bayes etc. Similarly, another MLP model was designed by Huve *et al.* [157] where he extracted data during three states of rest, cognitive activity, and vocabulary activity. The model achieved an accuracy of 66.48%. In another study the same author studied the binary classification capabilities of said model and got an accuracy of 66%. Chiarelli *et al.* [158] combined the EEG signal with a fNIRS scan for MI right left classification of EEG. The said study had a 16 lead system with eight leads from either (OxyHb and DeoxyHb) parts. Furthermore, Hiroyasu *et al.* [159] carried out gender detection using a D-AE as a denoising tool followed by a MLP for classification. The model has an accuracy of 81% over the local datasets. A corollary of this paper was that fNIRS was more affordable than PET (Positron Emission Tomography) scans.

fMRI

This tool is of great use in detecting brain impairment including both injury related damages as well as psychological and cognitive problems [160, 161].

In this case too CNN is the most prevalent with varying results. Havaei *et al.* [162] created a CNN based model that reads both local and global data to analyses brain tumors. Different filters have been used for different cases providing a more accurate result. In other diagnostics field, Sarraf *et al.* [163] implemented a deep CNN for the recognition of signs of Alzheimer's fMRI scans. The model obtained a score of 88% when applied on the BRATS dataset. Similarly, a CNN was applied by Hosseini *et al.* [164] for the detection of epileptic seizure using SVM classifiers. Moreover, Li *et al.* [165] combined fMRI to fill buttress the data from PET scans. In this model, two layered CNN mapped the connection between the two, which outperformed the non-combined model at 92.87% accuracy. In a different study, Koyamada *et al.* [166] extracted the features common to all subjects in the HCP (Human Connectome Project). Another aspect of these models is in the detection of diseases. Hu *et al.* [167] divided the brain in to 90 regions and converted the data derived from these regions into a correlation matrix which calculated the functional activity between the different segments. This use of fMRI allowed for the detection of Alzheimer's disease during early stages. Thereafter the system had been improved by the addition of a AE as a filter, which gave a net accuracy of 87.5%. Plis *et al.* [168] used a multi-layered DBN-RBM to extract features from an ICA processed fMRI signal achieving 90% average F1 scores across multiple datasets. Suk *et al.* [169] fed the fMRI data from a cognitively impaired source into an SVM to discover newer features. The SVM classifier after training gave an accuracy score of 72.58%. Similarly, Ortiz *et al.* [170] merged multiple SVM classifiers to achieve greater accuracy in analyzing fMRI data. Generative models in this field focus on the relation between a stimuli and the corresponding fMRI data. As such, Seeliger *et al.* [171] devised a convolutional GAD that was trained to generate the perceived visual image from the fMRI data. This type of studies has a lot of potential for helping people with disabilities in the future. Shen *et al.* [172] presented an alternative approach by mapping the relation of the fMRI to the distance of the target to the observer, at different distances. Han *et al.* [173] compared two different GAN, DCGAN (Deep Convolutional GAN) and WGAN (Wasserstein GAN) to conclude that DCGAN outperformed its opponent.

MEG
Cichy *et al.* [174] combined MEG with fMRI for object recognition. Shu *et al.* [175] demonstrated a newer approach if single word recognition using a sparse AE to decode the MEG. This however did not prove to be any better than the conventional means. Hasasneh *et al.* [176] used MLP to extract the features of a MEG read using a simple CNN. Garg *et al.* [177] streamlined the data in a MEG by refining the video and purging the unnecessary artifacts like blinking. A single level CNN decoded the

MEG messages which were read by ICA. On a local dataset, this model has shown a sensitivity of 85% and specificity of 96%.

2.4   Case Study: A Hybrid EEG-fNIRS BCI

The model in review is a multi-modal EEG-fNIRS combined with the Deep Learning Classification algorithm. The model involves a training using Left and Right hand Imagery with a 1 second frame difference. This model is then compared with similar models such as fNIRS, EEG and MI.

Equipment and Training
Brain activity was recorded using 128 channel EEG system at 50 imped-ance as per manufacturer recommendations. The HydroGel Geosics Sensor Node [178] provided a highly accurate value of signals. Real time EEG processing at 250 Hz was done with a window of 1 second. Brain hemodynamic activity was recorded using a standard NIRS system at the sensorimotor region. Optical fibers of 0.4 mm core and 3 mm core were used for the input and output channels respectively.

Training of the model was done by a group comprising of 15 volunteers who were free of psychoneurological diseases. The squeezing motion of the subject was recorded for both hands with a 5 sec active and 10 sec inactive phases. The hand was clenched during the active phase and the hand was relaxed during the inactive phase. The experiment recorded 200 training sets per subject to give a total of 3000 sets.

Classifiers
The DNN model was customized to incorporate a feed-forward network instead of backpropagation. The hidden layers perform ReLU function to remedy the gradient of errors seen in linear models. This is followed by the SoftMax layer which gives the output in the form of a prediction of right or right arm. The classifier was trained using a supervised learning approach with an adjusting parameter that could be modified based on the difference between desired and actual outputs.

Performance and Analysis
The model was tested thoroughly using a 10 fold validation using 200 tri-als of both the arms, with 20 sets per iteration. For comparison the other models (SVM, KNN) were trained with parameters equal to that of the experimental model.

2.5   Conclusion, Open Issues and Future Endeavors

Theoretically, Brain–Computer Interface community has seen many path breaking developments like, hybrid algorithms, state of art output devices, noise removal or robust filtering techniques [179, 180]. Some of open issues are listed below

1. Functional gaps in Implementation of the framework – A lot of functional gaps have been identified in the currently used brain signal capturing and implementation framework that utilizes EEG, ERP, and fMRI as brain signals and machine learning for feature processing along with classical filtering techniques for feature extraction or artifact removal [181]. Using Deep learning for feature extraction, feature precession and prediction processes could solve a lot of current challenges as it is capable of handling multiple features without over fitting, getting optimized results over a small dataset, adapting to the changing features of brain signals and continuous mapping the user feedback [182]. Past few years have seen some research to edify the same [183, 184], but using deep learning as feature extraction and feature processing is something still a nascent research domain.

2. Prospect Independent Brain signals processing or Signature dependent brain signal processing – The current stance of Brain–computer interface is focused on deliberating the signals detected or collated for a single person/prospect/entity. A single brain is analyzed for any present signature, features and then the intended action for that particular features are identifies. An open research area for future researchers to work *on is considering multiple prospects and their multiple features instead of deliberating a single one. This will help researchers map a particular signal to a specific activity back to its respective signature. Thereby, building a signature library, which will not only expedite the process of Brain–computer Interface but also create room for understanding the anatomy of human brain in fresh perspective. Moreover, the challenge of adapting to a prospects changing brain signals and then starting afresh with another prospect is also solved – providing research a process contingent view instead of a prospect contingent one [185].

3. Real time Brain signal processing – Present research set up mostly offline with previously collected data, that is later processed in the BCI units. But with advancing technology, almost everything works on real time data – web applications, Machine learning models even prosthetic systems also work with live streams of data continuously flowing in real time [186, 187]. It's the BCI set up that first collects the data then processes it later according to the availability of the processing units. Thus, a research domain open to future fellow researchers to work upon is implementing Brain–computer Interface set with online resources and live stream of data, i.e., brain signals are flowing in real time to the processing units to then feature extraction, filtration, processing and prediction straight to the output devices to perform intended actions [188].

4. Lightweight and flexible hardware – Most of Brain–computer interface require very heavy, complex and expensive hardware that is neither flexible nor easy to handle nor it is portable to other fellow devices or technical frameworks. The brain signal capturing devices are very heavy, ugly, and large – making users uncomfortable referred in Figure 2.7. In most cases users are very hesitant to wear such devices due to sheer fear or disgust.

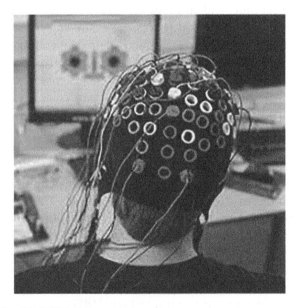

Figure 2.7 Wearable BCI devices.

References

1. Kumar, Y., Dewal, M.L., Anand, R.S., Relative wavelet energy and wavelet entropy based epileptic brain signals classification. *Biomed. Eng. Lett.*, 2, 3, 147–157, 2012.
2. Sanei, S., *Adaptive processing of brain signals*, John Wiley & Sons, 23–28, 2013.
3. Soon, C.S., Allefeld, C., Bogler, C., Heinzle, J., Haynes, J.D., Predictive brain signals best predict upcoming and not previous choices. *Front. Psychol.*, 5, 406, 2014.
4. Waldert, S., Invasive vs. non-invasive neuronal signals for brain-machine interfaces: Will one prevail? *Front. Neurosci.*, 10, 295, 2016.
5. Ball, T., Kern, M., Mutschler, I., Aertsen, A., Schulze-Bonhage, A., Signal quality of simultaneously recorded invasive and non-invasive EEG. *Neuroimage*, 46, 3, 708–716, 2009.
6. Schalk, G., McFarland, D.J., Hinterberger, T., Birbaumer, N., Wolpaw, J.R., BCI2000: a general-purpose brain–computer interface (BCI) system. *IEEE Trans. Biomed. Eng.*, 51, 6, 1034–1043, 2004.
7. Wolpaw, J.R., McFarland, D.J., Vaughan, T.M., Schalk, G., The Wadsworth Center brain–computer interface (BCI) research and development program. *IEEE Trans. Neural Syst. Rehabil. Eng.*, 11, 2, 1–4, 2003.
8. Curran, E.A. and Stokes, M.J., Learning to control brain activity: A review of the production and control of EEG components for driving brain–computer interface (BCI) systems. *Brain Cogn.*, 51, 3, 326–336, 2003.
9. Fabiani, G.E., McFarland, D.J., Wolpaw, J.R., Pfurtscheller, G., Conversion of EEG activity into cursor movement by a brain–computer interface (BCI). *IEEE Trans. Neural Syst. Rehabil. Eng.*, 12, 3, 331–338, 2004.
10. Sathyamoorthy, M., Kuppusamy, S., Dhanaraj, R.K. *et al.*, Improved K-means based Q learning algorithm for optimal clustering and node balancing in WSN. *Wirel. Pers. Commun.*, 122, 2745–2766, 2022.
11. Moore, M.M., Real-world applications for brain–computer interface technology. *IEEE Trans. Neural Syst. Rehabil. Eng.*, 11, 2, 162–165, 2003.
12. Jena, S.R., Shanmugam, R., Saini, K., Kumar, S., Cloud computing tools: Inside views and analysis. *Procedia Computer Science*, vol. 173, pp. 382–391, 2020.
13. Hwang, H.J., Kwon, K., Im, C.H., Neurofeedback-based motor imagery training for brain–computer interface (BCI). *J. Neurosci. Methods*, 179, 1, 150–156, 2009.
14. Pfurtscheller, G. and Neuper, C., Future prospects of ERD/ERS in the context of brain–computer interface (BCI) developments. *Prog. Brain Res.*, 159, 433–437, 2006.
15. Pfurtscheller, G., Müller-Putz, G.R., Scherer, R., Neuper, C., Rehabilitation with brain–computer interface systems. *Computer*, 41, 10, 58–65, 2008.
16. Fatourechi, M., Bashashati, A., Ward, R.K., Birch, G.E., EMG and EOG artifacts in brain computer interface systems: A survey. *Clin. Neurophysiol.*, 118, 3, 480–494, 2007.

17. Käthner, I., Ruf, C.A., Pasqualotto, E., Braun, C., Birbaumer, N., Halder, S., A portable auditory P300 brain–computer interface with directional cues. *Clin. Neurophysiol.*, 124, 2, 327–338, 2013.

18. İşcan, Z. and Nikulin, V.V., Steady state visual evoked potential (SSVEP) based brain–computer interface (BCI) performance under different perturbations. *PloS One*, 13, 1, e0191673, 2018.

19. Huang, D., Qian, K., Fei, D.Y., Jia, W., Chen, X., Bai, O., Electroencephalography (EEG)-based brain–computer interface+ (BCI): A 2-D virtual wheelchair control based on event-related desynchronization/synchronization and state control. *IEEE Trans. Neural Syst. Rehabil. Eng.*, 20, 3, 379–388, 2012.

20. Brouwer, A.M. and Van Erp, J.B., A tactile P300 brain–computer interface. *Front. Neurosci.*, 4, 19, 2010.

21. Donchin, E. and Coles, M.G., Is the P300 component a manifestation of context updating. *Behav. Brain Sci.*, 11, 3, 357–427, 1988.

22. Bayliss, J.D., Inverso, S.A., Tentler, A., Changing the P300 brain computer interface. *Cyber Psychol. Behav.*, 7, 6, 694–704, 2004.

23. Serby, H., Yom-Tov, E., Inbar, G.F., An improved P300-based brain–computer interface. *IEEE Trans. Neural Syst. Rehabil. Eng.*, 13, 1, 89–98, 2005.

24. Jin, J., Sellers, E.W., Zhou, S., Zhang, Y., Wang, X., Cichocki, A., A P300 brain–computer interface based on a modification of the mismatch negativity paradigm. *Int. J. Neural Syst.*, 25, 03, 1550011, 2015.

25. Münßinger, J., II, Halder, S., Kleih, S.C., Furdea, A., Raco, V., Hösle, A., Kubler, A., Brain painting: First evaluation of a new brain–computer interface application with ALS-patients and healthy volunteers. *Front. Neurosci.*, 4, 182, 2010.

26. Käthner, I., Ruf, C.A., Pasqualotto, E., Braun, C., Birbaumer, N., Halder, S., A portable auditory P300 brain–computer interface with directional cues. *Clin. Neurophysiol.*, 124, 2, 327–338, 2013.

27. Tong, J. and Zhu, D., Multi-phase cycle coding for SSVEP based brain–computer interfaces. *Biomed. Eng. Online*, 14, 1, 1–13, 2015.

28. Van Gerven, M., Farquhar, J., Schaefer, R., Vlek, R., Geuze, J., Nijholt, A., Desain, P., The brain–computer interface cycle. *J. Neural Eng.*, 6, 4, 041001, 2009.

29. Neuper, C., Scherer, R., Wriessnegger, S., Pfurtscheller, G., Motor imagery and action observation: Modulation of sensorimotor brain rhythms during mental control of a brain–computer interface. *Clin. Neurophysiol.*, 120, 2, 239–247, 2009.

30. Ramakrishnan, V., Chenniappan, P., Dhanaraj, R.K., Hsu, C.H., Xiao, Y., Al-Turjman, F., Bootstrap aggregative mean shift clustering for big data anti-pattern detection analytics in 5G/6G communication networks. *Comput. Electr. Eng.*, 95, 107380, 2021.

31. Birbaumer, N., Ghanayim, N., Hinterberger, T., Iversen, I., Kotchoubey, B., Kübler, A., Flor, H., 5 Freeing the mind: Brain communication that bypasses the body, in: *Pioneering studies in cognitive neuroscience*, vol. 67, 2009.

32. Hwang, H.J., Kwon, K., Im, C.H., Neurofeedback-based motor imagery training for brain–computer interface (BCI). *J. Neurosci. Methods*, 179, 1, 150–156, 2009.

33. Dhanaraj, R.K. *et al.*, Random forest bagging and x-means clustered antipattern detection from SQL query log for accessing secure mobile data. *Wirel. Commun. Mob. Comput.*, 3–7, 2021, 2021.

34. Jensen, O., Bahramisharif, A., Oostenveld, R., Klanke, S., Hadjipapas, A., Okazaki, Y.O., van Gerven, M.A., Using brain–computer interfaces and brain-state dependent stimulation as tools in cognitive neuroscience. *Front. Psychol.*, 2, 100, 2011.

35. Sellers, E.W., Kubler, A., Donchin, E., Brain–computer interface research at the University of South Florida Cognitive Psychophysiology Laboratory: The P300 speller. *IEEE Trans. Neural Syst. Rehabil. Eng.*, 14, 2, 221–224, 2006.

36. Palaniappan, R., Brain computer interface design using band powers extracted during mental tasks, in: *Conference Proceedings. 2nd International IEEE EMBS Conference on Neural Engineering, 2005*, IEEE, pp. 321–324, 2005, March.

37. Formisano, E., De Martino, F., Bonte, M., Goebel, R., Who" is saying" what"? Brain-based decoding of human voice and speech. *Science*, 322, 5903, 970–973, 2008.

38. Lotte, F., Congedo, M., Lécuyer, A., Lamarche, F., Arnaldi, B., A review of classification algorithms for EEG-based brain–computer interfaces. *J. Neural Eng.*, 4, 2, R1, 2007.

39. Scharnowski, F. and Weiskopf, N., Cognitive enhancement through real-time fMRI neurofeedback. *Curr. Opin. Behav. Sci.*, 4, 122–127, 2015.

40. Hinterberger, T., Veit, R., Wilhelm, B., Weiskopf, N., Vatine, J.J., Birbaumer, N., Neuronal mechanisms underlying control of a brain–computer interface. *Eur. J. Neurosci.*, 21, 11, 3169–3181, 2005.

41. Hinterberger, T., Veit, R., Lal, T.N., Birbaumer, N., Neural mechanisms underlying control of a Brain–Computer-Interface (BCI): Simultaneous recording of bold-response and EEG, in: *44th Annual Meeting of the Society for Psychophysiological Research*, Blackwell Publishing Inc, p. S100, 2004, September.

42. Carmena, J.M., Lebedev, M.A., Crist, R.E., O'Doherty, J.E., Santucci, D.M., Dimitrov, D.F., Nicolelis, M.A., Learning to control a brain–machine interface for reaching and grasping by primates. *PloS Biol.*, 1, 2, e42, 2003.

43. Musallam, S., Andersen, R.A., Corneil, B.D., Greger, B., Scherberger, H., U.S. Patent and Trademark Office, Washington, DC, 2010.

44. Hochberg, L.R., Serruya, M.D., Friehs, G.M., Mukand, J.A., Saleh, M., Caplan, A.H., Donoghue, J.P., Neuronal ensemble control of prosthetic devices by a human with tetraplegia. *Nature*, 442, 7099, 164–171, 2006.

45. Schwartz, A.B., Cortical neural prosthetics. *Annu. Rev. Neurosci.*, 27, 487–507, 2004.

46. Johnson, L.A., Blakely, T., Hermes, D., Hakimian, S., Ramsey, N.F., Ojemann, J.G., Sleep spindles are locally modulated by training on a brain–computer interface. *Proceedings of the National Academy of Sciences*, vol. 109, pp. 18583–18588, 2012.

47. Middendorf, M., McMillan, G., Calhoun, G., Jones, K.S., Brain–computer interfaces based on the steady-state visual-evoked response. *IEEE Trans. Rehabil. Eng.*, 8, 2, 211–214, 2000.

48. Petersen, S.E., Fox, P.T., Posner, M., II, Mintun, M., Raichle, M.E., Positron emission tomographic studies of the cortical anatomy of single-word processing. *Nature*, 331, 6157, 585–589, 1988.

49. McFarland, D.J. and Wolpaw, J.R., Sensorimotor rhythm-based brain–computer interface (BCI): Feature selection by regression improves performance. *IEEE Trans. Neural Syst. Rehabil. Eng.*, 13, 3, 372–379, 2005.

50. Kohlmorgen, J., Dornhege, G., Braun, M., Blankertz, B., Müller, K.R., Curio, G., Kincses, W., Improving human performance in a real operating environment through real-time mental workload detection. *Toward Brain–Comput. Interfacing*, 409422, 409–422, 2007.

51. Raina, R., Ng, A.Y., Koller, D., Constructing informative priors using transfer learning, in: *Proceedings of the 23rd international conference on Machine learning*, pp. 713–720, 2006, June.

52. van Gerven, M., Hesse, C., Jensen, O., Heskes, T., Interpreting single trial data using groupwise regularisation. *NeuroImage*, 46, 3, 665–676, 2009.

53. Sykacek, P., Roberts, S.J., Stokes, M., Adaptive BCI based on variational Bayesian Kalman filtering: an empirical evaluation. *IEEE Trans. Biomed. Eng.*, 51, 5, 719–727, 2004.

54. Vidaurre, C., Schlogl, A., Cabeza, R., Scherer, R., Pfurtscheller, G., A fully on-line adaptive BCI. *IEEE Trans. Biomed. Eng.*, 53, 6, 1214–1219, 2006.

55. Nijboer, F., Furdea, A., Gunst, I., Mellinger, J., McFarland, D.J., Birbaumer, N., Kübler, A., An auditory brain–computer interface (BCI). *J. Neurosci. Methods*, 167, 1, 43–50, 2008.

56. Birbaumer, N., Ghanayim, N., Hinterberger, T., Iversen, I., Kotchoubey, B., Kübler, A., Flor, H., A spelling device for the paralysed. *Nature*, 398, 6725, 297–298, 1999.

57. Nicolelis, M.A., Actions from thoughts. *Nature*, 409, 6818, 403–407, 2001.

58. Birbaumer, N. and Cohen, L.G., Brain–computer interfaces: Communication and restoration of movement in paralysis. *J. Physiol.*, 579, 3, 621–636, 2007.

59. Mason, S.G., Bashashati, A., Fatourechi, M., Navarro, K.F., Birch, G.E., A comprehensive survey of brain interface technology designs. *Ann. Biomed. Eng.*, 35, 2, 137–169, 2007.

60. Wolpaw, J.R. and McFarland, D.J., Control of a two-dimensional movement signal by a noninvasive brain–computer interface in humans. *Proceedings of the national academy of sciences*, vol. 101, pp. 17849–17854, 2004.

61. Yuan, Y., Xun, G., Ma, F., Suo, Q., Xue, H., Jia, K., Zhang, A., A novel channel-aware attention framework for multi-channel EEG seizure detection

via multi-view deep learning, in: *2018 IEEE EMBS International Conference on Biomedical & Health Informatics (BHI)*, IEEE, pp. 206–209, 2018, March.

62. Johansen, A.R., Jin, J., Maszczyk, T., Dauwels, J., Westover, M.B., Epileptiform spike detection via convolutional neural networks, in: *IEEE International Conference on Acoustics, Sp,* .

63. Morabito, F.C., Campolo, M., Ieracitano, C., Ebadi, J.M., Bonanno, L., Bramanti, A., Bramanti, P., Deep convolutional neural networks for classification of mild cognitive impaired and Alzheimer's disease patients from scalp EEG recordings, in: *2016 IEEE 2nd International Forum on Research and Technologies for Society and Industry Leveraging a better tomorrow (RTSI)*, IEEE, pp. 1–6, 2016, September.

64. Chu, L., Qiu, R., Liu, H., Ling, Z., Zhang, T., Wang, J., Individual recognition in schizophrenia using deep learning methods with random forest and voting classifiers: Insights from resting state EEG streams, in: *Computer Vision and Pattern Recognition v2, 2017*. arXiv preprint arXiv:1707.03467.U. R., 5, 2018.

65. Acharya, S.L.O., Hagiwara, Y., Tan, J.H., Adeli, H., Subha, D.P., Automated EEG-based screening of depression using deep convolutional neural network. *Comput. Methods Programs Biomed.*, 161, 103–113, 2018.

66. Ruffini, G., Ibañez, D., Castellano, M., Dunne, S., Soria-Frisch, A., EEG-driven RNN classification for prognosis of neurodegeneration in at-risk patients, in: *International Conference on Artificial Neural Networks*, Springer, Cham, pp. 306–313, 2016, September.

67. Hosseini, M.P., Soltanian-Zadeh, H., Elisevich, K., Pompili, D., Cloud-based deep learning of big EEG data for epileptic seizure prediction, in: *2016 IEEE global conference on signal and information processing (GlobalSIP)*, IEEE, pp. 1151–1155, 2016, December.

68. Lin, Q., Ye, S.Q., Huang, X.M., Li, S.Y., Zhang, M.Z., Xue, Y., Chen, W.S., Classification of epileptic EEG signals with stacked sparse autoencoder based on deep learning, in: *International Conference on Intelligent Computing*, Springer, Cham, pp. 802–810, 2016, August.

69. Page, A., Turner, J.T., Mohsenin, T., Oates, T., Comparing raw data and feature extraction for seizure detection with deep learning methods, in: *The Twenty-Seventh International Flairs Conference*, 2014, May.

70. Al-kaysi, A.M., Al-Ani, A., Boonstra, T.W., A multichannel deep belief network for the classification of EEG data, in: *International Conference on Neural Information Processing*, Springer, Cham, pp. 38–45, 2015, November.

71. Wang, Q., Hu, Y., Chen, H., Multi-channel EEG classification based on Fast convolutional feature extraction, in: *International Symposium on Neural Networks*, Springer, Cham, pp. 533–540, 2017, June.

72. Zhang, X., Yao, L., Huang, C., Sheng, Q.Z., Wang, X., Intent recognition in smart living through deep recurrent neural networks, in: *International Conference on Neural Information Processing*, Springer, Cham, pp. 748–758, 2017, November.

73. Lee, H.K. and Choi, Y.S., A convolution neural networks scheme for classification of motor imagery EEG based on wavelet time-frequency image, in: *2018 International Conference on Information Networking (ICOIN)*, IEEE, pp. 906–909, 2018, January.

74. Hartmann, K.G., Schirrmeister, R.T., Ball, T., Hierarchical internal representation of spectral features in deep convolutional networks trained for EEG decoding, in: *2018 6th International Conference on Brain–Computer Interface (BCI)*, IEEE, pp. 1–6, 2018, January.

75. Lu, N., Li, T., Ren, X., Miao, H., A deep learning scheme for motor imagery classification based on restricted Boltzmann machines. *IEEE Trans. Neural Syst. Rehabil. Eng.*, 25, 6, 566–576, 2016.

76. Li, J. and Cichocki, A., Deep learning of multifractal attributes from motor imagery induced EEG, in: *International Conference on Neural Information Processing*, Springer, Cham, pp. 503–510, 2014, November.

77. Ren, Y. and Wu, Y., Convolutional deep belief networks for feature extraction of EEG signal, in: *2014 International joint conference on neural networks (IJCNN)*, IEEE, pp. 2850–2853, 2014, July.

78. Zhang, X., Yao, L., Huang, C., Wang, S., Tan, M., Long, G., Wang, C., Multimodality sensor data classification with selective attention, in: *Computer Vision and Pattern Recognition*, arXiv preprint arXiv:1804.05493, 2018.

79. Zhang, X., Yao, L., Zhang, D., Wang, X., Sheng, Q.Z., Gu, T., Multi-person brain activity recognition via comprehensive EEG signal analysis, in: *Proceedings of the 14th EAI International Conference on Mobile and Ubiquitous Systems: Computing, Networking and Services*, pp. 28–37, 2017, November.

80. Nurse, E.S., Karoly, P.J., Grayden, D.B., Freestone, D.R., A generalizable brain–computer interface (BCI) using machine learning for feature discovery. *PloS One*, 10, 6, e0131328, 2015.

81. Redkar, S., Using deep learning for human computer interface via electroencephalography. *IAES Int. J. Robot. Automat.*, 4, 4, 2015.

82. Massa, R., de Saint-Martin, A., Hirsch, E., Marescaux, C., Motte, J., Seegmuller, C., Metz-Lutz, M.N., Landau–Kleffner syndrome: Sleep EEG characteristics at onset. *Clin. Neurophysiol.*, 111, S87–S93, 2000.

83. Kang, S.G., Mariani, S., Marvin, S.A., Ko, K.P., Redline, S., Winkelman, J.W., Sleep EEG spectral power is correlated with subjective-objective discrepancy of sleep onset latency in major depressive disorder. *Progress in Neuro-Psychopharmacology and Biological Psychiatry*, vol. 85, pp. 122–127, 2018.

84. Dahl, R.E., Ryan, N.D., Matty, M.K., Birmaher, B., Al-Shabbout, M., Williamson, D.E., Kupfer, D.J., Sleep onset abnormalities in depressed adolescents. *Biol. Psychiatry*, 39, 6, 400–410, 1996.

85. Sors, A., Bonnet, S., Mirek, S., Vercueil, L., Payen, J.F., A convolutional neural network for sleep stage scoring from raw single-channel EEG. *Biomed. Signal Process. Control*, 42, 107–114, 2018.

86. Vilamala, A., Madsen, K.H., Hansen, L.K., Deep convolutional neural networks for interpretable analysis of EEG sleep stage scoring, in: *2017 IEEE*

27th International Workshop on Machine Learning for Signal Processing (MLSP), IEEE, pp. 1–6, 2017, September.

87. Tan, D., Zhao, R., Sun, J., Qin, W., Sleep spindle detection using deep learning: a validation study based on crowdsourcing, in: *2015 37th Annual International Conference of the IEEE Engineering in Medicine and Biology Society (EMBC)*, IEEE, pp. 2828–2831, 2015, August.

88. Zhang, J., Wu, Y., Bai, J., Chen, F., Automatic sleep stage classification based on sparse deep belief net and combination of multiple classifiers. *Trans. Inst. Meas. Control*, 38, 4, 435–451, 2016.

89. Biswal, S., Kulas, J., Sun, H., Goparaju, B., Westover, M.B., Bianchi, M.T., Sun, J., SLEEPNET: Automated sleep staging system via deep learning, in: arXiv preprint arXiv:1707.08262, 2, 2017.

90. Tsiouris, K.M., Pezoulas, V.C., Zervakis, M., Konitsiotis, S., Koutsouris, D.D., Fotiadis, D., II, A long short-term memory deep learning network for the prediction of epileptic seizures using EEG signals. *Comput. Biol. Med.*, 99, 24–37, 2018.

91. Li, J., Zhang, Z., He, H., Implementation of eeg emotion recognition system based on hierarchical convolutional neural networks, in: *International Conference on Brain Inspired Cognitive Systems*, Springer, Cham, pp. 22–33, 2016, November.

92. Liu, W., Jiang, H., Lu, Y., Analyze EEG signals with convolutional neural network based on power spectrum feature selection. *Proceedings of Science*, 2017.

93. Frydenlund, A. and Rudzicz, F., Emotional affect estimation using video and EEG data in deep neural networks, in: *Canadian Conference on Artificial Intelligence*, Springer, Cham, pp. 273–280, 2015, June.

94. Zhang, T., Zheng, W., Cui, Z., Zong, Y., Li, Y., Spatial–temporal recurrent neural network for emotion recognition, in: *IEEE Trans. Cybern.*, 49, 3, 839–847, 2018.

95. Talathi, S.S., Deep recurrent neural networks for seizure detection and early seizure detection systems, 2017. arXiv preprint arXiv:1706.03283.

96. Wang, F., Zhong, S.H., Peng, J., Jiang, J., Liu, Y., Data augmentation for EEG-based emotion recognition with deep convolutional neural networks, in: *International Conference on Multimedia Modeling*, Springer, Cham, pp. 82–93, 2018, February.

97. Tang, H., Liu, W., Zheng, W.L., Lu, B.L., Multimodal emotion recognition using deep neural networks, in: *International Conference on Neural Information Processing*, Springer, Cham, pp. 811–819, 2017, November.

98. Chai, X., Wang, Q., Zhao, Y., Liu, X., Bai, O., Li, Y., Unsupervised domain adaptation techniques based on auto-encoder for non-stationary EEG-based emotion recognition. *Comput. Biol. Med.*, 79, 205–214, 2016.

99. Zheng, W.L., Zhu, J.Y., Peng, Y., Lu, B.L., EEG-based emotion classification using deep belief networks, in: *2014 IEEE International Conference on Multimedia and Expo (ICME)*, IEEE, pp. 1–6, 2014, July.

100. Zhao, Y. and He, L., Deep learning in the EEG diagnosis of Alzheimer's disease, in: *Asian conference on computer vision*, Springer, Cham, pp. 340–353, 2014, November.
101. Golmohammadi, M., Shah, V., Obeid, I., Picone, J., Deep learning approaches for automated seizure detection from scalp electroencephalograms, in: *Signal processing in medicine and biology*, pp. 235–276, Springer, Cham, 2020.
102. Golmohammadi, M., Ziyabari, S., Shah, V., de Diego, S.L., Obeid, I., Picone, J., Deep architectures for automated seizure detection in scalp EEGs, in: *2018 17th IEEE International Conference on Machine Learning and Applications (ICMLA)*, 745–750, IEEE, 2018.
103. Morabito, F.C., Campolo, M., Mammone, N., Versaci, M., Franceschetti, S., Tagliavini, F., Aguglia, U., Deep learning representation from electroencephalography of early-stage Creutzfeldt-Jakob disease and features for differentiation from rapidly progressive dementia. *Int. J. Neural Syst.*, 27, 02, 1650039, 2017.
104. Wen, T. and Zhang, Z., Deep convolution neural network and autoencoders-based unsupervised feature learning of EEG signals. *IEEE Access*, 6, 25399–25410, 2018.
105. Tan, C., Sun, F., Zhang, W., Chen, J., Liu, C., Multimodal classification with deep convolutional-recurrent neural networks for electroencephalography, in: *International Conference on Neural Information Processing*, Springer, Cham, pp. 767–776, 2017, November.
106. Tabar, Y.R. and Halici, U., A novel deep learning approach for classification of EEG motor imagery signals, in: *J. Neural Eng.*, 14, 1, 016003, 2016.
107. Dong, H., Supratak, A., Pan, W., Wu, C., Matthews, P.M., Guo, Y., Mixed neural network approach for temporal sleep stage classification. *IEEE Trans. Neural Syst. Rehabil. Eng.*, 26, 2, 324–333, 2017.
108. Manzano, M., Guillén, A., Rojas, I., Herrera, L.J., Combination of EEG data time and frequency representations in deep networks for sleep stage Classification, in: *International Conference on Intelligent Computing*, Springer, Cham, pp. 219–229, 2017, August.
109. Fraiwan, L. and Lweesy, K., Neonatal sleep state identification using deep learning autoencoders, in: *2017 IEEE 13th International Colloquium on Signal Processing & its Applications (CSPA)*, IEEE, pp. 228–231, 2017, March.
110. Supratak, A., Dong, H., Wu, C., Guo, Y., DeepSleepNet: A model for automatic sleep stage scoring based on raw single-channel EEG. *IEEE Trans. Neural Syst. Rehabil. Eng.*, 25, 11, 1998–2008, 2017.
111. Miranda-Correa, J.A. and Patras, I., A multi-task cascaded network for prediction of affect, personality, mood and social context using eeg signals, in: *2018 13th IEEE International Conference on Automatic Face & Gesture Recognition (FG 2018)*, IEEE, pp. 373–380, 2018, May.
112. Stober, S., Cameron, D.J., Grahn, J.A., Classifying EEG recordings of rhythm perception, in: *ISMIR*, pp. 649–654, 2014.

113. Sternin, A., Stober, S., Grahn, J.A., Owen, A.M., Tempo estimation from the eeg signal during perception and imagination of music, in: *International Workshop on Brain-Computer Music Interfacing/International Symposium on Computer Music Multidisciplinary Research (BCMI/CMMR)*, 2015.

114. Sternin, A., Stober, S., Grahn, J.A., Owen, A.M., Tempo estimation from the eeg signal during perception and imagination of music, in: *International Workshop on Brain-Computer Music Interfacing/International Symposium on Computer Music Multidisciplinary Research (BCMI/CMMR)*, 2015.

115. Shang, J., Zhang, W., Xiong, J., Liu, Q., Cognitive load recognition using multi-channel complex network method, in: *International Symposium on Neural Networks*, Springer, Cham, pp. 466–474, 2017, June.

116. Gordienko, Y., Stirenko, S., Kochura, Y., Alienin, O., Novotarskiy, M., Gordienko, N., Deep learning for fatigue estimation on the basis of multi-modal human-machine interactions, in: *Computers and Society 2017*, 6, 2017. arXiv preprint arXiv:1801.06048.

117. Bashivan, P., Yeasin, M., Bidelman, G.M., Single trial prediction of normal and excessive cognitive load through EEG feature fusion, in: *2015 IEEE Signal Processing in Medicine and Biology Symposium (SPMB)*, pp. 1–5, 2015, December.

118. Bashivan, P., Rish, I., Yeasin, M., Codella, N., Learning representations from EEG with deep recurrent-convolutional neural networks, in: *Published as a conference paper at ICLR 2016*, 3-4, 2015. arXiv preprint arXiv:1511.06448.

119. Li, P., Jiang, W., Su, F., Single-channel EEG-based mental fatigue detection based on deep belief network, in: *2016 38th Annual International Conference of the IEEE Engineering in Medicine and Biology Society (EMBC)*, IEEE, pp. 367–370, 2016, August.

120. Yin, Z. and Zhang, J., Cross-session classification of mental workload levels using EEG and an adaptive deep learning model. *Biomed. Signal Process. Control*, 33, 30–47, 2017.

121. Hung, Y.C., Wang, Y.K., Prasad, M., Lin, C.T., Brain dynamic states analysis based on 3D convolutional neural network, in: *2017 IEEE International Conference on Systems, Man, and Cybernetics (SMC)*, IEEE, pp. 222–227, 2017, October.

122. Hajinoroozi, M., Jung, T.P., Lin, C.T., Huang, Y., Feature extraction with deep belief networks for driver's cognitive states prediction from EEG data, in: *2015 IEEE China Summit and International Conference on Signal and Information Processing (ChinaSIP)*, IEEE, pp. 812–815, 2015, July.

123. San, P.P., Ling, S.H., Chai, R., Tran, Y., Craig, A., Nguyen, H., EEG-based driver fatigue detection using hybrid deep generic model, in: *2016 38th Annual International Conference of the IEEE Engineering in Medicine and Biology Society (EMBC)*, IEEE, pp. 800–803, 2016, August.

124. Almogbel, M.A., Dang, A.H., Kameyama, W., EEG-signals based cognitive workload detection of vehicle driver using deep learning, in: *2018 20th*

International Conference on Advanced Communication Technology (ICACT), IEEE, pp. 256–259, 2018, February.

125. Huang, D., Qian, K., Fei, D.Y., Jia, W., Chen, X., Bai, O., Electroencephalography (EEG)-based brain–computer interface (BCI): A 2-D virtual wheelchair control based on event-related desynchronization/synchronization and state control. *IEEE Trans.Neural Syst. Rehabil. Eng.,* 20, 3, 379–388, 2012.

126. Baltatzis, V., Bintsi, K.M., Apostolidis, G.K., Hadjileontiadis, L.J., Bullying incidences identification within an immersive environment using HD EEG-based analysis: A swarm decomposition and deep learning approach. *Sci. Rep.,* 7, 1, 1–8, 2017.

127. Völker, M., Schirrmeister, R.T., Fiederer, L.D., Burgard, W., Ball, T., Deep transfer learning for error decoding from non-invasive EEG, in: *2018 6th International Conference on Brain–Computer Interface (BCI),* IEEE, pp. 1–6, 2018, January.

128. Zhang, X., Yao, L., Huang, C., Kanhere, S.S., Zhang, D., Zhang, Y., Brain2Object: Printing your mind from brain signals with spatial correlation embedding, in: *Human-Computer Interaction (cs.HC),* 1, 2018. arXiv preprint arXiv:1810.02223.

129. Miranda-Correa, J.A. and Patras, I., A multi-task cascaded network for prediction of affect, personality, mood and social context using eeg signals, in: *2018 13th IEEE International Conference on Automatic Face & Gesture Recognition (FG 2018),* IEEE, pp. 373–380, 2018, May.

130. Van Putten, M.J., Olbrich, S., Arns, M., Predicting sex from brain rhythms with deep learning. *Sci. Rep.,* 8, 1, 1–7, 2018.

131. Hernández, L.G., Mozos, O.M., Ferrández, J.M., Antelis, J.M., EEG-based detection of braking intention under different car driving conditions. *Front. Neuroinform.,* 12, 29, 2018.

132. Lawhern, V.J., Solon, A.J., Waytowich, N.R., Gordon, S.M., Hung, C.P., Lance, B.J., EEGNet: A compact convolutional neural network for EEG-based brain–computer interfaces. *J. Neural. Eng.,* 15, 5, 056013, 2018.

133. Teo, J., Hou, C.L., Mountstephens, J., Deep learning for EEG-based preference classification, in: *AIP Conference Proceedings,* vol. 1891, AIP Publishing LLC, p. 020141, 2017, October.

134. Min, S., Lee, B., Yoon, S., Deep learning in bioinformatics. *Brief. Bioinform.,* 18, 5, 851–869, 2017.

135. Maddula, R., Stivers, J., Mousavi, M., Ravindran, S., de Sa, V., Deep recurrent convolutional neural networks for classifying P300 BCI signals. *GBCIC,* 201–202, 2017.

136. Liu, Q., Zhao, X.G., Hou, Z.G., Liu, H.G., Deep belief networks for EEG-based concealed information test, in: *International Symposium on Neural Networks,* Springer, Cham, pp. 498–506, 2017, June.

137. Gao, W., Guan, J.A., Gao, J., Zhou, D., Multi-ganglion ANN based feature learning with application to P300-BCI signal classification. *Biomed. Signal Process. Control,* 18, 127–137, 2015.

138. Cecotti, H., Convolutional neural networks for event-related potential detection: Impact of the architecture, in: *2017 39th Annual International Conference of the IEEE Engineering in Medicine and Biology Society (EMBC)*, IEEE, pp. 2031–2034, 2017, July.

139. Liu, M., Wu, W., Gu, Z., Yu, Z., Qi, F., Li, Y., Deep learning based on batch normalization for P300 signal detection. *Neurocomput.*, 275, 288–297, 2018.

140. Kawasaki, K., Yoshikawa, T., Furuhashi, T., Visualizing extracted feature by deep learning in P300 discrimination task, in: *2015 7th International Conference of Soft Computing and Pattern Recognition (SoCPaR)*, IEEE, pp. 149–154, 2015, November.

141. Carabez, E., Sugi, M., Nambu, I., Wada, Y., Identifying single trial event-related potentials in an earphone-based auditory brain–computer interface. *Appl. Sci.*, 7, 11, 1197, 2017.

142. Solon, A.J., Gordon, S.M., Lance, B.J., Lawhern, V.J., Deep learning approaches for P300 classification in image triage: Applications to the NAILS task, in: *Proceedings of the 13th NTCIR Conference on Evaluation of Information Access Technologies, NTCIR-13*, Tokyo, Japan, pp. 5–8, 2017, December.

143. Lin, Z., Zeng, Y., Tong, L., Zhang, H., Zhang, C., Yan, B., Method for enhancing single-trial P300 detection by introducing the complexity degree of image information in rapid serial visual presentation tasks. *PloS One*, 12, 12, e0184713, 2017.

144. Cecotti, H., Eckstein, M.P., Giesbrecht, B., Single-trial classification of event-related potentials in rapid serial visual presentation tasks using supervised spatial filtering. *IEEE Trans. Neurol. Netw. Learn. Syst.*, 25, 11, 2030–2042, 2014.

145. Mao, Z., *Deep learning for rapid serial visual presentation event from electroencephalography signal*, Doctoral dissertation, The University of Texas at San Antonio, 2016.

146. Mao, Z., Yao, W.X., Huang, Y., EEG-based biometric identification with deep learning, in: *2017 8th International IEEE/EMBS Conference on Neural Engineering (NER)*, IEEE, pp. 609–612, 2017, May.

147. Vařeka, L. and Mautner, P., Stacked autoencoders for the P300 component detection. *Front. Neurosci.*, 11, 302, 2017.

148. Manor, R., Mishali, L., Geva, A.B., Multimodal neural network for rapid serial visual presentation brain computer interface. *Front. Comput. Neurosci.*, 10, 130, 2016.

149. Attia, M., Hettiarachchi, I., Hossny, M., Nahavandi, S., A time domain classification of steady-state visual evoked potentials using deep recurrent-convolutional neural networks, in: *2018 IEEE 15th International Symposium on Biomedical Imaging (ISBI 2018)*, IEEE, pp. 766–769, 2018, April.

150. Waytowich, N., Lawhern, V.J., Garcia, J.O., Cummings, J., Faller, J., Sajda, P., Vettel, J.M., Compact convolutional neural networks for classification of asynchronous steady-state visual evoked potentials. *J. Neural. Eng.*, 15, 6, 066031, 2018.

151. Thomas, J., Maszczyk, T., Sinha, N., Kluge, T., Dauwels, J., Deep learning-based classification for brain–computer interfaces, in: *2017 IEEE International Conference on Systems, Man, and Cybernetics (SMC)*, IEEE, pp. 234–239, 2017, October.

152. Aznan, N.K.N., Bonner, S., Connolly, J., Al Moubayed, N., Breckon, T., On the classification of SSVEP-based dry-EEG signals via convolutional neural networks, in: *2018 IEEE International Conference on Systems, Man, and Cybernetics (SMC)*, IEEE, pp. 3726–3731, 2018, October.

153. Hachem, A., Khelifa, M.M.B., Alimi, A.M., Gorce, P., Arasu, S.V., Baulkani, S., Muthulakshmi, S.A., Effect of fatigue on ssvep during virtual wheelchair navigation. *J. Theor. Appl. Inform. Technol.*, 65, 1, 2014.

154. Kulasingham, J.P., Vibujithan, V., De Silva, A.C., Deep belief networks and stacked autoencoders for the p300 guilty knowledge test, in: *2016 IEEE EMBS Conference on Biomedical Engineering and Sciences (IECBES)*, IEEE, pp. 127–132, 2016, December.

155. Perez-Benitez, J.L., Perez-Benitez, J.A., Espina-Hernandez, J.H., Development of a brain computer interface using multi-frequency visual stimulation and deep neural networks, in: *2018 International Conference on Electronics, Communications and Computers (CONIELECOMP)*, IEEE, pp. 18–24, 2018, February.

156. Naseer, N., Qureshi, N.K., Noori, F.M., Hong, K.S., Analysis of different classification techniques for two-class functional near-infrared spectroscopy-based brain–computer interface. *Comput. Intell. Neurosci.*, 4–5, 2016.

157. Huve, G., Takahashi, K., Hashimoto, M., Brain activity recognition with a wearable fNIRS using neural networks, in: *2017 IEEE international conference on mechatronics and automation (ICMA)*, IEEE, pp. 1573–1578, 2017, August.

158. Chiarelli, A.M., Croce, P., Merla, A., Zappasodi, F., Deep learning for hybrid EEG-fNIRS brain–computer interface: Application to motor imagery classification. *J. Neural Eng.*, 15, 3, 036028, 2018.

159. Hiroyasu, T., Hanawa, K., Yamamoto, U., Gender classification of subjects from cerebral blood flow changes using deep learning, in: *2014 IEEE Symposium on Computational Intelligence and Data Mining (CIDM)*, IEEE, pp. 229–233, 2014, December.

160. Wen, D., Wei, Z., Zhou, Y., Li, G., Zhang, X., Han, W., Deep learning methods to process fMRI data and their application in the diagnosis of cognitive impairment: A brief overview and our opinion. *Front. Neuroinform.*, 12, 23, 2018.

161. Vieira, S., Pinaya, W.H., Mechelli, A., Using deep learning to investigate the neuroimaging correlates of psychiatric and neurological disorders: Methods and applications. *Neurosci. Biobehav. Rev.*, 74, 58–75, 2017.

162. Shreyas, V. and Pankajakshan, V., A deep learning architecture for brain tumor segmentation in MRI images, in: *2017 IEEE 19th International Workshop on Multimedia Signal Processing (MMSP)*, IEEE, pp. 1–6, 2017, October.

163. Sarraf, S., Tofighi, G., Alzheimer's disease neuroimaging initiative, DeepAD: Alzheimer's disease classification via deep convolutional neural networks using MRI and fMRI. in: *Cold Spring Harbour 2016 preprint*, 070441, 2016. BioRxiv.

164. Hosseini, M.P., Tran, T.X., Pompili, D., Elisevich, K., Soltanian-Zadeh, H., Deep learning with edge computing for localization of epileptogenicity using multimodal rs-fMRI and EEG big data, in: *2017 IEEE international conference on autonomic computing (ICAC)*, IEEE, pp. 83–92, 2017, July.

165. Li, R., Zhang, W., Suk, H., II, Wang, L., Li, J., Shen, D., Ji, S., Deep learning based imaging data completion for improved brain disease diagnosis, in: *International Conference on Medical Image Computing and Computer-Assisted Interventio*, Cham, Springer, pp. 305–312.

166. Koyamada, S., Shikauchi, Y., Nakae, K., Koyama, M., Ishii, S., Deep learning of fMRI big data: A novel approach to subject-transfer decoding, in: *Machine Learning (stat.ML)*, v3, 4, 2015. arXiv preprint arXiv:1502.00093.

167. Hu, C., Ju, R., Shen, Y., Zhou, P., Li, Q., Clinical decision support for Alzheimer's disease based on deep learning and brain network, in: *2016 IEEE International Conference on Communications (ICC)*, IEEE, pp. 1–6, 2016, May.

168. Plis, S.M., Hjelm, D.R., Salakhutdinov, R., Allen, E.A., Bockholt, H.J., Long, J.D., Calhoun, V.D., Deep learning for neuroimaging: A validation study. *Front. Neurosci.*, 8, 229, 2014.

169. Suk, H., II, Wee, C.Y., Lee, S.W., Shen, D., State-space model with deep learning for functional dynamics estimation in resting-state fMRI. *NeuroImage*, 129, 292–307, 2016.

170. Ortiz, A., Munilla, J., Gorriz, J.M., Ramirez, J., Ensembles of deep learning architectures for the early diagnosis of the Alzheimer's disease. *Int. J. Neurol. Syst.*, 26, 07, 1650025, 2016.

171. Seeliger, K., Güçlü, U., Ambrogioni, L., Güçlütürk, Y., van Gerven, M.A., Generative adversarial networks for reconstructing natural images from brain activity. *NeuroImage*, 181, 775–785, 2018.

172. Shen, G., Horikawa, T., Majima, K., Kamitani, Y., Deep image reconstruction from human brain activity. *PloS Comput. Biol.*, 15, 1, e1006633, 2019.

173. Han, C., Hayashi, H., Rundo, L., Araki, R., Shimoda, W., Muramatsu, S., Nakayama, H., GAN-based synthetic brain MR image generation, in: *2018 IEEE 15th International Symposium on Biomedical Imaging (ISBI 2018)*, IEEE, pp. 734–738, 2018, April.

174. Cichy, R.M., Khosla, A., Pantazis, D., Torralba, A., Oliva, A., Comparison of deep neural networks to spatio-temporal cortical dynamics of human visual object recognition reveals hierarchical correspondence. *Sci. Rep.*, 6, 1, 1–13, 2016.

175. Shu, M. and Fyshe, A., Sparse autoencoders for word decoding from magnetoencephalography, in: *Proceedings of the third NIPS Workshop on Machine Learning and Interpretation in NeuroImaging (MLINI)*, 2013.

176. Hasasneh, A., Kampel, N., Sripad, P., Shah, N.J., Dammers, J., Deep learning approach for automatic classification of ocular and cardiac artifacts in MEG data. *J. Eng.*, 5-7, 2018.

177. Garg, P., Davenport, E., Murugesan, G., Wagner, B., Whitlow, C., Maldjian, J., Montillo, A., Automatic 1D convolutional neural network-based detection of artifacts in MEG acquired without electrooculography or electrocardiography, in: *2017 International Workshop on Pattern Recognition in Neuroimaging (PRNI)*, IEEE, pp. 1-4, 2017, June.

178. Yuk, H., Lu, B., Zhao, X., Hydrogel bioelectronics. *Chem. Soc. Rev.*, 48, 6, 1642-1667, 2019.

179. Abdulkader, S.N., Atia, A., Mostafa, M.S.M., Brain computer interfacing: Applications and challenges. *Egypt. Inform. J.*, 16, 2, 213-230, 2015.

180. McCullagh, P., Lightbody, G., Zygierewicz, J., Kernohan, W.G., Ethical challenges associated with the development and deployment of brain computer interface technology. *Neuroethics*, 7, 2, 109-122, 2014.

181. Rashid, M., Sulaiman, N., Majeed, A.P.A., Musa, R.M., Nasir, A.F.A., Bari, B.S., Khatun, S., Current status, challenges, and possible solutions of EEG-based brain–computer interface: A comprehensive review. *Front. Neurobot.*, 14, 25, 2020.

182. Nagel, S. and Spüler, M., World's fastest brain–computer interface: Combining EEG2Code with deep learning. *PloS One*, 14, 9, e0221909, 2019.

183. Thomas, J., Maszczyk, T., Sinha, N., Kluge, T., Dauwels, J., Deep learning-based classification for brain–computer interfaces, in: *2017 IEEE International Conference on Systems, Man, and Cybernetics (SMC)*, IEEE, pp. 234-239, 2017, October.

184. Kwon, O.Y., Lee, M.H., Guan, C., Lee, S.W., Subject-independent brain–computer interfaces based on deep convolutional neural networks. *IEEE Trans. Neural Netw. Learn, Syst.*, 31, 10, 3839-3852, 2019.

185. Zheng, W.L. and Lu, B.L., Personalizing EEG-based affective models with transfer learning, in: *Proceedings of the twenty-fifth international joint conference on artificial intelligence*, pp. 2732-2738, 2016, July.

186. Kumar Dhanaraj, R., Krishnasamy, L. *et al.*, Black-hole attack mitigation in medical sensor networks using the enhanced gravitational search algorithm. *Int. J. Uncertain. Fuzz. Knowl.-Based Syst.*, 297-315, 2021, https://doi.org/10.1142/S021848852140016X.

187. Aliakbaryhosseinabadi, S., Kamavuako, E.N., Jiang, N., Farina, D., Mrachacz-Kersting, N., Online adaptive synchronous BCI system with attention variations, in: *Brain-computer interface research*, pp. 31-41, Springer, Cham, 2019.

188. Kalunga, E.K., Chevallier, S., Barthélemy, Q., Djouani, K., Monacelli, E., Hamam, Y., Online SSVEP-based BCI using Riemannian geometry. *Neurocomput.*, 191, 55-68, 2016.

3

Statistical Learning for Brain–Computer Interface

Lalit Kumar Gangwar, Ankit, John A.* and Rajesh E.

School of Computing Science and Engineering, Galgotias University, Greater Noida, India

Abstract

A BCI is a system that transforms brain impulses directly into motions for computer software, such as a word processor, or a device, such as a monitor. We describe who the target users of a BCI are and how a BCI works in this section. We also discuss the various forms of BCIs, with a particular emphasis on BCIs for those with acute disabilities.

A BCI is a system that comprises sensors for monitoring brain signals (typically in the form of 'electrodes,' an amplifier to enhance the feeble brain waves, and a computer that converts those signals into orders to operate software programs and devices. BCIs' components can be made portable or accessible. BCI-controlled gadgets range from assistive equipment for paralysed persons to internet-connected devices (such as a cellphone) for healthy individuals to basic videogames or entertainment tools.

Many groups are presently working on creating BCIs for a broad array of applications and user categories. Many of the apps are just designed for short-term usage and do not require permanent installation. Therapy devices to aid in the recovery of injured individuals, as well as remote controls for healthy individuals, are instances of this. Some BCIs are meant to replace a function that has been lost or degraded as a result of injuries or sickness (such as the loss of leg function due to stroke).

This paper discusses the BCI and Various techniques to BCI. A particular focus is placed on Machine learning techniques and Deep Learning techniques to BCI. Finally, we provide an overview of the Future Direction on BCI.

Keywords: BCI, techniques to BCI, machine learning, deep learning

*Corresponding author: johnmtech@gmail.com

M.G. Sumithra, Rajesh Kumar Dhanaraj, Mariofanna Milanova, Balamurugan Balusamy and Chandran Venkatesan (eds.) Brain-Computer Interface: Using Deep Learning Applications, (63–76) © 2023 Scrivener Publishing LLC

3.1   Introduction

"The BCI is also known as Neural Control Interface (NCI). BCI is a very interesting field, active and highly demanding topic now a day. A BCI is a direct contact between the brain and a device. The National Science Foundation funded research on BCI at the University of California, Los Angeles (UCLA) in the 1970s, which was followed by a contract with the Defence Advanced Research Projects Agency (DARPA). The BCI is a form of interface that allows users to communicate with computers. Only through the channel of Brain activity, which necessitated both connections between the Brain and the Computer program. There are several approaches for BCI, including non-invasive, semi-invasive, and invasive procedures. The National Science Foundation funded research on BCI at the University of California, Los Angeles (UCLA) in the 1970s, which was followed by a contract with the Defense Advanced Research Projects Agency (DARPA) [1]. Further in this, we are going to discuss these various forms of BCI Techniques. A BCI can help a paralyzed person to convey his/her thought to the computer application, e.g., let a person is paralyzed due to some reason and he/she will want to express his/her intention to the person but he/she is not able to express their intention that what he/she wants to express then the BCI role begins. We need to connect his/her Brain to the computer application after stabilizing the proper connection between both the Brain and computer application he/she can convey his/her thought to the other person.

The present paper represents the various techniques of BCI, with the main focus on Machine learning Techniques to BCI, Deep learning Techniques to BCI. In Deep learning Techniques to BCI, we are going to cover the topic Convolutional Neural Network Model (CNN) and Generative Deep Learning Models [2].

3.1.1   Various Techniques to BCI

The BCI Techniques are mainly divided into three parts which are mention below:

3.1.1.1   Non-Invasive

The BCI Sensors are placed on the scalp in the Non-invasive Technique is used to determine the electrical potentials produced by the brain Electroencephalography (EEG) or Magnetoencephalography (MEG). In Non-invasive, the Electroencephalography (EEG) signal takes place

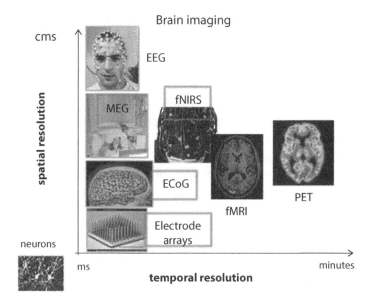

Figure 3.1 Different types of brain imaging techniques that are based on the comparison by spatial and sequential resolution.

electrodes kept on the scalp, on all the most external parts. The different types of representation techniques have been shown in Figure 3.1.

Because of the affordability and availability of technology, Electroencephalography (EEG) is the most widely used non-invasive approach for studying the human brain. The other Non-invasive techniques used to study the human brain are as follows:

- Magnetoencephalography (MEG)
- Electroencephalography (EEG)
- Positron Emission Tomography (PET)
- Functional Magnetic Resonance Imaging (fMRI)
- Near-Infrared Spectroscopy (fNIRS).

3.1.1.2   Semi-Invasive

The electrodes are kept on the exposed surface of the human brain in the Semi-invasive technique, the BCI. Electrocorticography (ECoG) or we can say that Electrocorticography (ECoG) uses electrodes kept on the surface of the human brain to calculate the electrical activity from the cerebral cortex. This method is used for the first time in the 1950s in the Montreal Neurological Institute [3]. This method is known as Semi-invasive however it still mandatory a craniotomy to set up the electrodes because of this reason it is necessary only when surgery is compulsory for medical reasons.

In the Semi-invasive Technique when the surgery took place the electrodes may be placed outside the epidural or under the subdural. The strip and the grid electrodes cover a huge area of the cortex approx. 4–256 electrodes. For more info see Figure 3.2.

There are also some positive sides of Electrocorticography (ECoG) which are mention below [4]:

- It has high spatial resolution and signals fidelity.
- It has a conflict with noise.
- It has low clinical risk and Robustness over a long recording period.
- It has a better-quality amplitude.

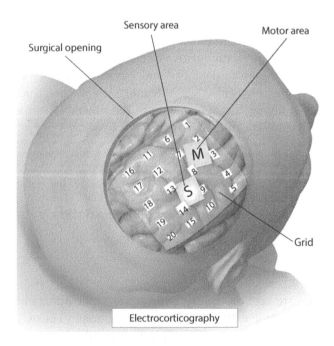

Figure 3.2 Electrocorticography is a kind of electrophysiological monitoring that records electrical impulses from the cerebral cortex using electrodes put directly on the accessible brain surface.

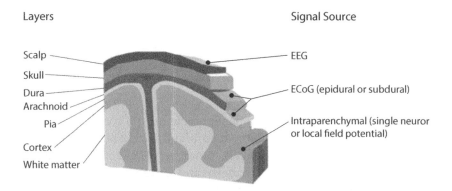

Layers   Signal Source

Scalp —   — EEG
Skull —
Dura —   — ECoG (epidural or subdural)
Arachnoid —
Pia —   Intraparenchymal (single neuror
                                                    or local field potential)
Cortex —
White matter —

Figure 3.3 Represents the different layers and signal sources.

3.1.1.3 *Invasive*

In the Invasive Technique, the BCI the micro-electrodes are kept directly into the cortex, to measure the activity of a particular neuron. In the Invasive technique, the Intraparenchymal signal is occupied directly to the implant electrodes in the cortex. The Invasive Technique of the BCI is implanted directly into the human brain during neurosurgery. In the Invasive technique after neurosurgery, there are distributed into two units of BCI which are "Single unit BCIs" and "Multiunit BCIs". The main distinction between these two, BCIs and multiunit BCIs is that single-unit BCIs detect signals from a single region of a brain cell, whereas multiunit BCIs detect signals from many areas of the brain cell [5]. The different layers and signal sources of the brain's structure have been shown in Figure 3.3.

3.2 Machine Learning Techniques to BCI

Machine Learning Techniques play a huge role in the field of BCI. We all know that the human brain itself is a very complex system. The signals collected from sensors reading levels of voltage are as indirect to the real brain interfacing that we will get. But at present, it's the best we can do without an invasive scheme that needs electrodes that go beneath the scalp. We know that every human brain structure is different to each other. Any single solution which we will find according to the interfacing problem will not work for everyone's brain. The human brains are not having a high level of logical understanding of that level of complexity, because of which we will employ machine learning technique algorithms to give an approx.

Figure 3.4 Brain signal is the "Input wave" whereas Move right is the "category".

evaluation of the solution of the difficult problems with comparative speed and accuracy. As compare to the human brain machines are good at the rules to identify a pattern in difficult scenarios [6]. Scientists have developed different techniques to find patterns and features that cannot be done by human beings easily, e.g., assume that we are watching a cricket game and we paused the television on an exact shot. What if wanted to predict the shot at which we have paused the television is going to be six, four. How could we do this? The easiest way is to draw a structure between the shot and the direction where the ball is going and at which speed. A machine can work in any dimension or many dimensions at a single time whereas a human brain can't.

In this, Classifier receives the Brain signal as Input wave and indicates label on it or we can say put it in the category with the label Move right have been represented in Figure 3.4.

There are many different types of Machine learning algorithms are available but we are going to discuss only two machine learning algorithms which are the most common algorithm for the BCI which are mention below:

Figure 3.5 This figure represents the easiest way to find the solution to classify two different items, like the two teams according to the example is to draw a line between them.

3.2.1 Support Vector Machine (SVM)

In everyday terms, the Support Vector Machine (SVM) algorithms, very much like other machine learning procedures, mean to characterize a curve fit for separating two unmistakable classes of information. In a higher-dimensional space, this curve is known as a hyperplane. To track down the right hyperplane, the algorithm goes through an enhancement interaction where the quantities of misclassified occurrences (players, in the above model) are limited. This interaction is the thing that we call "preparing the algorithm" and we'll turn out how to do it later in this instructional exercise [7].

Just keep in mind that the easiest way to find the solution to classify two different items, like the two teams according to the example is to draw a line between them as shown in Figure 3.5.

Few important points will be kept in mind well-implanting SVM algorithm which is mention below:

- The features of the SVM method should always be numerical.
- When the features in the SVM algorithm are normalized and standardized, the SVM method's performance improves significantly.

3.2.2 Neural Networks

There's nothing more appropriate to figure out how to tackle an issue than a brain. The neurons fire in grouping and further reason a chain response

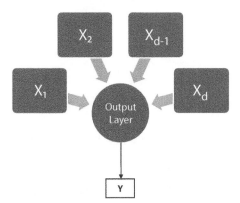

Figure 3.6 The value X_1, X_2, X_{d-1}, X_d is the input layers. The Neural networks are small in amount as compare to the sheer size of the structures which are found in the brain. Only a few neurons cells are used to encode the input layer and the output layer. This type of neural network can only able to solve linear problems [9].

of different neurons terminating which thusly makes a course impact and results, on the whole, the things that a mind can achieve. Neural organizations are designed according to this conduct and endeavor to recreate the capacity of a human mind to figure out how to take care of an issue [8]. The input layers and output layers of the design of the brain using linear structure are shown in Figure 3.6.

The following is next to each other of the primary legitimate portrayal of neurons and the neural organization we make in this instructional exercise. It's not difficult to see the likeness of their designs.

3.3   Deep Learning Techniques Used in BCI

Deep learning is a classification tool that is used in several daily applications, for example, speech recognition, machine vision, computer vision, and natural language processing using a BCI [1, 10].

BCI is a kind of interface that is used to translate brain signals in form of messages or commands to communicate with other devices or other brains.

Designing a BCI, on the other hand, is an extremely complicated undertaking that needs the expertise of several areas, including computer science and engineering, neurology, neural networks, and signal processing.

Mainly two phases are required to construct such complex BCI (Figure 3.7),

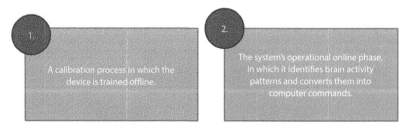

Figure 3.7 Phases required to construct such complex BCI.

Because SNR is unpleasant, due to which calibration is challenging in BCI.

The main difficulty of BCI is correctly identifying human intents. The reality is that BCI's real-world implementation is constrained by both low classification accuracy and poor generalization potential [11].

Deep learning and brain knowledge have been employed in recent years to solve such problems. Unlike traditional machine learning algorithms, deep learning can learn complex high-level features from brain signals without the need for manual feature selection, and its accuracy scales well with the size of the training set. Furthermore, Deep learning algorithms have been utilized to investigate a wide range of BCI signals (e.g., ERP, fMRI, spontaneous EEG).

Why DL is Used for BCI?

First, multiple biological, and environmental artifacts can quickly corrupt brain signals.

Working with electroencephalogram (EEG) presents several challenges. Since the primary goal of BCI is to recognize brain signals, the most common and efficient algorithms are discriminative deep learning models.

A brain signal that goes from neurons interacting with one another via the skull and scalp, and just slightly into the EEG sensor, is difficult to explain. Because EEG data is notoriously noisy, it is difficult to extract a coherent signal for a particular purpose [1, 12].

As a result, extracting meaningful information from distorted brain impulses and developing a reliable BCI mechanism that works in a range of settings are important. Furthermore, because electrochemical mind impulses are non-stationary, BCI has a poor SNR [13].

Although several pre-processing and feature development methods have been developed to minimize noise, they are time demanding and may result in information loss in the resulting features (e.g., feature extraction and selection in the time and frequency domains).

Third, feature engineering is heavily dependent on human domain information. Human knowledge can aid in capturing characteristics in some specific aspects, but it is inadequate in more general situations. As a result, a technique is needed to extract representative features automatically [14].

DL is one of the best ways for extracting distinguishable characteristics automatically.

Furthermore, since the bulk of recent machine learning research relies on static data, it is unable to correctly interpret dynamically evolving brain signals. In BCI applications, working with dynamical data sources necessitates the use of novel learning methods.

There are three benefits of deep learning:

1. First, it uses back-propagation to obtain identifiable insights from unstructured brain impulses, skipping the time-consuming pre-processing and function engineering steps.
2. Deep neural networks may also employ deep structures to collect simultaneously representational rising characteristics and hidden relationships.

3. Finally, DL algorithms outperform traditional classifiers such as SVM and LDA.

It stands to reason that nearly any BCI problem may be classed as a categorization problem.

3.3.1   Convolutional Neural Network Model (CNN)

CNN is an artificial intelligence neural net related to the visual cortex. To decrease classification mistakes, it may automatically know the proper features from the data by improving the weight values of each filter via front and backpropagation. The features extraction and classification using CNN has been presented in the Figure 3.8.

The auditory cortex, like the visual cortex, is arranged hierarchically. A hierarchical organization of brain regions performs various sorts of processing on sensory information as it enters the system. Former regions, often described as the "main visual cortex," react to fundamental characteristics such as color and orientation. More sophisticated functions, such as object recognition, will be available in the future [14].

Deep learning approaches have the benefit of not requiring any pre-processing, allowing optimum configurations to be mastered automatically. In the case of CNN's, attribute features extraction are combined into a single, dynamically optimized structure. Furthermore, fNIRS time series data from human participants were input into the CNN. Because the convolution is done in a sliding display way, the CNN function extraction technique maintains the temporal features of the time – series acquired by fNIRS.

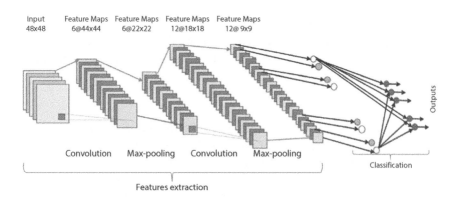

Figure 3.8 Features extraction and classification.

3.3.2 Generative DL Models

Most of the time, Generative DL models are employed to generate training datasets or to augment findings. In other words, Generative DL models aid in increasing the quality and amount of training data in the brain signal area. After the data has been augmented, discriminative models can be performed to evaluate the data. This method was created to increase the robustness and efficacy of trained dl networks, particularly when the training set is limited.

In a nutshell, generative models accept input and produce a bunch of identical data. In this part, we'll look at the two prominent generative dl methods: Variational Autoencoder (VAE) and Generative Adversarial Networks (GAN).

3.4 Future Direction

The BCI is an important medium for users and applications to communicate. To issue commands and complete the interaction, no external devices or muscle involvement is needed. BCIs were originally designed with healthcare applications in mind, resulting in the development of assistive devices. They also aided in the restoration of mobility capacity and the replacement of damaged motor functionality for visually disabled or locked-in people. The bright future expected for BCI has inspired researchers to explore how BCI can be used to better the lives of non-paralyzed people through medical applications.

The research's focus, however, has been expanded to cover non-medical uses. The latest experiments have focused on average users, exploring the use of BCIs as a novel input interface and the creation of hands-free apps.

Communication and Control
BCI technologies bridge the gap between the human mind and the outside world, eliminating the requirement for traditional information transmission methods. They are in charge of transmitting and receiving signals from human minds, as well as decoding their silent thoughts. As a result, they can assist handicapped individuals with communicating and writing down their thoughts and feelings through some approaches, such as spelling applications, semantic categorization, or silent voice exchange.

Medical Applications
The medical sector has a wide range of applications that could benefit from brain impulses in all stages of treatment, including avoidance, identification, diagnosis, recovery, and reconstruction.

User State Monitoring

Initially, BCI technologies primarily focused on handicapped persons with mobility or speech issues. They aimed to provide a means for specific people to connect uniquely. However, BCI finally finds its way into the realm of safe people. It serves as a physiological measurement instrument that retrieves and uses data about a person's mental, cognitive, and affective state.

Advertisement and Neuromarketing

The marketing sector has also inspired BCI researchers' attention. The benefits of using EEG assessment for TV ads in both commercial and political fields were explained in the study. The created attention that comes with watching activity is calculated using BCI.

Entertainment and Games

Because of leisure and gaming applications, nonmedical brain-machine interfaces are now available. Several videogames are given, including one in which aeroplanes are rendered to navigate to a specific place in a virtual world, either in 2D or 3D. Many studies have been conducted on combining the functionality of existing games with brain controlling capabilities, to provide a multi-brain gaming experience.

3.5   Conclusion

The goal of BCI is just to translate brain activity into computer instruction. One of the most difficult parts of the BCI study is the non-stationarity of brain impulses. Because of the non-stationary, identifying consistent patterns in the signals is difficult for a classifier, resulting in low classification outcomes. When combined with the CNN and RL agent or other feedback methods, this might improve learning efficiency for operating a BCI and reduce training time.

BCI technology is rapidly evolving. They are developing methods for recording and distinguishing brain cell signals. BCI combined with caring AI can help disabled people communicate, monitor their environment, and regain their mobility. Allow paralyzed people to use their minds to operate prosthetic limbs. Will deliver auditory data to a deaf person's head, enabling them to understand. It has a wide variety of non-medical uses. Despite its initial success, however, brain-machine interfacing poses various challenges.

References

1. Alom, M.Z., Taha, T.M., Yakopcic, C., Westberg, S., Sidike, P., Nasrin, M.S., Hasan, M., Van Essen, B.C., Awwal, A.A.S., Asari, V.K., A state-of-the-art survey on deep learning theory and architectures. *Electronics*, 8, 3, 292, 2019.

2. Chaudhary, U., Birbaumer, N., Ramos-Murguialday, A., Brain–computer interfaces for communication and rehabilitation. *Nat. Rev. Neurol.*, 12, 9, 513–525, 2016.

3. He, Y., Phat Luu, T., Nathan, K., Nakagome, S., Contreras-Vidal, J.L., A mobile brain-body imaging dataset recorded during treadmill walking with a brain–computer interface. *Sci. Data*, 5, 1, 1–10, 2018.

4. Carabez, E., Sugi, M., Nambu, I., Wada, Y., Identifying single trial event-related potentials in an earphone-based auditory brain–computer interface. *Appl. Sci.*, 7, 11, 1197, 2017.

5. Müller, K.-R., Krauledat, M., Dornhege, G., Curio, G., Blankertz, B., Machine learning techniques for brain–computer interfaces. *Biomed. Tech.*, 49, 1, 11–22, 2004.

6. Gonfalonieri, A., A beginner's guide to brain–computer interface and convolutional neural networks, *Towards Data Science*, November 25 2018.

7. Rajesh Kumar, D. and Shanmugam, A., A hyper heuristic localization based cloned node detection technique using GSA based simulated annealing in sensor networks. *Cognitive computing for big data systems over IoT*, Springer, Cham, pp.307-335, 2018.

8. Silvoni, S., Ramos-Murguialday, A., Cavinato, M., Volpato, C., Cisotto, G., Turolla, A., Piccione, F., Birbaumer, N., Brain–computer interface in stroke: A review of progress. *Clin. EEG Neurosci.*, 42, 4, 245–252, 2011.

9. Nijholt, A., Brain–computer interfaces and human-computer interaction, in: *Brain–Computer Interfaces*, pp. 3–19, Springer, London, 2010.

10. Dhiviya, S., Malathy, S., Kumar, D.R., Internet of Things (IoT) elements, trends and applications. *J. Comput. Theor. Nanosci.*, 15, 5, 1639–1643, 2018.

11. Santhanam, G., Ryu, S., II, Yu, B.M., Afshar, A., Shenoy, K.V., A high-performance brain–computer interface. *Nature*, 442, 7099, 195–198, 2006.

12. Graimann, B., Allison, B.Z., Pfurtscheller, G., Brain-computer interfaces: Revolutionizing human-computer interaction. 1st ed. Berlin Heidelber: Springer Verlag, 2010.

13. Krishnasamy, L. A. L. I. T. H. A., *et al.* A geodesic deployment and radial shaped clustering (RSC) algorithm with statistical aggregation in sensor networks. *Turk. J. Electr. Eng.*, 29.3, 1464–1478, 2021.

14. King, C.E., Wang, P.T., Chui, L.A., Do, A.H., Nenadic, Z., Operation of a brain–computer interface walking simulator for individuals with spinal cord injury. *J. Neuroeng. Rehabil.*, 10, 1–14, 2013.

4

The Impact of Brain–Computer Interface on Lifestyle of Elderly People

Zahra Alidousti Shahraki[1]* and Mohsen Aghabozorgi Nafchi[2]

[1]Department of Computer Engineering, University of Isfahan, Isfahan, Iran
[2]School of Electrical and Computer Engineering, Shiraz University, Shiraz, Iran

Abstract

Today, the interface between the brain and the computer can be designed using intelligent tools. This two-way communication that is named the Brain–computer interface can make new changes in the world of science. Today, with the development of smartphones, the use of applications and social networks has formed an important part of people's communication. Therefore, the tools must be designed in such a way as to cover the needs of all members of society. For example, for improving the quality of living of aged people, they need to use these facilities with other people. So designing intelligence tools should be such that they can be implemented with the mental decision of people. Also as aging has some effects on activities of daily routines or the human body and their brains, it's important to settle the difficulties in communicating, walking, drive safely, the lifestyle of people, and their health. In this research, the challenging discussion of the effect of a brain–computer interface technology on aged people's life system is discussed and the role of the user interface is examined. Also, deep learning is one of the most important algorithms to make the patterns of subjects. Robots to feed elderly people, intelligent wheelchairs that are controlled by mental decisions, applications to make decisions and help to memorizing information for elderly people with Alzheimer, cameras to synthesize eye movements for aged people with vision disorder people, devices that help to make decisions for elderly people who have had a stroke and getting communication disorders, are high-tech devices that help to people who are suffering from cognition errors or physical disability. The BCI applications which are based on deep learning algorithms can monitor brain activity. They have programmed signals that can make better decisions in different

---

*Corresponding author: Zahra_alidousti@yahoo.com

M.G. Sumithra, Rajesh Kumar Dhanaraj, Mariofanna Milanova, Balamurugan Balusamy and Chandran Venkatesan (eds.) Brain-Computer Interface: Using Deep Learning Applications, (77–100) © 2023 Scrivener Publishing LLC

situations and can help to decrease the decision timing and improve the level of confidence and create a balance between different levels of people in society. Creating a balance between people improves the level of quality in every society and helps to increase the healthy life in society. In this chapter, we explore the relationship between the BCI applications which are based on deep learning algorithms and their applications for elderly people.

Keywords: Brain Computer Interface (BCI), diseases, intelligence application, mental decisions, machine learning, AI in health, elderly people, disability, cognitive science

4.1   Introduction

The aging process occurs in all humans over the age of 60. With age, physical, psychological, and social changes over time are identified [55]. Today, the results show that one of the biggest risk factors for most diseases occurs in the elderly [59]. Most of the daily deaths in the world are due to old age and the diseases that the elderly face. In modern countries, the mortality rate of older people is higher than that of young people [60, 61]. Age can lead to visual impairment and consequently reduced non-verbal communication [62], which is likely to cause depression and isolation among the elderly. Therefore, it is necessary to research the factors that cause disability faster and provide solutions to prevent premature aging and premature diseases in people. A society that faces premature aging has a very low rate of social vitality and life expectancy, and ultimately growth and development.

The majority or a significant number of people experience some of the characteristics of aging during their lifetime. Therefore, with the obtained experiences, aging can be reduced by presenting methods and factors affecting it. One of the consequences of increasing age from childhood to old age is decreasing of auditory and visual ability. Teens' or young children's ability to hear high-frequency sounds is lost [56]. Approximately half of the people over the age of 75 have hearing loss or presbyopia, which inhibits speech communication [57]. Decreased brain function also occurs with age and therefore dementia increases with age. According to statistics, approximately 3% of people aged 65–74 years and about 19% of people between 75 and 84 years, and also about half of the people over 85 years of age suffer from dementia [58].

As mentioned, maintaining social vitality and life expectancy among members of society is essential. People who have problems or illnesses for various reasons should be able to enjoy the same facilities as other people in the community. Therefore, with the development of technology and the design of smart tools, it is possible to help all members of society, especially the elderly and those with disabilities. The use of the "brain–computer interface (BCI)" seems to have been first coined by Jacques Vidal in 1973 [54]. BCI system is defined as the natural neural pathways to the output signal that bypasses the brain and translates into new types of output.

BCI to control external systems uses neural responses. BCI applications are the new way to improve the ability of doing daily works for disability people and the needy [8]. By new methods using on the applications, it is possible to help more and more [9]. Using different methods and algorithms can create a versatile smart tool.

4.2 Diagnosing Diseases

Neural networks can help in diagnosing patients' problems. In fact, people with physical and mental disabilities have some of the nerve signals that carry commands to the brain and cannot function properly. Most elderly also suffer from this physical and mental problem. Their physical problem is due to old age and inability to walk and pain in their limbs and other parts of their body, and their mental problem is due to diseases such as Alzheimer's or mental illness that they suffer from. These problems are due to the fact that over the years, their muscles have been weakened and over time they have faced weakness of the nerves. In this regard in [1], it is examined and proved that the design of applications based on neural networks have an important role in the care and health of the elderly. It seems that by examining neural algorithms, we can design applications that stimulate neural signals and see the result in the elderly.

Using of convolutional neural networks [10] is for image processing and vision processing, and also because medical image processing and disease diagnosis is one of the most important and challenging issues, this neural networks can be used to diagnosing diseases using the BCI applications [11]. Especially for the elderly who are more prone to physical injury, the use of accurate medical image processing methods is effective in diagnosing their disease. Older people may not be able to understand and express their problem for a variety of reasons.

Visual impairment or misunderstanding of conditions due to dementia or Alzheimer's cause's misdiagnosis of environmental conditions, so using convolutional neural networks can help detecting of eye movement of them. By recognizing eye movement, one can identify the purpose and needs of people who are unable to speak. Elderly people who cannot speak and don't have the brain disability to understand can show their goal by looking and eye movement and detection of eye movement by BCI applications is one of the most important points that should be considered in designing applications.

Optimization algorithms can help to make better choices and clustering and prioritize the various commands that are created in the brain. Three-dimensional (3D) convolutional neural networks (CNN) is a model of convolutional in 3D that allow us in real time to process the information contained in a neural signal channels and also information is stored in the communication between a channel and its neighbors [14]. The final feature representation combines information from all channels [15], and creates a targeted BCI application.

In [2], some models to prevent harm to the elderly are presented. The role of airbags [2] in reducing the incidence of injury to the individual is significant. The elderly are at risk due to physical weakness and sometimes poor eyesight. They may be injured and fall while walking and doing daily activities. Therefore in designing BCI applications for the elderly, important factors such as calculating body temperature and heart rate should always be considered. In most cases, the increasing or decreasing heart rate occurred by falling or damage. Also, improper nutrition or forgetfulness in taking their medications create symptoms such as discoloration of the face and low blood sugar or other cases. Deep learning algorithms and color recognition algorithms can play an effective role in preventing this damage from happening. Momentary changes in the patient's skin color, as well as the instantaneous recording of the patient's pressure and temperature, are effective by BCI applications. Deep learning algorithms can recorded any changes in the applications and then the right decision is made for each patient. Decreased or increased blood sugar causes a change in heart rate or darkening of the skin or lips. Also, high blood sugar causes a dry throat and a feeling of thirst in the patient, which is determined by the patient's facial expressions and eye conditions. The signals of the human brain react differently to these symptoms. So clustering techniques for the reactions and decision-making algorithms can help diagnose and solve the elderly person's problem. So, it is necessary for sending calculated information to doctors by the real-time sensors, and in case of any changes, the patient should be transferred to the medical center immediately. Activating the GPS sensors is one of the most important sensors that should be considered in the BCI applications. Deep learning and the use of clustering algorithms with GPS sensors have significant effects in selecting the best performance at the moment of injury to the patient. Using of deep learning techniques in BCI applications can reduce injury to the patient in real-time by activating the detection sensors. We can prioritize methods that reduce injury by selecting and clustering several factors.

In [3], it is examined and implemented the measures such as the height of elderly, distance and the angle of them to the ground. Due to the fact that older people fall more due to physical disability, changes in the angle of the legs and back of the elderly person should be recorded in real-time sensors. It seems that in order to perform accurate calculations, the person's height and scales such as the amount of curvature of the elderly person must be calculated, so that as soon as any changes occur in these situations, it can be photographed in 3D-positions and then alarmed to health centers. Hereon, using of intelligent learning methods helps in diagnosis. The measurement of the patient's heart rate or behaviors in the elderly after a fall should be carefully measured. If there is a problem such as shortness of breath, smart devices should be activated around the elderly.

Anemia is one of the most common diseases among the elderly. This disease has various complications such as dizziness, lack of concentration, distraction, etc. [20]. Diagnosis of anemia can also be recognized by a person's appearance. Symptoms such as discoloration of the face and nails, etc. are the first signs of anemia. In diagnosing various problems of anemia and trying to solve the problems of the elderly, it is necessary to carefully examine various factors. The combination of genetic algorithm and machine learning and neural networks and also clustering methods [19] can create a complete model that helps physicians to make more accurate decisions. These algorithms that are implemented on the BCI application activate the system in case of any problems. Optimizing the BCI algorithms that can evaluate the usability for hand therapy will help the World Health Organization (WHO) to provide better services [21]. The use of evolutionary methods can have important effects on achieving better results in this field.

Using optimization algorithms can make the best results by recording and examining the elderly person's condition. In this method, various factors should be defined as parameters of the algorithm and also the relationship of factors with each other, such as the relationship between facial discolorations with decreasing or increasing blood pressure. Rising or falling heart rate due to falling as a function should be defined. Changing each parameter at different times can determine the patient's condition at any time.

Because older people have heart problems or have had heart surgery, accurate diagnosis of heart rate among them is a crucial issue that needs to be evaluated more carefully, so activating heart rate sensors must be very accurate. Segmentation of heart rate sound using evolutionary algorithms can help in the optimal evaluated of heart rate [22].

The use of genetic algorithms in convolutional neural networks has shown that the detection and analysis of brain images have better results [28]. Various changes due to injury to the patient cause changes in brain signals. Brain signal processing along with brain image processing and facial image processing simultaneously can show excellent results from the patient's condition and eventually the use of deep learning methods can evaluate the results and make the decision right after each event.

The "silent speech BCI system" [29] is an interesting definition for recognizing sounds. Using clustering and segmentation methods based on images on this system has shown that brain signals have a better response than comprehension. In general, it is critical to use patterns that analyze nerve signals. Any changes in mood, behavior, and speech cause a change in nerve signals. This is not just about the elderly. Everyone reacts differently to each event based on their age. Therefore, data analysis of nerve signals in the elderly can make better decisions for the elderly.

Data mining and the application of semantic data patterns play an important role in recognizing the meaning of signals.

Every person at any age reacts differently to changes in heart rate. Of course, it is very important to note that some reactions or pain in parts of the body are similar, but it should be considered that data mining methods can categorize the reactions of the elderly or the mentally retarded or people with Alzheimer's. Hence it made a different decision for each person by intelligent applications. Systems that work with this technology also recognize limb images. It seems that this technology can have positive results for the elderly. Brain commands can be activated by displaying images of words. For example, by showing news or question sentences to the elderly who do not have good brain activity, it can be challenged. If the elderly do not have the ability to speak or talk, the brain command is displayed on the monitor. It seems that such BCI applications can be very useful in the future for many patients who have lost their speech due to any reason, especially due to stroke reason. Stroke was one of the most common causes of death in the world in 2011, which according to statistics is occurred about 6.2 million deaths [63]. A stroke occurs at any age, even in childhood, but the risk of developing this disease increases from the age of 30 and its cause varies according to age [64]. In the elderly and people over 45 years, various risk factors for stroke are higher [65]. According to the obtained results, it is necessary to design smart applications that can detect the symptoms of stroke among people, especially the elderly and those who are not able to express the problem and have in special condition. A number of symptoms at the time of stroke are common to all people that need to be considered in all applications, but due to different special conditions, especially the elderly who have different and more problems, stroke may have other complications or even with other symptoms may occur. Applications should offer different solutions for each age group to reduce the risk of serious injury or death. Intelligent clustering techniques combined with deep learning methods can help to identify and provide solutions tailored to each individual situation.

Patients with Alzheimer's disease may also have their brain signals stimulated and their exacerbation delayed. One of the first signs in the diagnosis of Alzheimer's is forgetting the latest events [66]. As the disease progresses, symptoms can include speech problems, getting lost in walking paths, mood swings, and loss of hope and motivation [66, 67]. Over time, the person at risk of injury often withdraws from family and society [66]. Gradually, the body's functions are destroyed and eventually causes death [68]. Although the rate of progression of this disease can vary between individuals, life expectancy after diagnosis and providing solutions to prevent the rapid growth of this disease is about three to nine years [69, 70]. In these patients, their psychological symptoms should be further investigated. Most seniors who develop Alzheimer's have this problem due to old age, getting away from the community, and reduced communication with others. Of course, part of this disease is inherited but this can be delayed with new methods in the age of technology. In this regard, it is necessary to implement an idea with cognitive sciences and a combination of cognitive and behavioral patterns to help people who are at the risk of Alzheimer's disease for do not suffering from dementia. By challenging the minds of older people, the nervous systems are stimulated and brain activity does not cause aging and the destruction of the nervous system.

EEG (electroencephalography) can detect brain function using electrodes attached to the scalp. EEG is commonly used to diagnose brain disorders, especially epilepsy or seizures and other brain disorders. Brain cells function in all conditions, even when the person is asleep, and are identified by electrodes as wavy lines on the EEG.

EEG analysis is performed using data analysis and calculation methods that help researchers to better understand brain function and physicians in selecting and diagnosing the brain–computer interface (BCI) [71]. Also it creates a new communication channel [72].

Epilepsy causes the death of nerve cells. People with the disease are exposed to other diseases. With the loss of nerve cells, people may develop speech disorders or Alzheimer's or other problems. Older people who are more prone to injury should avoid the factors that cause this problem. Regular monitoring of blood pressure and blood sugar regulation should be a priority for the elderly. A healthy diet should be considered for the elderly according to their body condition. Detection of symptoms related to epilepsy or seizures by detection algorithms can prevent the disease. The activities of brain cells can be examined and the results of brain cell function on the BCI application can be determined by the EEG analysis. In case of cell dysfunction, the BCI application should specify the patient's condition. Pattern detection method and intelligent learning algorithms help to assess the patient's condition.

One of the most common diseases among the elderly is dementia (mild cognition impairment). In [4], the types of dementia have been studied and using clustering methods has been identified to detect the dementia types and measurement items. The elderly with this disease have been divided into different groups. Using machine learning techniques for accurate division helps to select groups accurately. Each group receives applications tailored to them due to the different disabilities they have in their brains. For example, by conducting a study, elderly who talk difficulty and expressing words with delay or spelling-error distance value (SEDV) [5] can be placed in one group and it can be examined what other problems they may have, then it is provided other tools to strengthen their other problems too. By using deep learning algorithms, detecting dementia types with specific problems by brain–computer interfaces can be done and it helps to solve the patient's problem by providing services through BCI applications.

4.3   Movement Control

Another problem that older people face is using a wheelchair to get around and do their daily activities. Nowadays, with the advancement of technology, using of electronic wheelchairs has become popular. The wheelchair can move easily without the need to use a hand or without pushing another person [6]. The main base of electronic wheelchairs is to detect the behavior and reactions of the brain signals. In [7], designing intelligence wheelchair using deep learning patterns is presented. It is necessary to determine the path with instructions that are made through the patient's voice or eye movement towards the target. The use of noise detection algorithms, as well as the detection of brain commands according to the reactions that occur in the brain, helps to build ultra-intelligent wheelchairs.

Designing systems for remote object identification [16], and accurate delay calculation play an important role in route detection to prevent obstacles. Also using three-dimensional path detection algorithms [17] and RGB image processing using neural networks [18] to detect the objects or obstacles have crucial important. It seems that this architecture [17] can be implemented on the design of wheelchairs that work with the BCI application. Detection of an object in the path of the wheelchair is especially important for the elderly who are disabled to change the way by eyesight movement. In BCI applications it should be considered in real-time that if it doesn't any receiving to brain signals, the section of path detection in BCI will be able. Various features must be considered for accurate real-time detection. Clustering algorithms can help with the right choice and using the optimization algorithm can make the best choice at the real-time.

A brain-inspired neural network [12] is a potential approach that can learn the signal in different directions with high time accuracy by estimating the complexity of movements. Deep learning and the use of the BI-SNN method can help correlate changes in body muscles and changes in brain signals in BCI programs [13]. Using BI-SNN technique on EEG in BCI applications can have better results in real-time reactions.

4.4   IoT

The Internet of Things is a new intelligence technique for making objects smarter. In this technology, with wireless networks and the Internet, home appliances can be moved or turned on and off without the need of human-to-human or human-to-computer. An important part of the application of this technology is in healthcare and for people who are disabled. It has a significant impact on improving the quality of their lives. The advantages of this technology are much higher than its disadvantages and it seeks to eliminate the disadvantages and especially increase the security in this technology. The internet of Health things (IHT) for monitoring the vital signs of patients in the hospital [23] is introduced. The available data are collected from patients. According to the vital signs that are present in the patient, the diagnosis is made to solve the problem. It is useful for the elderly. The elderly should have a more accurate data set because they have different problems than others. Designing this method of using the application can help the elderly more. The issue of IoT security in medicine is pointed [24] and Internet of Medical things (IoMT) provides a solution that can store data more securely. If this method is provided in the BCI application, it can help to maintain the patient's health [25]. Elderly people with various diseases can use their own BCI applications. Depending on the symptoms, each person should use their own smart objects. Someone with Alzheimer's should use reminder BCI application and someone with speech disorders or has had a heart attack or his brain cells have been destroyed due to old age should use smart objects that can control a person's function. At the moment that the elderly needs help, smart objects should be used according to the specific situation. Activation of the smart object is done using detection techniques based on the target signals.

4.5   Cognitive Science

The elderly live mostly in quiet and unchangeable environments. They cannot go out of the house because of their disabilities. So it's an important point to address in terms of psychology for improving the quality of their lifestyle. Knowing the mental state of each patient [27] and providing an environment that is in accordance with the taste of each patient can help increase self-confidence and raise the morale of the elderly and thus help the longevity of the elderly. Influence of interior design elements is a positive point for the elderly and it is seemed it is needed to empower the BCI applications [26]. We can use the cognitive science to learn more about the elderly in terms of their favorite color tastes. Cognitive scientists focus on how the nervous system, intelligence and behavior are studied. Designing intelligent systems and using the Internet of Things using cognitive science can be effective in designing a quality system.

By recognizing the facial moods, it is possible to identify the different situations of aging people. Detecting a state of happiness, sadness and even detecting the changing in the face color that can be the symbol of a problem in the patient's body is essential with the highest accuracy rate [30]. Designing a face recognition BCI application that can achieve face images and the symptoms of any problem with high efficiency is one of the essential points in designing BCI applications. Using cognitive algorithms can have important role in designing of this tools.

Cognitive health is one of the topics in general brain health that discusses the ability of the elderly to think, learn and remember information. One of the most important daily tasks of people in order to take care of physical health is cognitive health. Dividing each person's moods using clustering methods based on the age and gender criteria of each elderly person can help to provide a solution for his health. Therefore, different learning tools must be implemented according to the specific conditions. So it can provide services to everyone according to its own conditions. Designing smart objects smarter in order to recognize and provide services to each person using deep learning algorithms can be a positive point in making smart systems and applications smarter.

Applications games should also be designed for educational purposes. Brain games that can challenge the mind, are useful for every ages. Children increase their analytical power with games. In the same way, designing games that are appropriate for the age of young people or the elderly promotes their mind and especially using games in the many diseases of elderly can be prevented. Alzheimer's disease or lack of self-confidence in the elderly due to their distance from technology are factors that should be considered in designing game ideas. Online games have the best ideas for gaming that expand communication between people. There are several benefits to designing online gaming applications for the elderly. MindGameku game [31] has been presented using convolutional neural network technique and deep learning and the acceptance of this game has increased by reviewing the results. It can be used for the elderly by examining this game and expanding it.

The GO game is a two-player game designed using deep neural networks [32]. It has important challenging effects on mind and will can use for elderly. Go is a strategy game that try to encircle the further territory. This game is one of the first board games that still has many fans [33]. If this game is presented in multiplayer, it can attract many people and also positive results will be obtained. This game with a special application for the elderly can be very useful for them.

Smart games should be tailored to the needs of the elderly and they challenge the minds of the elderly. The challenge of smart games should change daily. It should have aimed at improving and strengthening the patient mentally and physically. Elderly people who are sedentary can change their lifestyle with attractive and cheerful intelligence games. The elderly who are physically disabled can use daily challenging games that are related to their minds. Choosing the best intelligence game and changing the style of play by deep learning methods can be effective in the direction of the elderly lifestyle.

Games that are written or visual should be designed for older people with different conditions. Those who have hearing problems should use intelligence video games and those who have vision problems should use online games with audio techniques. Providing different methods in games allow most people to use. It seems that it is possible to design BCI applications that provide each game in a various multimedia technology [35] at the same time. The role of graphics and animations in designing game is very influential [34]. The most important advantage of these BCI games is that the elderly with different conditions can enjoy playing together at the same time, and the impacts of the services is very great for the elderly. Not separating people from each other because of certain problems they have, especially in the elderly or disabled, makes them live together actively and motivated.

4.6 Olfactory System

The human olfactory system is one of the essential systems in the human body [38]. The olfactory nerves may be damaged for a variety of reasons. These changes are more common in the elderly [36, 39]. One of the causes that has occurred in the last years is Covid19 disease. It effects on the olfactory loss of individuals [40]. Usually people with Alzheimer's lose their sense of smell or sometimes their sense of smell changes [37]. Olfactory memory is an odor-evoked memory that is used on elderly and can used to detect some odor impairments [46]. Using of intelligent methods in the accurate diagnosis of this problem is effective. The applications that can monitor a patient's olfactory impairment based on brain cell function can be a good option for diagnosing the disease.

An important discussion is to create conditions for the elderly who have olfactory disorders and may be harmed. The harms of this situation, which was very enjoyable for them in their youth, are not enjoying the smell of food.

Lack of sense of smell, in addition to not enjoying the taste and aroma, has other health effects. For example, Gas leaks [41] are one of the most dangerous things that can happen in homes. Gas leaks are one of the most common causes of death in homes, which can be prevented by rapid detection of gas odor. People with olfactory problems are more at risk. Elderly people with olfactory problems or physical disabilities cannot protect themselves in the event of an accident and they are vulnerable to lack of sense of smell. Therefore, by designing powerful applications, such problems should be prevented.

The use of smart sensors in detecting environmental conditions can prevent this from happening and also using of smart sensors in smartphones. Applications can alert health centers in the event of changes in temperature and odor. Intelligent olfactory system [42] is a very useful and excellent technology that can be useful for people who have an olfactory problem for any reason. This system with its conditions can simulate the olfactory nerves and the patient can understand the sense of smell around him. This system can reduce the disadvantages of lack of sense of smell to some extent. Neural networks have a significant impact on the development of intelligent olfactory systems [44]. In the design of intelligence systems, deep learning [43] and graph theories [45] and pattern recognition and clustering on olfactory intelligence systems [47] help to analyze various parameters. It provides better models for more accurate intelligent olfactory system design.

Wireless systems can be a good option for designing applications that are widely used. These systems use radio wave technology and can be activated via Bluetooth or the Internet. Using wireless systems in BCI applications is very useful. Designing BCI wireless applications [48] is a good option for applications used by the elderly. Maybe there are advantages and disadvantages to these applications. The advantage of these systems is the lack of physical connection and the disadvantage is that the elderly may not be able to active this application. The challenging issue that seems to be debated is whether these systems have negative influences on the functioning brains of the elderly because of the waves they have or not. Due to the effects that waves have on the brain, the use of wireless applications should be designed based on the conditions of each elderly person. Diagnosis of the use of wireless systems is selected with criteria. The program should be taught by clustering algorithms and deep learning what commands to execute according to each person's situation.

The olfactory system using Wi-Fi can maintain high-quality olfactory signals for a limited time [53]. Designing a BCI application that can understand the environmental conditions by recording and maintaining signals can be useful for the elderly or disabled.

4.7   Brain-to-Brain (B2B) Communication Systems

Brain-to-brain (B2B) communication systems can facilitate the exchange of information between people by transmitting signals with non-invasive interface [50]. Also the multi-person brain-to-brain system [52] is more able to make more conversation. The systems learn to trust the signals sent [49]. The B2B social network [51] can be designed to make conversations between people. These systems transmit waves through the scalp and they are a way of hyper-interaction. It seems that the using of this system in applications is very necessary. This system can help to improve the condition of the elderly by communicating between people. B2B social networks help to communicate between people. The best conditions can be established in the design of these systems using different criteria. Depending on the circumstances of each individual and the clustering of individuals based on similar criteria, the interaction between individuals is created. The method of clustering in selecting relief centers can play an effective role in improving the situation of people in need. Implemented algorithms can be a good choice in this system based on the objective function. Patterns based on learning functions can also be used.

4.8 Hearing

A hearing aid is a device that helps hearing-impaired people to hear sound in its entirety or with higher quality. According to the results, hearing loss and aging are related. With age, the problem of hearing loss increases among the elderly. This problem has other negative consequences [77].

Research has shown that a small number of people with hearing loss use hearing aids [74]. It seems that the high cost and lack of health insurance for patients makes it impossible for them to use hearing aids.

With hearing loss, the communication between people decreases. The resulting is social isolation and depression, which reduces the quality of life. To reduce these injuries, using a hearing aid [73] can be helpful.

Smartphones played an important role in the design of modern hearing aids [79]. Early hearing aids guided sounds in front of the ear and blocked all other sounds. These hearing aids were placed behind or inside the ear. Modern devices try to make the sound audible by changing the ambient sound. These devices use signal processing to improve auditory and speech performance. The use of signal processing algorithms to reduce noise and reduce the frequency of sound plays an important role in the performance of these devices. User-friendly is also one of the important features that should be considered [78]. Also, using of the devices can be expanded the signal processing methods and also aging cause's changes in the auditory nerves [103]. Therefore, choosing a hearing aid suitable for the age and condition of people helps to improve their condition.

Using smart hearing aids and hearing aids that work with Bluetooth or Wi-Fi can be a step towards smart hearing aids. Of course, it must be considered whether the waves that are in direct contact with the nerves of the ear based on the on or off of Wi-Fi cause more damage or not. All the efforts that researchers make to design the tools smarter are for the welfare of the people. It should be noted that modernization does not reduce the health of the elderly or disabled or those who are more at risk.

One of the things that can have a positive effect on the elderly is the intelligent operation of applications, in a way that changes the sound of music according to the level of hearing. So that people can easily hear the sound of movies or music or radio. This automatic change of sound according to the person's hearing threshold should be so intelligent that no disturbance is felt in the person's hearing. Designing BCI applications according to the hearing of an elderly person can help to create their vitality. Deep learning algorithms with cognitive methods on detecting a person's moods provide them with situational selection patterns according to each person's circumstances to motivate and make the person feel good.

Most elderly have hearing loss problems and use hearing aids or cochlear implants. They also use magnetic resonance imaging (MRI) more than other people. According to studies [82], MRI imaging is not suitable for those who have cochlear implants due to its waves and causes damage to their health. Because MRI is essential for the elderly, it is necessary to use another method to reduce their hearing problems to reduce damage to their health. Using some applications can be an alternative to cochlear implants [83]. BCI applications based on visual can have influences impacts on helping hearing loss [84]. Improving the performance of this auditory BCI and controlling the processing of hearing aids is essential.

An important point is that the popularity of using smart devices is growing among the elderly. Also a number of people with various problems have welcomed the use of smart controls that can make their work easier. Using voice interfaces in BCI applications can increase the usefulness of the application [80].

One of the most important points in hearing aids should be the usual combination with auditory attention detection (AAD) in BCI applications. This technology can be used to play music for hearing impaired people or people who have cochlear implants [81].

Most BCI systems based on visual stimuli use a number of auditory stimuli. These systems can be a good choice for people with visual or physical disabilities because they are not dependent on vision [85]. Synchronous or asynchronous in BCI applications can make differences in their performance. These systems are divided into two categories of synchronous and non-synchronous according to the response time and accuracy [86]. Devices that need to respond quickly to a function are a priority.

4.9   Diabetes

Diabetes is one of the hundreds of common diseases that the elderly suffer from. It should be detected and controlled using smart tools. Diagnosing diabetes by using applications can reduce the incidence of the problem. Introducing algorithms along with intelligent learning methods [87, 88] can help control this disease. Smart phones can help patients and medical centers by detecting and notifications for taking medications with reliable apps.

The symptoms of diabetes diseases can be diagnosed for patients who have only diabetes. But the elderly who have problems other than diabetes such as Alzheimer's or speech impairment may be more at risk.

Diabetes in elderly people is often diagnosed with symptoms dementia and urinary incontinence [90]. The risk of cardiovascular disease in older people with diabetes is more than double that of non-diabetics. Therapeutic goals for controlling blood sugar, blood pressure, and cholesterol should be considered in the elderly [91].

4.10   Urinary Incontinence

Designing multipurpose applications is critical for these people. Using of neural signals, clustering methods and convolution neural networks can be effective in designing the applications [89].

In [75], it has been shown that some elderly people have urinary incontinence. One of the most common causes of incontinence is due to overactive bladder and stress, which disrupts the life system of people with the disease [76].

Urinary incontinence is more common among the elderly. Various factors affect this disease. Old age and lack of concentration and even sneezing and coughing can cause this to happen [93]. Strategies for controlling urinary incontinence have been identified [92]. It seem to alleviate this problem to some extent. Controlling urinary incontinence can have a positive effect on mood and positive life trends in the elderly. The methods of managing urinary incontinence using smart applications is examined [94]. These applications must meet several important criteria. Including respect for user privacy and maintaining psychological security between the patient and the medical center are the most important factors. It seems that providing an application that can calm the minds of people, especially the elderly who are more prone to psychological trauma, can play a role in treatment and control or prevention.

Improper closure of the bladder can cause problems called stress urinary incontinence (SUI). Stress incontinence is commonly seen in men after prostate surgery [96], and also in pregnant women, childbirth, obesity, and menopause. It is often with weak pelvic floor. It is leading to inadequate closure and stress incontinence [97–99]. Also the incidence of post-menopausal stress incontinence increases. It is especially in older women [100].

It is necessary to reduce the incidence of this problem by managing other problems, due to the various problems that cause urinary incontinence in the elderly.

Exercise can be effective in reducing stress and then reducing urinary incontinence. Exercise related to this problem in the elderly increases their physical vitality. "Kegel exercise", known as pelvic floor exercise, causes the muscles to contract and relax constantly, thereby restoring the strength of the pelvic floor muscles [101]. This exercise should be performed simultaneously for several minutes several times during the day and its effect is determined about one to three months after the start of exercise [102]. They have profound influences for treatment the elderly. Using BCI applications to training and checking how to exercise can be advantaged for elderly. The effect of using applications in controlling incontinence on the improvement of pelvic floor muscles has been identified and it is hoped that the use of these applications will have a positive effect on reducing the disease and improving the patient's health [95]. It is necessary to use of learning patterns that can help in designing a smart application. By diagnosing the person's condition and recognizing the symptoms related to stress that are result the urinary incontinence, different ways should be offered to the person. The solutions should be according to the ability of the elderly by cognitive methods. Therefore, super-intelligent patterns can bring good results for the elderly.

4.11   Conclusion

The elderly are an important part of society their needs to be addressed. A society that can protect its elderly can thrive on science and technology and healthy living. Symptoms that develop over time due to old age should be identified and prevented or treated. These symptoms can be detected using modern methods. Designing smart programs that can detect physical or mental harm to the elderly can help to prevent it. In this chapter, the factors that are determined by old age were examined and methods and applications that could examine different criteria were introduced. It is possible to monitor the physical or mental disabilities of the elderly by designing BCI applications. It can help these people in case of injury. These applications also help to improve the physical and mental condition of the elderly by providing services.

References

1. Mansoor, A., Usman, M.W., Jamil, N., Naeem, M.A., Deep learning algorithm for brain–computer interface. *Sci. Program.*, 2020, Article ID 5762149, 2020.

2. Guo, S., Xie, Y., Li, Y., Research on the prediction model of elderly fall, in: *MATEC Web of Conferences, EDP Sciences*, vol. 336, p. 07019, 2021.

3. Mahdi, S.Q., Gharghan, S.K., Hasan, M.A., FPGA-based neural network for accurate distance estimation of elderly falls using WSN in an indoor environment. *Measurement*, 167, 108276, 2021.

4. Fukushima, A., Morooka, R., Tanaka, H., Kentaro, H., Tugawa, A., Hanyu, H., Classification of dementia type using the brain–computer interface. *Artif. Life Robot.*, 26, 2, 216–221, 2021.

5. Kurihara, R., Tanaka, H., Umahara, T., BCI character input characteristics in patients with mild dementia, in: *Human Interface Symposium*, 2017.

6. Xin, L., Gao, S., Tang, J., Xu, X., Design of a brain controlled wheelchair, in: *2018 IEEE 4th International Conference on Control Science and Systems Engineering (ICCSSE)*, IEEE, pp. 112–116, 2018.

7. Zubair, Z.R.S., A deep learning based optimization model for based computer interface of wheelchair directional control. *Tikrit J. Pure Sci.*, 26, 1, 108–112, 2021.

8. Belkacem, A.N., Jamil, N., Palmer, J.A., Ouhbi, S., Chen, C., Brain computer interfaces for improving the quality of life of older adults and elderly patients. *Front. Neurosci.*, 14, 692, 2020.

9. Saha, S., Mamun, K.A., Ahmed, K., II, Mostafa, R., Naik, G.R., Darvishi, S., Khandoker, A.H., Baumert, M., Progress in brain computer interface: Challenges and potentials. *Front. Syst. Neurosci.*, 15, 4, 2021.

10. Le Cun, Y., LeNet-5, convolutional neural networks. 20, 5, 14, 2015. URL: http://yann. lecun. com/exdb/lenet.

11. Kwon, J. and Im, C.-H., Subject-independent functional near-infrared spectroscopy-based brain–computer interfaces based on convolutional neural networks. *Front. Hum. Neurosci.*, 15, 121, 2021.

12. Ionescu, M., Paun, G., Yokomori, T., Spiking neural P systems. *Fundam. Inform.*, 71, 2, 3, 279–308, 2006.

13. Kumarasinghe, K., Kasabov, N., Taylor, D., Brain-inspired spiking neural networks for decoding and understanding muscle activity and kinematics from electroencephalography signals during hand movements. *Sci. Rep.*, 11, 1, 1–15, 2021.

14. Valenti, A., Barsotti, M., Bacciu, D., Ascari, L., A deep classifier for upper-limbs motor anticipation tasks in an online BCI setting. *Bioengineering*, 8, 2, 21, 2021.

15. Ji, S., Xu, W., Yang, M., Yu, K., 3D convolutional neural networks for human action recognition. *IEEE Trans. Pattern Anal. Mach. Intell.*, 35, 1, 221–231, 2012.

16. Arnold, E., Omar, Y., Al-Jarrah, M.D., Fallah, S., Oxtoby, D., Mouzakitis, A., A survey on 3D object detection methods for autonomous driving applications. *IEEE Trans. Intell. Transport. Syst.*, 20, 10, 3782–3795, 2019.

17. Bird's eye view LiDAR point cloud based real-time 3D object detection for autonomous driving, in: *2021 IEEE International Intelligent Transportation Systems Conference (ITSC)*, 2809-2815, IEEE, 2021.

18. Shrivastava, S., VR3Dense: Voxel representation learning for 3D object detection and monocular dense depth reconstruction. arXiv preprint arXiv:2104.05932, 2021.

19. Kilicarslan, S., Celik, M., Sahin, Ş., Hybrid models based on genetic algorithm and deep learning algorithms for nutritional anemia disease classification. *Biomed. Signal Process. Control*, 63, 102231, 2021.

20. Gambhir, I.S., Jain, A., Pujar, D., Srivastava, A., Chakrabarti, S.S., Prasad, S., Iron deficiency anemia in elderly patients-A cross-sectional study from a tertiary teaching and research hospital in North India. *The Indian Journal of Gerontology, XXIX, I-IV*. ISSN-0971-8060: 27.

21. Zulauf-Czaja, A., Al-Taleb, M.K.H., Purcell, M., Petric-Gray, N., Cloughley, J., Vuckovic, A., On the way home: A BCI-FES hand therapy self-managed by sub-acute SCI participants and their caregivers: A usability study. *J. Neuro Eng. Rehab.*, 18, 1, 1–18, 2021.

22. Alonso-Arévalo, M.A., Cruz-Gutiérrez, A., Ibarra-Hernández, R.F., García-Canseco, E., Conte-Galván, R., Robust heart sound segmentation based on spectral change detection and genetic algorithms. *Biomed. Signal Process. Control*, 63, 102208, 2021.

23. Da Costa, C.A., Pasluosta, C.F., Eskofier, B., Da Silva, D.B., Rosa Righi, R., Internet of Health Things: Toward intelligent vital signs monitoring in hospital wards. *Artif. Intell. Med.*, 89, 61–69, 2018.

24. Gatouillat, A., Badr, Y., Massot, B., Sejdić, E., Internet of medical things: A review of recent contributions dealing with cyber-physical systems in medicine. *IEEE J. Internet Things*, 5, 5, 3810–3822, 2018.

25. Park, S., Cha, H.-S., Kwon, J., Kim, H., Im, C.-H., Development of an online home appliance control system using augmented reality and an ssvep-based brain–computer interface, in: *2020 8th International Winter Conference on Brain–Computer Interface (BCI)*, IEEE, pp. 1–2, 2020.

26. Engineer, A., Sternberg, E.M., Najafi, B., Designing interiors to mitigate physical and cognitive deficits related to aging and to promote longevity in older adults: A review. *Gerontology*, 64, 6, 612–622, 2018.

27. Kadakkuzha, B.M., Akhmedov, K., Capo, T.R., Carvalloza, A.C., Fallahi, M., Puthanveettil, S.V., Age-associated bidirectional modulation of gene expression in single identified R15 neuron of aplysia. *BMC Genom.*, 141, 1–14, 2013.

28. Lee, S., Kim, J., Kang, H., Kang, D.-Y., Park, J., Genetic algorithm based deep learning neural network structure and hyperparameter optimization. *Appl. Sci.*, 11, 2, 744, 2021.

29. Min, B., Kim, J., Park, H.-J., Lee, B., Vowel imagery decoding toward silent speech BCI using extreme learning machine with electroencephalogram. *Biomed Res. Int.*, 2016, Article ID 2618265, 2016.

30. Zhi, H. and Liu, S., Face recognition based on genetic algorithm. *J. Vis. Commun. Image Rep.*, 58, 495–502, 2019.
31. Li, M., Li, F., Pan, J., Zhang, D., Zhao, S., Li, J., Wang, F., The MindGomoku: An online P300 BCI game based on Bayesian deep learning. *Sensors*, 21, 5, 1613, 2021.
32. Clark, C. and Storkey, A., Training deep convolutional neural networks to play go, in: *International conference on machine learning*, PMLR, pp. 1766–1774, 2015.
33. Shotwell, P., The game of go: Speculations on its origins and symbolism in ancient China. *Changes*, 2008, 1–62, 1994.
34. Cattan, G., The use of brain–computer interfaces in games is not ready for the general public. *Front. Comput. Sci.*, 3, 628773, 2021.
35. Kuang, Z. and Tie, X., A survey of multimedia technologies and robust algorithms, 2021. arXiv preprint arXiv:2103.13477.
36. Doty, R.L. and Kamath, V., The influences of age on olfaction: A review. *Front. Physcol.*, 5, 20, 2014.
37. Vilensky, J.A., Robertson, W., Suarez-Quian, C.A., *The clinical anatomy of the cranial nerves: The nerves of "on old olympus towering top"*, John Wiley & Sons, Wiley-Blackwell, 2015.
38. Saladin, K.S. and Miller, L., *Anatomy & physiology*, WCB/McGraw-Hill, New York, 1998.
39. Makowska, I., Kloszewska, I., Grabowska, A., Szatkowska, I., Rymarczyk, K., Olfactory deficits in normal aging and Alzheimer's disease in the polish elderly population. *Arch. Clin. Neuropsychol.*, 26, 3, 270–279, 2011.
40. Whitcroft, K.L. and Hummel, T., Olfactory dysfunction in COVID-19: Diagnosis and management. *JAMA*, 323, 24, 2512–2514, 2020.
41. Kletz, T.A., Learning from accidents: Routledge, 978-0-7506-4883-7, 2007.
42. Gao, Z., Chen, S., Li, R., Lou, Z., Han, W., Jiang, K., Qu, F., Shen, G., An artificial olfactory system with sensing, memory and self-protection capabilities. *Nano Energy*, 86, 106078, 2021.
43. Zhang, J., Tian, T., Wang, S., Liu, X., Shu, X., Wang, Y., Research on an olfactory neural system model and its applications based on deep learning. *Neural Comput. Appl.*, 32, 10, 5713–5724, 2020.
44. Gardner, J.W., Hines, E.L., Wilkinson, M., Application of artificial neural networks to an electronic olfactory system. *Meas. Sci. Technol.*, 1, 5, 446, 1990.
45. Meunier, D., Fonlupt, P., Saive, A.-L., Plailly, J., Ravel, N., Royet, J.-P., Modular structure of functional networks in olfactory memory. *Neuroimage*, 95, 264–275, 2014.
46. Tzeng, W.-Y., Figarella, K., Garaschuk, O., Olfactory impairment in men and mice related to aging and amyloid-induced pathology. *Pflügers Archiv-Eur. J. Physiol.*, 473, 5, 805–821, 2021.
47. Sankaran, S., Khot, L.R., Panigrahi, S., Biology and applications of olfactory sensing system: A review. *Sens. Actuators B: Chem.*, 171, 1–17, 2012.

48. Lee, S., Shin, Y., Woo, S., Kim, K., Lee, H.-N., Review of wireless brain–computer interface systems. Brain-computer interface systems-recent progress and future prospects, 215–238, 2013.

49. Jiang, L., Stocco, A., Losey, D.M., Abernethy, J.A., Prat, C.S., Rao, R.P.N., BrainNet: A multi-person brain-to-brain interface for direct collaboration between brains. *Sci. Rep.*, 9, 1, 1–11, 2019.

50. Grau, C., Ginhoux, R., Riera, A., Nguyen, T.L., Chauvat, H., Berg, M., Amengual, J.L., Pascual-Leone, A., Ruffini, G., Conscious brain-to-brain communication in humans using non-invasive technologies. *PloS One*, 9, 8, e105225, 2014.

51. Hasson, U., Ghazanfar, A.A., Galantucci, B., Garrod, S., Keysers, C., Brain-to-brain coupling: A mechanism for creating and sharing a social world. *Trends Cogn. Sci.*, 16, 2, 114–121, 2012.

52. Hildt, E., Multi-person brain-to-brain interfaces: Ethical issues. *Front. Neurosci.*, 13, 1177, 2019.

53. Zhang, B., Zhuang, L., Qin, Z., Wei, X., Yuan, Q., Qin, C., Wang, P., A wearable system for olfactory electrophysiological recording and animal motion control. *J. Neurosci. Method.*, 307, 221–229, 2018.

54. Vidal, J.J., Toward direct brain–computer communication. *Annu. Rev. Biophys. Bioeng.*, 2, 1, 157–180, 1973.

55. Bowen, R.L. and Atwood, C.S., Living and dying for sex. *Gerontology*, 50, 5, 265–290, 2004.

56. Rodríguez Valiente, A., Trinidad, A., García Berrocal, J.R., Górriz, C., Ramírez Camacho, R., Extended high-frequency (9–20 kHz) audiometry reference thresholds in 645 healthy subjects. *Int. J. Audiol.*, 53, 8, 531–545, 2014.

57. Walling, A. and Dickson, G., Hearing loss in older adults. *Am. Family Phys.*, 85, 12, 1150–1156, 2012.

58. Larson, E.B., Yaffe, K., Langa, K.M., New insights into the dementia epidemic. *New Engl. J. Med.*, 369, 24, 2275, 2013.

59. Belikov, A.V., Age-related diseases as vicious cycles. *Ageing Res. Res.*, 49, 11–26, 2019.

60. Saravanakumar Pichumani, T.V.P., Sundararajan, R.K.D., Nam, Y., Kadry, S., Ruzicka indexed regressive homomorphic ephemeral key Benaloh cryptography for secure data aggregation in WSN. *J. Internet Technol.*, 22, 6, 1287–1297, Nov. 2021.

61. Guevvera, Y., World Health Organisation: Neonatal and perinatal mortality: Country, regional and global estimates. *WHO Cebu: Sun*, 9241563206, 2006.

62. Worrall, L.E. and Hickson, L.M.H., Communication disability in aging: From prevention to intervention, 0-7693-0015-4, 2003.

63. Tilwani, K., Jangid, P., Tilwani, R.K., Nagal, M., Comparative study of carotid-femoral pulse wave velocity and carotid intima-media thickness with age & gender in cerebrovascular accident (CVA) patients and healthy control individual. *Int. J. Basic Appl. Physiol.*, 8, 1, 62, 2019.

64. Ellekjær, H., Holmen, J., Indredavik, B., Terent, A., *Epidemiology* of *stroke* in: *Innherred, Norway, 1994* to *1996: Incidence and 30-day case-fatality rate. Stroke, 28*, 11, 2180–2184, 1997.

65. Feldman, E.L., Cornblath, D.R., Porter, J., Dworkin, R., Scherer, S., National Institute of Neurological Disorders and Stroke (NINDS), in: *Advances in understanding and treating neuropathy*, 2008, 1–6, Bethesda, Maryland, 24–25 October 2006.

66. Burns, A and Iliffe, S., Alzheimer's disease. *BMJ*, 338, b158, 2009.

67. Revi, M., Alzheimer's disease therapeutic approaches, in: *Genedis*, 2018, pp. 105–116, Springer, Cham, 2020.

68. Dhanaraj, R.K., Krishnasamy, L., Geman, O., Izdrui, D.R., *Black hole and sink hole attack detection in wireless body area networks. Comput. Mater. Continua,* 68, 2, 1949–1965, 2021.

69. Querzfurth, H.W., Review article. Mechanism of disease Alzheimer's disease. *New Engl. J. Med.*, 362, 329–344, 2010.

70. Todd, S., Barr, S., Roberts, M., Passmore, A.P., Survival in dementia and predictors of mortality: A review. *Int. J. Geriatr. Psychiatry*, 28, 11, 1109–1124, 2013.

71. Pardey, J., Roberts, S., Tarassenko, L., A review of parametric modelling techniques for EEG analysis. *Med. Eng. Phys.*, 181, 2–11, 1996.

72. Ramoser, H., Muller-Gerking, J., Pfurtscheller, G., Optimal spatial filtering of single trial EEG during imagined hand movement. *IEEE Trans. Rehabil. Eng.*, 8, 4, 441–446, 2000.

73. MacDonald, A.A., Joyson, A., Lee, R., Seymour, D.G., Soiza, R.L., The effect of hearing augmentation on cognitive assessment scales at admission to hospital. *Am. J. Geriatr. Psychiatry*, 20, 4, 355–361, 2012.

74. Popelka, M.M., Cruickshanks, K.J., Wiley, T.L., Tweed, T.S., Klein, B.E.K., Klein, R., Low prevalence of hearing aid use among older adults with hearing loss: The epidemiology of hearing loss study. *J. Am.Geriatr. Soc.*, 46, 9, 1075–1078, 1998.

75. Shah, D. and Badlani, G., Treatment of overactive bladder and incontinence in the elderly. *Rev. Urol.*, 4, Suppl 4, S38, 2002.

76. Sims, J., Browning, C., Lundgren-Lindquist, B., Kendig, H., Urinary incontinence in a community sample of older adults: Prevalence and impact on quality of life. *Disabil. Rehabil.*, 33, 15–16, 1389–1398, 2011.

77. Jaul, E. and Barron, J., Age-related diseases and clinical and public health implications for the 85 years old and over population. *Public Health Front.*, 5, 335, 2017.

78. Wei, Q., *et al.* Develop a low price wireless binaural hearing device using 2.4 GHz GFSK method., 3-06, 2012.

79. Mills, M., Hearing aids and the history of electronics miniaturization. *IEEE Ann. Hist. Comput.*, 33, 2, 24–45, 2011.

80. Kopeć, W., Kowalski, J., Paluch, J., Jaskulska, A., Skorupska, K.H., Niewiński, M., Krzywicki, M., Biele, C., Older adults and brain–computer interface:

An exploratory study, in: *Extended Abstracts of the 2021 CHI Conference on Human Factors in Computing Systems*, pp. 1–5, 2021.

81. Belo, J., Clerc, M., Schön, D., EEG-based auditory attention detection and its possible future applications for passive BCI. *Front. Comput. Sci.*, 3, 661178, 2021.

82. Fierens, G., Standaert, N., Peeters, R., Glorieux, C., Verhaert, N., Safety of active auditory implants in magnetic resonance imaging. *J. Otol.*, 16, 3, 185–198, 2021.

83. Rutkowski, T.M. and Mori, H., Tactile and bone-conduction auditory brain computer interface for vision and hearing impaired users. *J. Neurosci. Methods*, 244, 45–51, 2015.

84. Krishnasamy, L., Ramasamy, T., Dhanaraj, R., CHinnasamy, P., A geodesic deployment and radial shaped clustering (RSC) algorithm with statistical aggregation in sensor networks. *Turk. J. Elec. Eng. Comput. Sci.*, 29, 3, 1464–1478, 2021.

85. da Silva Souto, C., Lüddemann, H., Lipski, S., Dietz, M., Kollmeier, B., Influence of attention on speech-rhythm evoked potentials: First steps towards an auditory brain–computer interface driven by speech. *Biomed. Phys. Eng. Express*, 2, 6, 065009, 2016.

86. Bonci, A., Fiori, S., Higashi, H., Tanaka, T., Verdini, F., An introductory tutorial on brain–computer interfaces and their applications. *Electronics*, 10, 5, 560, 2021.

87. Abaker, A.A. and Fakhreldeen, A.S., A comparative analysis of machine learning algorithms to build a predictive model for detecting diabetes complications. *Informatica*, 45, 1, 2021.

88. Bharadwaj, H.K., Agarwal, A., Chamola, V., Lakkaniga, N.R., Hassija, V., Guizani, M., Sikdar, B., A review on the role of machine learning in enabling IoT based healthcare applications. *IEEE Access*, 9, 38859–38890, 2021.

89. Swapna, G., Vinayakumar, R., Soman, K.P., Diabetes detection using deep learning algorithms. *ICT Express*, 4, 4, 243–246, 2018.

90. Mordarska, K. and Godziejewska-Zawada, M., Diabetes in the elderly. *Prz. Menopauzalny= Menopause Rev.*, 16, 2, 38, 2017.

91. Kilvert, A. and Fox, C., Diagnosis and management of diabetes in older people. *Pract. Diabetes*, 34, 6, 195–199, 2017.

92. Si Ching, L., II, Managing the elderly with urinary incontinence and dementia. *Int. Arch. Urol. Complic.*, 3, 027, 2017.

93. Dhanaraj, R.K. *et al.*, Random forest bagging and x-means clustered antipattern detection from SQL query log for accessing secure mobile data. *Wirel. Commun. Mobil. Comput.*, 2021, Article ID 2730246, 9 pages, 2021.

94. Dantas, L.O., Carvalho, C., de Jesus Santos, B.L., Ferreira, C.H.J., Bo, K., Driusso, P., Mobile health technologies for the management of urinary incontinence: A systematic review of online stores in Brazil. *Braz. J. Phys. Ther.*, 25, 4, 387–395, 2021.

95. Nagib, L., Bellotto, A., Riccetto, C., Martinho, N.M., Camargos Pennisi, P.R., Blumenberg, C., Paranhos, L.R., Botelho, S., Use of mobile apps for controlling of the urinary incontinence: A systematic review. *Neurourol. Urodyn.*, 39, 4, 1036–1048, 2020.

96. Nitti, V.W., The prevalence of urinary incontinence. *Rev. Urol.*, 3, Suppl 1, S2, 2001.

97. Ramasamy, M.D., Periasamy, K., Krishnasamy, L., Dhanaraj, R.K., Kadry, S., Nam, Y., Multi-disease classification model using Strassen's half of threshold (SHoT) training algorithm in healthcare sector. *IEEE Access*, 9, 112624–112636, 2021.

98. Rortveit, G., Hannestad, Y.S., Daltveit, A.K., Hunskaar, S., Age- and type-dependent effects of parity on urinary incontinence: The Norwegian EPINCONT study. *Obstet. Gynecol.*, 98, 6, 1004–10, 2001 Dec.

99. Lukacz, E.S., Lawrence, J.M., Contreras, R., Nager, C.W., Luber, K.M., Parity, mode of delivery, and pelvic floor disorders. *Obstet. Gynecol.*, 107, 6, 1253–60, 2006 Jun.

100. Crepin, G., Biserte, J., Cosson, M., Duchene, F., Appareil génital féminin et sport de haut niveau, in: *[The female urogenital system and high level sports]*, vol. 190, pp. 1479–91, discussion 1491–3, October 2006.

101. Dumoulin, C., Cacciari, L.P., Hay-Smith, E.J.C., Pelvic floor muscle training versus no treatment, or inactive control treatments, for urinary incontinence in women. *Cochrane Database Syst. Rev.*, 10, CD005654, 2018-10-04.

102. Ramakrishnan, V., Chenniappan, P., Dhanaraj, R.K., Hsu, C.H., Xiao, Y., Al-Turjman, F., Bootstrap aggregative mean shift clustering for big data anti-pattern detection analytics in 5G/6G communication networks. *Comput. Electr. Eng.*, 95, 107380, 2021.

103. Wang, M., Zhang, C., Lin, S., Wang, Y., Seicol, B.J., Ariss, R.W., Xie, R., Biased auditory nerve central synaptopathy is associated with age-related hearing loss. *J. Physiol.*, 599, 6, 1833–1854, 2021.

5

A Review of Innovation to Human Augmentation in Brain-Machine Interface – Potential, Limitation, and Incorporation of AI

T. Graceshalini[1*], S. Rathnamala[2†] and M. Prabhanantha Kumar[3]

1Vellammal College of Engineering and Technology, Madurai, Tamilnadu, India
2Sethu Institute of Technology, Virudhunagar, Tamilnadu, India
3Vellore Institute of Technology, Vellore, Tamilnadu, India

Abstract

The beginning of Industrial Revolution in late 1700s manifested a revolving fact in the history of humans: a phase for effective and increasing human beings/machinery interactions. In the coming decades, there were many more inventions followed, which gave rise to an increasing sense of interest and a need for imagination. Several areas of human capacity development were addressed. These are (i) neurotechnology, (ii) nootropics, (iii) genetic engineering, and (iv) brain-computer interfaces, ordered by increasing the possibility of implementation in the global economy. Brain-machine interface (BMI) utilizes existing neuroscience and engineering expertise to enable voluntary, thought-oriented control of external machines. This study underlines the increasing ability of BMI and BMI technologies to be introduced into our sector. The study also shows the limitations needed to push BMI technology out of infancy and incorporate it into artificial intelligence.

Keywords: Human augmentation, neurotechnology, brain-computer interfaces, global economy, brain-computer interfacing, artificial intelligence

Corresponding author: tgs@vcet.ac.in
†*Corresponding author:* rathnamala@sethu.ac.in

M.G. Sumithra, Rajesh Kumar Dhanaraj, Mariofanna Milanova, Balamurugan Balusamy and Chandran Venkatesan (eds.) Brain-Computer Interface: Using Deep Learning Applications, (101–126) © 2023 Scrivener Publishing LLC

5.1   Introduction

A fusion of technical capabilities enables the creation of "intelligent" brain-machine interface (BMI) [1] designs using machine learning and artificial intelligence (AI). The goal of this current technological wave is to interact in ways that foster relationship learning and adapting to new practical needs. It involves both restore-based disruptive neuronal behavior and non-invasive indicators mechanisms such as neural prosthesis electroencephalography (EEGs) [2]. Advances in BMI nanoengineering capabilities in computers, hardware, and algorithms that learn and evolve qualitatively are exploited. Finally, they are capable of understanding and adapting in (near) real-time to external environmental and physiological needs. Finally, the idea is to create a human experience for applications such as gaming, allowing the device to adapt and react in different clinical circumstances to changing events. In this comment, the ability, reasons, and technological state of the gadgets to produce them are discussed. We currently discuss a multitude of themes and difficulties in technology. Brain and Brain-computer interfaces are systems meant to connect with the central nervous system, including the brain, spinal cord, and sensory neural retina, which can be interchangeably used in this context. In addition to conducting preprogrammed neural control via an outside computer, or for brain stimulation, brain pulses are frequently acquired and clinically evaluated to restore brain activity following damage or discomfort, according to the purpose and aim of the technology. Any method, whether biochemical or through patient direction and desires, uses feedback to increase performance [3]. Furthermore, there is an increasing list of non-invasive brain interface technologies, the majority of which are funded by innovative start-ups and are not designed for therapeutic purposes. These strategies are being applied to enhance the user experience and control interfaces in sports augmented reality (AR), and virtual reality (VR). While this is an important demand, it is distinct from technology used to treat and recover patients' health functions and quality of life [4]. Not least because it can pave the way for scientifically relevant studies. Advances in neurophysiology, computational biology, signal processing, and hardware statistical and engineering dimensions, for example, will have a major effect on the gaming, medical device, and neural prosthesis industries. The market for brain-machine engagement is projected to hit $1.46 billion by 2020, with a CAGR of 11.5 percent expected to reach $1.72 billion by 2022, with a further provision for a CAGR of 11.5 percent between 2012 and 2022. Because of the expected expansion of all of these non-invasive technologies, the game industry has almost surpassed medical applications as a market leader [5]. Despite their importance, these predictions largely represent the interaction between neural controllers and sensory experiments with robots. They are not chances that have been inserted into the craft's present condition. BMI that can learn and evolve represents cutting-edge advances in what is possible through BMI technology integration, including nano-technologies, artificial learning, and AI. AI can be used to create "intelligent" BMIs that can learn and adapt to evolving functional demands and needs [6].

This allows for interaction with human gamers and AR/VR [7], as well as the enhancement and creation of therapeutic applications for patients with chronic diseases. This last point cannot be overstated, since not only are the medical needs of various neurological diseases met, but it is also important to customize BMI to patients' needs. It would also contribute to changing the technology for people's disease evolution over time. The idea that both have one size is the primary fault of the present state-of-the-art BMI and neural prosthesis. This means that all patients can be treated correctly with a technology that operates within a particular collection or spectrum of features. Although we do not know of a system or technology which mirrors the upgraded inclusion of BMI machine learning and nan-otechnology, we argued that this topic is worth exploring because of its potential and effect. All is now [8] employed in the design and functioning of BMI and neural prosthesis on its own, machine learning and nanotech-nology in a series of ways that match the vision we presented here.

5.2 Technologies in Neuroscience for Recording and Influencing Brain Activity

[9] In developing new neuronal acquisition strategies and activation, cognitive processes such as vision, recollection, concentration, and preparation and execution of actions have evolved. The effects on cognitive improvement, neural interpretable control, and/or stimulation of particular target areas of the brain, but also a host of other related variables, are not the only contingent. This includes the extent to which technology needs instrumentation into the body, as well as other functional factors such as how compact and costly devices are, which affect its usefulness for human cognitive enhancement in daily life [10]. We will analyze these innovations in the following parts with their advantages and disadvantages.

5.2.1   Brain Activity Recording Technologies

5.2.1.1   A Non-Invasive Recording Methodology

[11] EEG (Electroencephalography) and near-infrared functional spectroscopy are the most widely utilized noninvasive methods for recording neural activity. EEG monitors electrical electrodes mounted on the scalp. One of the key benefits of EEG is that it has very high temporal precision, is comparatively affordable and portable to use when it comes to outdoor use for cognitive enrichment compared with other non-invasive recording techniques. However, usually, spatial resolution is limited [12]. The FMRI detects variations in blood supply (hemodynamic reaction) in the brain, monitors brain function. The spatial resolution is much better on comparing EEG, but the temporal resolution is small. Sadly, for signal acquisition fMRI requires large and costly facilities. For these purposes, it is usually unsuitable for human augmentation applications despite little effort to use it for contact. fNIRS, like fMRI, uses the hemodynamic response to assess the location and duration of brain activity. Its key advantages are its compact size, lower cost than fMRI, and lower sensitivity to electrical noise than EEG. These technologies have enhanced cognitive enhancement technology, particularly when coupled with technologies such as brain stimulation, to improve spatial work memory. FNIRS does, however, have poor space and time resolutions. MEG, which is commonly used to assess the functions of certain brain areas, locate regions impacted by anatomy as well as other diagnostic uses, is another non-invasive technology. Similar to fMRI, however, MEGs are bulky, need a magnetically shielded laboratory, and are costly [13]. For these purposes, MEG is not practicable for human increase, although some implementations are suggested based on this.

5.2.1.2   An Invasive Recording Methodology

Invasive devices use electrodes that are mounted either on the brain or the surface of the brain [8]. Therefore, recordings with a decent temporal and spatial resolution are usually less influenced by noise and distortions caused by the skull and the scalp. Implanting electrodes, however, involves brain operation to make these procedures costly and to present future ethical problems. Electrocardiograph (ECoG) [14] is an invasive technique like EEG in which neuronally produced electrode testing is performed directly on a brain, unlike EEG electrodes. EcoG screens are often just a very small region of the brain for neural activity. However, ECoG-dependent applications for cognitive human development exist. The brain microelectrode needle-shaped clusters are other invasive tools. They emit powerful but only minimal, accurate noise signals (i.e., the entire electrode measures the electrical activities of one or more neurons). For example, Gerhardt and his colleagues build invasive electrodes with ceramic foundations. Due to their extensive layout and the presence of many pads on their surface, the electrodes provide high-density, high-precision multiple recordings in deep brain areas and electrical stimulation. Invasive recording methods have the downside of only penetrating small portions of the brain, but modern developments have allowed us to look at even wider areas [15]. Due to the dangers of neurosurgery (although see [16]) and its related ethical problems, most research on non-human primates through the use of microelectrodes has been performed. Research on humans, particularly people with motor disorders and cognitive enhancement, has only been much less commonly carried out. Figure 5.1 represents the basic anatomy of the brain and its related functions.

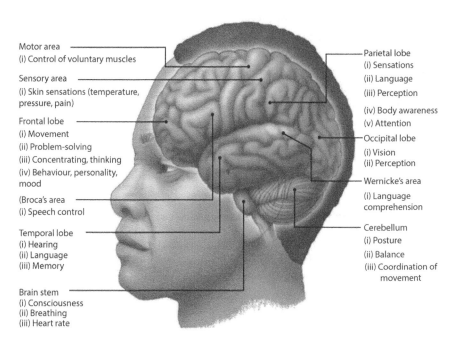

Figure 5.1 Anatomy of the brain and its functions.

5.3   Neuroscience Technology Applications for Human Augmentation

This segment examines the key applications of human cognitive increase neuroscience technology. Many of the applications come within two general areas: Neuroergonomics and brain-computer interfaces (BCIs). Neuroergonome studies and uses this expertise to develop structures that allow people to perform more safely, more efficiently, and efficiently in daily activities and workplaces [17]. Instead, BCIs have historically focused more attention on offering ways of compensating people with serious motor impairments for lack or lost mobility, for instance enabling them to operate appliances like wheelchairs or screen cursors or to connect when the natural communication method has been badly lost. There is a substantial correlation between BCIs and neuro ergonomic systems as a broad concept of human cognitive augmentation considering any increase over the functionality currently available to a person [17, 18]. The key distinctions are the user class and program fields of concern for these users. These distinctions, however, are becoming less clear: neuroergonomics for recovery, for instance, and BCIs were used to enhance decision-making incompetent people [19, 20].

Moreover, with BCI technologies developing further, BCI spellers and pointer control systems, which are still usable for seriously challenged people, maybe "competitive" with products used currently by customers [21]. Moreover, a random control (i.e. not specifically caused by the BCI) and behavior of new BCI variations, such as passive BCIs, now fill the divide between neuroergonomics and BCIs. For these reasons, we will not attempt to distinguish neuroergonomics from BCI-related applications and will not exclude applications based on their user base size and architecture [22]. We would instead concentrate on what cognitive functions each implementation wants to enhance, as mentioned above.

5.3.1   Need for BMI

The brain-based technology interface is a growing topic, and many companies have been focused on innovating and facilitating daily chores. One of the concerns that emerge is why BMI systems are needed? BMI is a sophisticated technique, but it certainly leads to an easier existence. The reasons for focusing on this technology are as follows [23]:

1. Device control may be simpler by our ideas

2. It takes a little time to choose a task, whereas it is easier to run an appliance by using ideas or our brain waves technically
3. Re-establish communication lines of brain and assist persons artificial limbs related to brain

5.3.1.1 Need of BMI Individuals for Re-Establishing the Control and Communication of Motor

The huge range of neurological disorders like engine neurons and backbone injuries, might cause severe motor muscular paralysis, restricting patients to artificial devices controlled by a few muscles, thereby being referred to as a 'locking in.' The normal channel from the brain to the limb is damaged, and BMI is used to re-establish connection alternately. BMI systems can even be used by a healthy person to operate applications in a range of user activities via the brain signal [24].

5.3.1.2 Brain-Computer Interface Noninvasive Research at Wadsworth Center

The Wadsworth Center study has explored numerous ways employed by the BMI to control a computer cursor to analyze its advantages and inconveniences, including sensory rhythm direct, which is adaptable to the potential created by motor imaging and linear regression by employing the choice of frequency-domain characteristics [25]. The other option was the cursor P300, which focuses on the sign and provides a matrix in which stimuli of varying durations may be produced. The method of Linear regression is employed for allowing those signals, like a control input, to move the cursor. The study revealed that the BMI is a methodology applied and fully user-driven; the EEG characteristics regulate speed, precision, bit rate, and usefulness of the BMI system. The sensor motor rhythms are a method that uses superior results in screen control management activities, but the P300-BCI system was lent than SMR-BMI [26].

5.3.1.3 An Interface of Berlin Brain-Computer: Machine Learning-Dependent of User-Specific Brain States Detection

The scientists at the brain-computer Berlin interface active sensory-motor rhythms, such as moving the right or the left hand and utilizing the system to determine the user's particular brain states. When tested for their trained models, they reached a data transmission rate of over 35 bits per minute, and the total spelled output was 4.5 letters per minute (including error correction, an EEG 128-Channel, and a feedback check for unapprenticed users) [27, 28].

5.4　History of BMI

The history of BMIs is tied directly to the quest for creating new electrophysiological methods for recording the extracellular electrical activity of huge neural populations with the use of multi-electrodes [29]. Studies already mentioned in the introduction In the 1950s, a pioneer of the present BMI design was John Cunningham Lilly, then a principal investigator of the national health institutes. On or on the surface of the pial cortex, Lilly was able to implant 25–610 electrodes in adult rhesus monkeys [30] (Figure 5.2).

Besides capturing field potential (25 channels at a time), Lilly also used electronic current via these electrodes to elicit movement both in anesthetic and eave monkeys, where animals demonstrated a range of competencies and states (arm motions, sleep, etc.) [31]. He observes that there are several cortical locations, including M1 and S1, that engine responses can be called up. Lilly determined that the distinction between cortical areas was not distinct, supposed to be alone motor or sensory. Instead, he proposed to identify these sections as sensor motors. The following intermediate stage in developing the BMI idea is the advent of "EEG biofeedback"

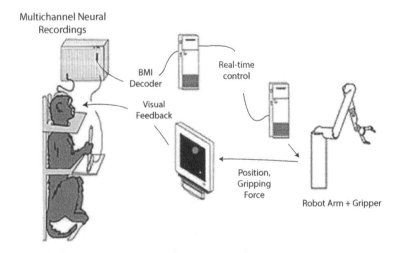

Figure 5.2 Adult rhesus monkey experiment over BMI.

or "neuro-feedback," particularly popular in many experimental environments in the 1960s and 1970s. The studies indicated participants about their brain activity such as auditory or visual feedback from EEG data which helped their self-regulation. In animal and human patients, David Nowlis, and Joe Kamiya [32] recorded and turned EEGs to sound. These types of neurofeedback assisted those who gained control of their EEG activities. Maurice Sterman [33] has transformed and accomplished seizure reduction using this kind of neurofeedback training EEGs for epilepsy patients in light and color. In 1963, Gray Walter [34] presented the first experiment in which humans provided brain impulses for an outside device in discussions with the Osler Society at Oxford University. It may not be fully true or verifiable Dennett's version, as Walter did not publish the speech himself. Nevertheless, published literature shows that Walter and his colleagues implanted and utilized multiple electrodes (up to 1000) in the cortex in neurological implants for several months to measure cortical field potential. In the tests reported by Dennett, Walters recorded the potentials of motor cortex preparedness before motions, which are also categorized as 'Bereit shafts potentials'. Pressing the button was automatic [35]. The possibility for ready led the movement around a half-second and was powerful enough to be identified by the recording equipment from Walter. Walter then managed to establish a direct connection between the motor cortex of each patient and the projector. The key was electrically unplugged from the projector and the slides were forwarded by the motor cortical readiness capabilities in this experimental situation which we now would name the brain control. The patients were surprised that even before physically initiating motion, the projector reacted to their intent. While Walter's tests may be seen as the earliest demonstration of a possible BMI construction idea, he never published or interpreted these results in the BMI context, even though he researched artificial brain robots in his previous career in the 1950s [36, 37]. In the late 1960s, researchers at the NIH Neural Control Laboratory started experimenting with the option of using cortical neuron recording to control artificial actuators [38]. They also aimed to use direct links between brains and external equipment to restore hearing to the surviving person, paraplegic person, and blind person [39]. The study took place at specific universities and medical schools, with the cooperation of subcontractors. "We will focus on creating concepts and methods for the operation of external devices such as predictive devices, communications equipment, telecommunication operators, and perhaps even nervous system information computers." said Karl Frank, the NIH Laboratory Chief [40]. The NIH team initially put into the primary motor cortex five microelectrodes (M1) that featured signals and then saw the action potential generated by 3–8 M1 neurons [41]. Since these neural impulses were eventually translated into the motion of an outside device, the researchers examined whether the recorded activity of tiny neural populations might anticipate wrist motions in the process. As a prediction algorithm, they used multiple linear regression. Neuronal rates were used as inputs and movie cinematic rates returned to their output. After 10 years of investigation, it demonstrated in real-time the movement of a cursor on the LED-screen by a Rhesus monkey using its nerve activity as a direct motor source with a size of 12 microelectrodes implanted in M1 at 37 mph. At the end of the '60s, when they used the electrical activity of individual neurons as neurofeedback's in monkey M1, Eberhard Fetz, and his colleague researchers took place [42]. With this system, the monkeys learned how to control their neuron activity. Normally, one neuron was tested at the same time. Feedback from the audience (click for each point) or visual feedback (transferred to the rate of neuronal activity). Monkeys learned to control each M1 neuron's activity willingly to achieve a certain firing level needed for a reward. Brindley and Craggs have employed epidural recordings of cortical field potential in the frequency range of 80 to 250 Hz in children to investigate the possibilities of developing engine neuroprosthetic treatment that detects the unique arm and leg generating action [43]. Craggs also used mid-thoracic baboons with complete transections of the backbone as a model for human paraplegia and recorded commands from direct cortical foot images separated from the spinal cord projection region [44]. These laboratories have also researched the extraction and/or creation of neurofeedback from the motor signals of the brain, an area that focused on the provision of information to the brain, both on the peripheral and central nervous system, via electric stimulation [45–47]. This discovery resulted in early attempts to create sensory BMI's to restore normal perceptions to those with neurological problems that produced substantial sensory deficits. Finally, this pioneering research has yielded the most remarkable results on cochlear implants (Figure 5.3).

At the same time, certain progress was made in the creation of a cortical visual prosthesis spearheaded by the Brindley and Dobelle groups [48]. These researchers used electric current in surface electrode grids for the visual cortex of blind people. With this device, blind people may sense light spots, phosphenes, and distinguish basic, multifunctional visual objects. Bach-y-Rita and his colleagues began developing blind visual replacement systems in the 1960s, based on tactile stimulation of the skin on the back of the patient [49]. This approach was called tactile image projection vision replacement. The equipment used comprised 400 solenoid stimulators, which were arranged into a range of 20 by 20. The tactile stimulation was

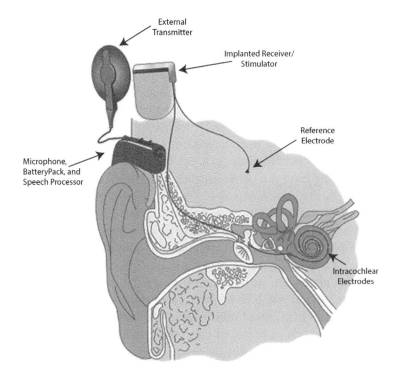

Figure 5.3 Cochlear BMI.

used to recreate visual pictures acquired by a video camera, using a sense of touch, on the surface of the patient's back. After training for 10 hours, blind patients learned to distinguish items and their positioning in space and attractions, such as the entrance frame of the room.

5.5   BMI Interpretation of Machine Learning Integration

Brain-Machine Interfaces (BMIs), to build real-time bidirectional inter-connections between live brains and artificial actuators in order, integrate methodologies, ideas, and concepts originating from neurophysiology, informatics, and technology. While certain theoretical proposals and con-ceptual experimentation with the direct connection of brains to machines originate from the early 1960s, BMI's research only started toward the end of the 1990s when the new neurophysiology technologies for large-scale brain activity monitoring were intimately related to these concepts [50].

BMIs have as their primary aim (1) the detection and use of operating principles and flexible qualities of the brain's distributed and dynamic circuits and (2) the establishment of innovative treatments to restore movement and sensations for seriously damaged people. A vast array of BMI applications has arisen in the last decade, significantly broadening these basic objectives. BMI research has revealed that robots and virtual actuators exert brain control over motions that perform both upper and lower limb activities. BMIs also include ways of returning sensory inputs from external brain drives. BMI Research has led to several neurophysiologic results, including evidence of the feasibility of integrating artificial instruments through the continuous use of the monkey's brain system. Work on BMIs has helped to discover novel techniques to retrain neurologists. This effort led to partial neurological recovery from the long-term continuous use of BMI in individuals with spinal cord injury [51]. The knowledge given by input and hardware telemetry is used to recall this algorithm. This may provide data on the current status or external data on system output settings calculated by the BMI sensors. In response to stimuli, for example, physiological measures of other algorithms outside the BMI-machine learning system, such as haptic or computer visual responses or internal parameters for current stimulus or device tracking photosystems. In the internal parameters of the algorithms, they continuously view variables such as pulse length and amplitude, stimulus rates, the use of energy in the system, the stimulation or registration density, the electrical properties (resistances, impedances) of neural tissues, and the persistent or almost permanent amounts of biochemical factors such as neurotransmission. Not one of them excludes one another, of course. Most information types and streams should be submitted in addition to the sampling resolutions, but they are likely to differ. So that the BMI produces the optimum results, which change dynamically as demands from outside contexts, machine learning algorithms can recognize subtle and no proliferating patterns and phenomena (e.g. therapeutic or operational). This includes offline architectures and algorithms, their implementation, and testing in the BMI architecture. Inappropriate parameter spaces algorithms should be able to distinguish patterns in online data. The algorithms mentioned below will decide if these data will be used separately. This step is not part of the brain interface scheme and can be accomplished using cloud algorithms if the bandwidth is necessary. However, machine-learning algorithms that classify designs inside data will undoubtedly be used in real-time to determine the board. Data transmission times and insufficient capacity would be eliminated [52]. Due to physical limitations, fewer data may also be required on the machine than can physically be preserved. To make a machine autonomous decision, the data can only be recorded for a limited time, normally as a moving window that corresponds to the processing power of the algorithm. This may also be helpful or necessary, however, the BMI system may not be necessary for offline analysis to store certain data or types of data. For example, to understand offline why machines make decisions and the health outcomes of those decisions. This step completes the closing process: the algorithms are supplied with knowledge and learned, pattern recognition, and autonomous executable decisions that in turn alter the brain-computer interface's performance dynamically and how it communicates with the outside world [53]. In neural prostheses, a noninvasive BMI is a connector to an AR or VR system which may be the brain itself recovers the therapeutic function or device. Several research groups recognized the promise early on and are investigating how computer training can influence and combine neural stimulation with feedback. Jerbi and collaborators have created a systematic technique for recognizing motor-related signals using stochastic learning, specifically for BMI applications [54]. Most notably, the BMI training classifier does not need to be pre-programmed with comprehensive information. They were superior to other Berlin BMI IV 2008 datasets and were tested on EEG data sets with high accuracy. Their algorithms were superior. Different preprocessing methods and neural network architectures were explored in a recent analysis for EEG classification tasks. Interestingly, the data analysis in conjunction with a preprocessing phase studying the electrode system's spectral energy conservation characteristics has been deemed appropriate in a reasonably easy networking architecture. They were in linear regression with a single convolution sheet, relationship layer, and single classifier [55]. They were able to co-adapt data training through their approach to achieve online classification. Another research has a connected methodology. The ability of the computer to learn to modulate in real-time and almost real-time the result of physiological and other internal device inputs such as the feedback of other internal processing algorithms may be one of BMI's main advantages. Most BMIs have a decoder that decodes and makes sense of neural signals for executable or actionable output. This usually requires intensive supervised training to refine the representation of neural signals that are captured until the decoder can equate detected signals correctly with expected outputs and commands. This teaching has historically involved supervised guidance from a human on the loop. This usually involves a technician or clinician who also receives the patient's feedback. Eventual training and modifications are rarely carried out daily and require time. In addition, neural signals that map outputs are limited to the training data which is exposed to the system during training. This significantly reduces the capacity of the BMI to respond in reality to variable particular conditions. Their versatility will then be drastically reduced to patients when complications occur. Early work was based on external sensor references input to calculate an error between the device output and the intended controlled objective. Visual and auditory signs were used. Although these methods are however strictly restricted since they involve the continued feedback of an arbitrary reference goal to change the mapping to BMI output. More recently, some of these inconveniences have been solved by the adjustment of output metrics of unattended learning approaches such as Bavarian mathematical methods and improved learning that are not externally referenced. But in most instances, they require substantial periods of preparation. Latest studies can specifically investigate and adapt endogenous neuronal signals in iterative closed feedback loops using the BMI as a training source. Chavariagga and colleagues are, for example, exploring a technique called act-critical strengthening learning that doesn't require a supervised error signal [56].

In general, machine learning is still under consideration in the area of BMI and neural prostheses in particular. One challenge is the absence of the right solution to the constraints set by the BMI by main modern approaches, such as deep learning, which have had great success in other applications. Panuccio *et al.* (2018) also published an excellent report in a recent article which outlines the current state and challenges of neural engineering, aiming to restore the neural function, including a range of related criteria outlined in this report, which will need to address new algorithms and machine learning to construct an adaptive IMO. The probability of creating BMIs which can react to the space and time conditions needed to achieve realistic results is a significant factor, since such machine learning techniques make other approaches impossible. The optimal strength of the stimuli required for a goal response in neurons is a complex factor for neural stimulation and may not be the highest stimulation density possible for the system [57]. The density of stimuli can be responded in a complicated manner, which depends also on fundamental physiology and pathology. In certain cases, it is impossible to understand the right relaxing density. In addition, the optimum density of stimuli can differ from one person to another and under a common illness and, with the transition in physiology and the adaptation of the body to modified conditions, the disease can change considerably in a particular patient. This may be due to age or exogenous factors such as the patient's response to other medications, diet, and psychiatric disorders. Another factor to remember is hardware and other algorithms that use known or calculated neural knowledge to communicate with the brain, which has various scaling requirements. It depends on the external problem and how neural data are used. The technical capacities and limitations of external data requiring technology are represented. The sample can lead to a deceptive or false AR/VR experience or a patient without a disability cannot communicate accurately or in a timely. The results are also available. Excess sampling will take time and resources for computation. The empirically defined precision of a computer model of how the theory is evaluated and understood may be impacted by data scaling problems in a testing setting. Treatment or other therapeutic choices may have a clinical effect. The change in the time and space scaling parameters needed by exogenous BMI considers situational issues, which cannot yet be considered substantially by the current state of the art. Integrating computer training and AI with the nanotechnology BMI enables you to consider, develop and respond to environmentally challenging questions like complex scaling criteria to address these challenges technically [58]. (For example: see Figure 5.4 Brain-machine interface schematics).

The extracellular activity of several hundred neurons in several cortical zones involving motor control of arm and moving is measured using intracranial recordings. A set of decoders that pull system parameters from

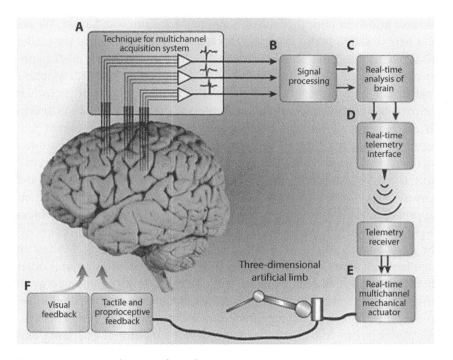

Figure 5.4 Brain-machine interface schematics.

the brain signal process the combined action of cortical neuronal ensembles in real-time. The decoder outputs are utilized to control the robot arm motions which enable human patients to carry out arm movements [59].

The interface phases of the brain-computer system include:

(1) Brain measurement/BMI recorder
(2) Preprocessing
(3) Feature extraction
(4) Implementation and classification Machine Learning
(5) Signal control translation

5.6   Beyond Current Existing Methodologies: Nanomachine Learning BMI Supported

The study on nanotechnology designed to communicate and interact with the brain and central nervous system, in general, has increased in the last few years. Recently, a substantial attempt was made to record and induce high densities in the brain using nanoscale neurotechnology. The brain initiative and the Human brain project have had a major impact on federal science efforts in both the United States and the European Union. We are not here to examine this extensive literature, but rather to guide the reader to references and publications in general. Machine learning, BMI nano-engineered, and neuro-prosthesis have not yet been combined. Machine learning is becoming particularly important in other areas of molecular science and nanotechnology (for example, see the review by [60]. Albrecht *et al.*, for example, published a tutorial on using near-transparent networks to analyze or derive molecular data from DNA sequence studies demonstrated in previous years how to improve Si-Si and Si-Ge thermal interfacial conduction using an atomic version of the mechanism and Green's function optimization. In a library of over 60,000 candidates, their approach was able to define optimal structures. Also, existing techniques were able to create an extensive research framework built and optimized by deep learning on a 3 D-pressed Diffractive Deep Neural Network in another remarkable recent study (D2NN). Their classification and other imaging operations were possible without using or using any energy in their structures other than input light. Computer training capability (i.e. model identification and interpretation) is the capacity of BMI and neural prosthesis to consult and improve device output and operating efficiency through the use of extremely detailed physical and chemical data from sensors. However, as previously said, it is critical to recognize that the most recent computer and AI algorithms are insufficient for these requirements. Many people who can detect and use nanotechnological BMI devices can deliberately create machine learning algorithms. Current machine-learning methods, especially deep artificial neural networks (ANNs), are extremely effective. What is perhaps more disturbing is that these types of the mathematical downgrade are the foundational principles that lead to ANN's current state-of-the-art and performance. However, theoretical and practical constraints remain, just as they do in every other framework. As a result, the data on which they function must be able to satisfy these constraints. Current algorithms, in particular, rely on exposure to large data sets to learn properly(a form of model bias). Only existing data will contain correlations and trends (model bias again). There is always a risk that a small training set would generalize (model overfitting). In these circumstances, they show nearly full strength and the potential to adapt beyond their training sets. New information cannot be learned further (model saturation). And these reasons are why these approaches are not available (data sparseness problem). Finally, they take vast computer resources and an item of enormous energy expenditure to classify learning patterns properly. These approaches are constrained by several key problems inherent in mathematical learning engineering. However, even with that drawback and the entire buzz surrounding machines and AI at the moment, the achievements of these methods are difficult not to be impressed. If data and resources are adequate to fulfill the task of the algorithms, these proceedings will be remarkably effective, with efforts at replacing new methods likely unworkable (and even unnecessary) for the near future at least. Machine learning is suited to the present state of the art of the BMI in some ways. BMI may possess a large number of data and physiological signals, relaxation parameters, and functional densities which are sufficiently well understood to determine for extremes, at least, are operational conditions. Thus, the current machine can properly learn algorithms for decision-making to adjust the BMI to its targets, based on proven and practical physiological ranges of activity. Indeed, in a monogeneric brain-computer interface, the degree of controlling synthesis over the material or the device and space and time relaxation resolutions and the recording density can be designed. Nanogenerated BMI will deliver the output and a lot of experience, combined with the level of nanoscale Functional Control Engineering, which is particularly appropriate for using state-of-the-art machine learning and AI for smart, embedded BMIs. But it's important to ask, whether BMIs can provide a certain amount of functionality and incorporation in machinery and AI architectures that are programmed to learn differently from existing algorithms. Machines that model complex neurobiological properties mathematically and abstractly. Specifically, empirical (i.e., data-driven) statistics perform best on problems where distortion, sparsity, and saturation do not (or cannot) restrain learning. However, outside of these boundaries, the mammalian brain is excellently understood [61]. The capacity of the brain to adjust and extrapolate beyond the outcome and its unbelievable physical and computing capability is particularly crucial. These characteristics go beyond existing computer training levels but they may be critical for the development of BMI in the brain. The human brain varies greatly from how modern neural artificial networks, deep learning, and algorithm "read" methods result from patterns. The brain much of the time is learned through analogy and a rundown. It adapts robustly to various circumstances and environments that it could not have met with an unbelievable degree of plasticity. Brain stability, adaptability, and strength of computing are higher than any existing computer. An extremes example of the extraordinary robustness of the human brain and its adaptability is a rare pediatric chronic inflammatory neurological disease, known as Rasmussen's encephalitis, that usually affects one hemisphere. It normally has seizures that cause muscle coordination, speech loss, hemiparesis, encephalitis, and cognitive dysfunction and are very frequent. The bulk of cases are medical refractory (stop reacting). Hemispherectomy is both the first and only efficient cure for epilepsy. Part or whole of the cerebral hemisphere is separated from the unintended hemisphere by surgery. The corpus callosum is the "ribbon thread," which divides the two ends of the brain. However, the other patients' brains will take over the roles of the cerebral tissue excised to different degrees. In certain cases, the patients will almost naturally function psychologically and cognitively, with the volume of brain removal into consideration. (You can also compare what would happen when you uninstall any transistors or circuits on a device.) With about 20W electricity, the brain can do anything for computing efficiency and energy efficiency - insufficient for powering a dim light bulb, the "wetware" is around 3lbs, equivalent to a 2liter soda bottle. Finally, although the computational characteristics and learning ability are available, that means that we don't have to reverse brain engineer to the point where we model or simulate a portion of how biology executes internal brain algorithms. One solution is to abstract biological knowledge and document the main algorithms, namely the legislation behind the BMI property or scheme. The result is that mathematical models are separate from fundamental bio details, but they catch realistic features to an algorithmic imitation. Of necessity, it can be more science than art if this line of abstraction is drawn.

5.7   Challenges and Open Issues

In this last part, we will present briefly some of the problems and challenges in implementing the vision above. We do not detail this text, but let the parties consult and discuss it further. First, the majority of recent attempts in developing neurotechnologies for the tracking or relaxation of high density have concentrated on the mechanics, chemistry, and engineering of key nanotechnology. This can be understood because the basic technology required to allow for activation or recording at the actual brain interface must arrive first. The data and knowledge supplied by these technologies must precede all methods or technologies for changing or using them. To ensure reliable recording or relaxation, above and above the real interface, mechanical and operating stability and long-term system durability are crucial. For instance, as the electrodes turn, or exaggerated reactive gliosis exists, they will seriously affect the efficiency and precision of the machines, making any machine learning algorithms monitoring or adaptation meaningless. These represent fundamental problems in engineering that have drawn considerable work. And though much has been achieved, very active areas of study are still available.

In addition to these familiar problems concerning the manufacturing and functionality of BMI products, there are relatively less focused, transparent problems. Questions on how to view and use data from these machines, which are of interest in any debate on incorporating machine education into the system as a whole, are of special importance. The density to record or boost can be so high on a nanoscale that the telemetry dilemma about how all these signals are to be detected is a problem. In other words, how do you monitor where signals originate and where (when records are made) (in the case of stimulation). The standard microscale method of the person 'read out' is physically impossible for high-density recordings, for instance, several thousand signals. Many nanotechnologies are designed into such drastic densities as standalone nano-scale instruments, which then can be used in large quantities. But, while each system can truly track local signals, how is the information collected globally over the entire sensor community, and how is this data meaningful? This issue is crucial in the case of applications requiring spatial "corticotopic" detail. We have no definitive response yet, but we cannot overestimate the impact of the issue. Whatever the answers, a mixture of nanotechnology, algorithms, and methods of data analysis are almost definitely needed. How do you selectively focus nanoscale electrodes on and on according to the specified programmed protocols, in regulated and organized spatial and temporal combinations, to create the most effective clinically significant stimulation paradigms, i.e. turning on and off. This will probably range from one patient to the next and develop in the same patient over time. As discussed above. The learning and adaptation processes used in the BMI and neural prosthesis could be at the center of the learning process to handle certain improvements. The architecture of BMI systems should comply with the installation and incorporation of machining, which is designed to operate within the overall framework from a material and engineering perspective.

Other critical aspects are wider topics that go beyond simply nanoengineered, specific, and important BMI integration with AI. For example, the neurophysiology, neural code, and purpose of neural signals are not well understood in processing information. This makes it difficult or impossible to create practical BMI learning algorithms. This makes it difficult. While neural stimulation or interface recording technologies have been mastered and efficient learning of machinery to monitor closed-loop feedback can still be developed, what we will optimize is not clear. We simply don't understand how well the brain functions. It is the brain that adapts to engineered technology and not the opposite to modern technology for a neural prosthesis. Other open topics show open innovation challenges beyond and beyond neuroscience. How can machine learning and AI performance be extended to the device itself in terms of limited form factors and local computing capability? If access to vital computing services in the cloud is required, appropriate bandwidth access should be ensured, especially in clinically sensitive circumstances.

5.8   Conclusion

Finally, the ethical problems posed by the implementation and application of these innovations must be recognized and considered. The ethical implications of neurotechnologies and AI on their own are significant. And at least one recent commentary simultaneously addressed ethical issues in psychiatry, neurotechnology, and AI. The authors defined four concepts to be followed and respected by those technologies: anonymity, identification, agency, and equity. There must be a continuous and changing dialogue that follows technological change. The possible threats to be ignored or deferred are too high. The integration of the brain network and the brain programming interfaces of machine learning and AI provides the possibility of important neurotechnological developments. BMIs that can learn and respond to environmental and situational pressures of external demands provide enormous opportunities to dramatically transform patients' care and quality of life. It also provides possibilities for non-invasive human-machine encounters and collaborations that are present only within the field of science fiction.

We might imagine an age of customized human journeys, impacting both clinical and non-clinical applications. As for all advancement that changes in disruption and paradigm, there are, of course, many technological problems to address, many of which are not straightforward and are serious ethical issues to consider and navigate with consideration. However, it cannot be avoided the opportunities, how we collaborate, use technology and machinery, and the evolving effect on the quality of life and well-being of the most beneficial patients. We argued that the use of modern neural Algorithms and modern machinery architectures should be taken into consideration in modeling cognitive science and neurosciences processes in machine learning and in the AI algorithms necessary to reach the interface of "smart" nano-engineered brain machines. For this reason, we have not argued for the need for general artificial intelligence (AGI) and are by no means obvious. The use of sophisticated algorithms is likely to be advanced applications such as smart adaptive BMI based on experimental evidence on current mathematical models and hypotheses. These independent algorithms are however not AGI from a context (although they could conceivably contribute to it). Substantial analyses, pattern analysis, education, and decision-making may take place in these algorithms, but only in the context and embodiment of neurotechnology. The concept of a self-aware machine or a conscious computer should not be confused with those technical considerations currently needed in this paper, namely, the subject. This is a fundamental distinction, as the regulatory questions and the continuing AGI discussions are very different from neurotechnology's societal and ethical concerns.

References

1. Galiautdinov, R. and Mkrttchian, V., Brain Machine Interface for Avatar Control and Estimation for Educational Purposes Based on Neural AI Plugs: Theoretical and Methodological Aspects, in: *Avatar-Based Control, Estimation, Communications, and Development of Neuron Multi-Functional Technology Platforms*, pp. 294–316, IGI Global, 2020.
2. Jebari, K.J.N., Brain machine interface and human enhancement–An ethical review. 6, 3, 617–625, Springer, New York, USA, 2013.
3. Galiautdinov, R.J., II, Brain machine interface: The accurate interpretation of neurotransmitter signals targeting muscles. *International Journal of Applied*

Research in Bioinformatics (IJARB), 10, 1, 26–36, IGI Global, Pennsylvania, USA, 2020.

4. Silva, G.A.J.F., II, A new frontier: The convergence of nanotechnology, brain machine interfaces, and artificial intelligence. *Front. Neurosci.*, 12, 843, 2018.

5. Hortal, E., Iáñez, E., Úbeda, A., Perez-Vidal, C., Azorin, J.M.J.R., Systems, A., Combining a brain–machine interface and an electrooculography interface to perform pick and place tasks with a robotic arm. *Rob. Auton. Syst.*, 72, 181–188, 2015.

6. Chen, X., Chen, J., Cheng, G., Gong, T.J.P.O., Topics and trends in artificial intelligence assisted human brain research. *PLoS ONE*, 15, 4, e0231192, 2020.

7. Jones, C., Novitzky, M., Korpela, C., AR/VR Tutorial System for Human-Robot Teaming, in: *2021 IEEE 11th Annual Computing and Communication Workshop and Conference (CCWC)*, pp. 0878–0882, IEEE, New York, USA, 2021.

8. Musk, E. J. J. O. M., II, An integrated brain-machine interface platform with thousands of channels. 21, 10, e16194, 2019.

9. Chen, R., Canales, A., Anikeeva, P. J. N. R. M., Neural recording and modulation technologies. 2, 2, 1–16, 2017.

10. Liu, D. *et al.*, Interactive brain activity: Review and progress on EEG-based hyperscanning in social interactions. *bioRxiv*, 9, 1862, 4, 545–564, 2018.

11. Formento, E., Botros, P., Carmena, J.J.B., A non-invasive brain-machine interface via independent control of individual motor units, 2021.

12. Ito, H., Fujiki, S., Mori, Y., Kansaku, K.J.N.R., Self-reorganization of neuronal activation patterns in the cortex under brain-machine interface and neural operant conditioning. 156, 279–292, 2020.

13. Prasad, G. J. L. M. A. H. O. R., II and Systems, B., Brain-machine interfaces. 461–470, 2018.

14. Benabid, A.L. *et al.*, An exoskeleton controlled by an epidural wireless brain–machine interface in a tetraplegic patient: A proof-of-concept demonstration. 18, 12, 1112–1122, 2019.

15. Niketeghad, S. and Pouratian, N.J.N., Brain machine interfaces for vision restoration: The current state of cortical visual prosthetics. 16, 1, 134–143, 2019.

16. Waldert, S.J.F., II, Invasive vs. non-invasive neuronal signals for brain-machine interfaces: Will one prevail? 10, 295, 2016.

17. Liao, L.-D. *et al.*, Biosensor technologies for augmented brain–computer interfaces in the next decades. 100, 1553–1566, 2012.

18. Farah, M.J. and Wolpe, P. R. J. T. H. C. R., Monitoring and manipulating brain function: New neuroscience technologies and their ethical implications. 34, 3, 35–45, 2004.

19. Li, Z., Ruan, M., Fang, Y.J.N.B., Major depressive disorder: Advances in neuroscience research and translational applications. 1–18, 2021.

20. Yeung, A.W.K. *et al.*, Virtual and augmented reality applications in medicine: analysis of the scientific literature. 23, 2, e25499, 2021.

21. Xu, W., Dainoff, M.J., Ge, L., Gao, Z. J. A. P. A., From human-computer interaction to human-ai interaction: New challenges and opportunities for enabling human-centered AI, 2021.
22. Rao, R.P., *Brain-computer interfacing: An introduction*, Cambridge University Press, Cambridge, England, 2013.
23. Kapoor, N., Furler, J., Paul, T.V., Thomas, N., Oldenburg, B. J. J. B. S., The BMI-adiposity conundrum in South Asian populations: Need for further research. 51, 4, 619–621, 2019.
24. Chaudhary, U., Mrachacz-Kersting, N., Birbaumer, N. J. T. J. O.P., Neuropsychological and neurophysiological aspects of brain-computer-interface (BCI) control in paralysis. 599, 9, 2351–2359, 2021.
25. Alonso-Valerdi, L.M. and González-Garrido, A. A. J. D. C., A. Computational neuroscience: Principles, and L. applications, IntechOpen, in: *Characterizing Motor System to Improve Training Protocols Used in Brain-Machine Interfaces Based on Motor Imagery*, pp. 57–76, 2018.
26. Leuthardt, E.C., Moran, D.W., Mullen, T.R.J.F., II, Defining surgical terminology and risk for brain computer interface technologies. 15, 172, 2021.
27. Abiri, R., Borhani, S., Sellers, E.W., Jiang, Y., Zhao, X. J. J. O. N. E., A comprehensive review of EEG-based brain–computer interface paradigms. 16, 1, 011001, 2019.
28. Lebedev, M.A., Opris, I., Casanova, M.F., Augmentation of brain function: Facts, fiction and controversy. *Front. Syst. Neurosci.*, 12, 45, 2018.
29. McMullen, D.P. *et al.*, Demonstration of a semi-autonomous hybrid brain–machine interface using human intracranial EEG, eye tracking, and computer vision to control a robotic upper limb prosthetic. 22, 4, 784–796, 2013.
30. Lebedev, M.A. and Nicolelis, M. A. J. P. R., Brain-machine interfaces: From basic science to neuroprostheses and neurorehabilitation. 97, 2, 767–837, 2017.
31. Ifft, P.J., Shokur, S., Li, Z., Lebedev, M.A., Nicolelis, M. A. J. S. T. M., A brain-machine interface enables bimanual arm movements in monkeys. 5, 210, 210ra154–210ra154, 2013.
32. Nowlis, D.P. and Kamiya, J.J.P., The control of electroencephalographic alpha rhythms through auditory feedback and the associated mental activity. 6, 4, 476–484, 1970.
33. Lucido, M.J., *Effects of neurofeedback on neuropsychological functioning in an adult with autism*, Walden University, Minneapolis, Minnesota, USA, 2012.
34. Soekadar, S.R. and Birbaumer, N. J. C. P. N. D., Clinical brain-machine interfaces. 83, 347, 172–179, 2014. https://www.sciencedirect.com/journal/neurobiology-of-disease/vol/83/suppl/C
35. Lorentz, H., Mach, E., Poe, E. A. J. T. B. F., II, An unmistakable difference exists between spatial and temporal concepts. 241, 2019.
36. Walter, W. G. J. S. A., An imitation of life. 182, 5, 42–45, 1950.
37. Hurst, F., *Imitation of life*, Duke University Press, North Carolina, USA, 2004.

38. Seo, D., Carmena, J.M., Rabaey, J.M., Maharbiz, M.M., Alon, E. J. J. O. N. M., Model validation of untethered, ultrasonic neural dust motes for cortical recording. 244, 114–122, 2015.

39. Schmidt, E.M., Cortical control of robotic devices and neuromuscular stimulators, in: *Neurobionics*, pp. 289–295, Elsevier, Netherlands, 1993.

40. Frank, K. J. A. O. O., LXII Some approaches to the technical problem of chronic excitation of peripheral nerve. *Rhinol. Laryngol.*, 77, 4, 761–771, 1968.

41. Humphrey, D.R., Schmidt, E., Thompson, W.J.S., Predicting measures of motor performance from multiple cortical spike trains. 170, 3959, 758–762, 1970.

42. Sharif, S. and Ali, S. M. J. W. N., I Felt the Ball"–The Future of Spine Injury Recovery. 140, 602–613, 2020.

43. Grahn, P.J., Strategies to advance intraspinal microstimulation toward therapeutic application for restoring function following spinal cord injury. *College of Medicine-Mayo Clinic*, 2015.

44. Urbin, M., Royston, D.A., Weber, D.J., Boninger, M.L., Collinger, J. L. J. N. O. D., What is the functional relevance of reorganization in primary motor cortex after spinal cord injury? 121, 286–295, 2019.

45. Brindley, G. and Craggs, M. J. T. J. O. P., The electrical activity in the motor cortex that accompanies voluntary movement. 223, 1, 28P–29P, 1972.

46. Brindley, G. and Lewin, W. J. T. J. O. P., The visual sensations produced by electrical stimulation of the medial occipital cortex. 194, 2, 54–5P, 1968.

47. Libet, B., Alberts, W.W., Wright, E., Delattre, L., Levin, G., Feinstein, B., Production of threshold levels of conscious sensation by electrical stimulation of human somatosensory cortex, in: *Neurophysiology of Consciousness*, pp. 1–34, Springer, USA, 1993.

48. Dhanaraj, R.K., Krishnasamy, L. *et al.*, Black-hole attack mitigation in medical sensor networks using the enhanced gravitational search algorithm. *Int. J. Uncertain. Fuzz. Knowl.-Based Syst.* 1968, 196, 2, 479–493.

49. Sharif, S. and Ali, S.M., Spine health special section. *World Neurosurg.*, 140, 602–613, 2020.

50. Zhang, S. *et al.*, Pain control by co-adaptive learning in a brain-machine interface. *Curr. Biol.*, 30, 20, 3935–3944, 2020.

51. Myszczynska, M.A. *et al.*, Applications of machine learning to diagnosis and treatment of neurodegenerative diseases. *Nat. Rev. Neurol.*, 16, 8, 440–456, 2020.

52. Samek, W., Montavon, G., Lapuschkin, S., Anders, C.J., Müller, K.-R., Toward interpretable machine learning: Transparent deep neural networks and beyond, 2020. arXiv preprint arXiv:2003.07631.

53. Trajkovic, L., Brain-machine interface systems. *IEEE Syst. Man Cybern. Mag.*, 6, 3, 4–8, 2020.

54. Jerbi, K. *et al.*, Inferring hand movement kinematics from MEG, EEG and intracranial EEG: From brain-machine interfaces to motor rehabilitation. *IRBM*, 32, 1, 8–18, 2011.
55. Dhanaraj, R.K., Krishnasamy, L., Geman, O., Izdrui, D.R., Black hole and sink hole attack detection in wireless body area networks. *Comput. Mater. Continua*, 68, 2, 1949–1965, 2021.
56. Chavarriaga, R., Sobolewski, A., Millán, J.D.R., Errare machinale est: The use of error-related potentials in brain-machine interfaces. *Front. Neurosci.*, 8, 208, 2014.
57. Shepherd, G.M., Corticostriatal connectivity and its role in disease. *Nat. Rev. Neurosci.*, 14, 4, 278–291, 2013.
58. Chaudhary, P. and Agrawal, R., Brain Computer Interface: A new pathway to human brain, in: *Cognitive computing in human cognition*, pp. 99–125, Springer, USA, 2020.
59. Dhiviya, S., Malathy, S., Kumar, D.R., Internet of Things (IoT) elements, trends and applications. *J. Comput. Theor. Nanosci.*, 15, 5, 1639–1643, 2018.
60. Wiecha, P.R., Arbouet, A., Girard, C., Muskens, O.L., Deep learning in nano-photonics: Inverse design and beyond. *Photon. Res.*, 9, 5, B182–B200, 2021.
61. Angehrn, Z. *et al.*, Artificial intelligence and machine learning applied at the point of care. *Front. Pharmacol.*, 11, 10–15, 2020.

6

Resting-State fMRI: Large Data Analysis in Neuroimaging

M. Menagadevi[1]*, S. Mangai[2], S. Sudha[2] and D. Thiyagarajan[3]

[1]Department of Biomedical Engineering, Dr. NGP Institute of Technology, Coimbatore, TN, India
[2]Department of Biomedical Engineering, Velalar College of Engineering and Technology, Erode, TN, India
[3]Department of Artificial Intelligence and Machine Learning, School of Engineering, Malla Reddy University, Hyderabad, Telangana, India

Abstract

Recent advancements in brain imaging have considerably improved to detect pathophysiological variation in the brain network. Structural and functional characteristics of the brain is understood using different imaging techniques such as angiography, midline ultrasonography, skull radiography, Computed Tomography (CT), Positron Emission Tomography (PET), Magnetic Resonance Imaging (MRI) etc. All the imaging modalities have their unique advantages and limitations. However, among these modalities, resting-state functional Magnetic Resonance Imaging (rfMRI) is the best technique to find brain disorders by measuring the brain connectivity. A huge amount of data is required to explore this complex connectivity network. Recent innovations in imaging techniques, the rfMRI have a unique methodological approach to analyze the big data related to neurological disorders. To find the brain of complex cognitive operations, large set of rfMRI data is required. The development of fMRI in medical applications provides an opportunity to use this exciting modality in the field of pathophysiology, diagnostic uncertainty, identify mechanisms of therapeutic action. This chapter focus on different connectivity of resting-state functional neuroimaging, database descriptions, sharing, infrastructure, analysis methods and clinical applications and also focus on the advanced research challenges and opportunities toward

*Corresponding author: menaga1961988@gmail.com

M.G. Sumithra, Rajesh Kumar Dhanaraj, Mariofanna Milanova, Balamurugan Balusamy and Chandran Venkatesan (eds.) Brain-Computer Interface: Using Deep Learning Applications, (127–156) © 2023 Scrivener Publishing LLC

neuroimaging. Big data forms a framework for current technology to have data integration, learning capability and multidiscipline research.

Keywords: Brain connectivity, rfMRI dataset, data analysis, clinical applications

6.1   Introduction

6.1.1   Principles of Functional Magnetic Resonance Imaging (fMRI)

fMRI is commonly used for brain imaging technique, it detects the activity of brain by measuring the changes occur during blood flow. This technique measures the brain cerebral blood flow and neuronal activity. fMRI detects the neuronal changes in the brain, and it gives unique information in both basic and clinical neurosciences. Difference between brain tissue resonances is measured based on these functionally dependent levels of blood oxygen, that is called as Blood Oxygen Level Dependent (BOLD) signal. This BOLD signal depends on Cerebral Blood Flow, Blood Volume and Metabolic rate of Oxygen. The brain uses 20% of the oxygen from the body. Energy to the brain is supplied by glucose molecules present in the oxygen. Oxygen consumption is increase due to increase in blood flow and glucose level. When the oxygen content increased during the consumption, the oxygen level in the blood can be identified using fMRI [12, 19].

Cubical region in the brain which measure the BOLD signal is called voxels. Activity of the neuron in the brain is measured by using BOLD signal. During brain activation, neurons in a voxel become active, so that the BOLD signal will vary over time. It helps the neuroscientist to characterize the brain function using BOLD signal changes. During the neural activity of the brain bold signal value peaks from 4 to 6 seconds after which it decreases back to baseline, again it shoots for 8–12 seconds after onset of brain signals. If there is no additional neural activity for 20 seconds it again returns to baseline this is called Hemodynamic Response Function (HRF).

6.1.2   Resting State fMRI (rsfMRI) for Neuroimaging

rsfMRI imaging is used to study the functional connectivity in different region of the brain. This method identifies approximately 0.01–0.1 Hz low-frequency variations of the BOLD signal, which represents the activity of the brain. Because of changes in deoxygenated hemoglobin and contract agent, the low magnetic field BOLD signal, is measured using rsfMRI.

Blood oxygenation level increases due to increase in CBF and its rapidity increase the rsfMRI signal. The widely used methods for Resting State study are the whole brain investigation and the Region-of-Interest (ROI) analysis. By the BOLD signal detection, the ROI correlates the brain voxels and time sequence of an existing ROI [1, 14].

Brain connectivity is important to analyze the human brain network. Brain connectivity of is investigated through rsfMRI, and it is analyzed in terms of similarities in the temporal region. Several neuronal activities of the brain are measured through changes in a BOLD signal in resting state. Main advantage of rsfMRI includes better signal-to-noise ratio, simplicity of the procedure, and lesser period of acquisition time. rsfMRI examine numerous brain networks at one time. Complex cognitive processes in the brain are occurred during the transmission of information between different areas in the brain, which is examined by functional connectivity analyzes in rsfMRI [8, 11, 15].

6.1.3 The Measurement of Fully Connected and Construction of Default Mode Network (DMN)

To measure a fully connected region in the brain, the brain is separated into 90 regions. Average time series of all the region in the brain is measured by the time series average of all voxel. The correlation among two regions was measured. Correlation matrix of dimension 90*90 of Fully connected network was built and calculated the average correlation matrix. DMN was constructed using Seed region [2, 4]. Seed region is located in bilateral medial, inferior temporal gyrus and precuneus region of the brain. Threshold of DMN is set using Standard deviation of sub-network [11, 20].

6.2 Brain Connectivity

Functional and Anatomical connectivity is very important to analyze the neural activity of the brain [1, 3].

6.2.1 Anatomical Connectivity

Physical connections among neural units are called anatomical connectivity of the brain. Anatomical connections are relatively stable over few minutes or seconds; it undergoes significant morphological change on large timescale. These static images help the neurologist to identify the microstructure underlying the brain [6].

6.2.2   Functional Connectivity

Electroencephalogram (EEG), Spectroscopy, rsfMRI used to analyze the brain functional connectivity. Functional connectivity information can be determined by measuring correlation of brain region in the temporal domain [23]. All the elements of the system are measured by direct or indirect structural links. Inherent activity of the functional network causes more than 60% of brain metabolic activity. This intrinsic activity is examined using low BOLD frequency signals [6, 8].

6.3   Better Image Availability

Brain region and its functional connections can be identified using functional rsfMRI, to explore this complex network large amounts of data are necessary. An era of big data analysis is obtained by combining neuroimaging techniques with new approach of rsfMRI. By using preprocessing techniques artifacts are reduced in the data, after preprocessing analytic technique is applied on rsfMRI dataset to align the data in the time series [4, 16].

Large data's of rsfMRI are essential to form new cognitive operations in the human brain. More number of data sets are preferred to increase reliability and accuracy of the complex problems compare to small datasets. Due to the recent advancement in technology is an unrestricted sharing of data and able to get more number of neuroimaging data through open access datasets. Functional and Human Connectomes Project are two big data sharing projects for neuroimaging. 1300 rfMRI images were collected from 33 international institutions and centers in 2009 using FCP. All images are available and user can use the image upon the registration. Information provided in the datasets are unnamed and limited to age and gender. In Human Connectome Project, studies are carried out under the age of 22–35 by healthy twins and non-twin siblings. All neuroimaging data are accessible through the registration in www.humanconnectome. org. The Laboratory of Neuro Imaging (LONI) has Alzheimer's disease (AD) population around 1000 data. Consortium for Reliability and Reproducibility (CoRR) has 1629 healthy resting-state fMRI (rsfMRI) data. The Neuroimaging Informatics Tools and Resources Clearinghouse (NITRC) has 6845 imaging data. Beijing Enhanced dataset have 180 healthy images using different data modalities like MRI (Magnetic Resonance Imaging), rsFMRI, DW-MRI (Diffusion Weighted Magnetic Resonance Imaging). Nathan Kline Institute (NKI) dataset has 207 healthy rfMRI, MRI, DW-MRI images obtained from the ages of 4–85 years old. Mind-Brain-Body Dataset is available in Max Planck Institute Leipzig has 194 healthy subject includes structural and resting-state fMRI data acquisition. 580 healthy cross-sectional images were provided by Southwest University Longitudinal Imaging Multimodal (SLIM) Data Repository. 494 healthy adult multimodel images such as structural MRI, rsfMRI and behavioral images are available in Southwest University Adult Lifespan Dataset (SALD). Child Mind Institute healthy brain network has 1551 healthy children and adolescents MRI, rsfMRI, natural stimulus fMRI, DWMRI images. Dallas Lifespan Brain Study (DLBS) contain 350 healthy adults MRI, tfMRI, rsfMRI, DW-MRI images, aged 20–89 categorized in terms of perception, brain structure and function. rsfMRI images of Early and late Mild Cognitive impairment is available in Neuroimaging Initiative of Alzheimer's disease.550 rsfMRI images of healthy, mild cognitive impairment and Alzheimer disease subjects are available in ADIN (Alzheimer Disease Neuroimaging Initiative) 2 and Open Access Series of Imaging Studies (OASIS). Autisum Brain Imaging Data Exchange (ADIDE 1 and 2) contain 1112,521 rsfMRI images of healthy and Autism disorder patients. Center for biomedical research contain 147 healthy and schizophrenia images [21]. Publically available rsfMRI dataset are listed in the Table 6.1.

Currently available datasets is given in the link https://sites.google.com/site/publicdatadatabase/. Due to the increase in the size of functional neuroimaging databases, the quality of the images acquired is improved by

- Higher spatially and temporally image resolution
- Imaging modalities
- Imaging sessions
- Specific target populations

6.3.1   Large Data Analysis in Neuroimaging

Recent advances in neuroimaging technology offer major progress in the analysis of human brain to develop the research in medicine, neuroscience and psychology. This advancement in technology provides a large volume of brain data with its functional and structural components. In the growth of advanced treatments in the neurological disorder and disease, large image databases are required. Billions of neurons and their connectivity are captured through the imaging techniques. So this large amount

Table 6.1 Publically available rsfMRI dataset.

Name of the dataset	Number of subject	Populations
1000 Functional Connectomes Project	1288	Healthy
Human Connectome Project	1200	Healthy
Laboratory of Neuro Imaging	1000	Alzheimer's disease
Consortium for Reliability and Reproducibility (CoRR)	1629	Healthy
Beijing Enhanced	180	Healthy
Nathan Kline Institute	207	Healthy
Max Planck Institut Leipzig Mind-Brain-Body Dataset	194	Healthy
Southwest University Longitudinal Imaging Multimodal	580	Healthy
Southwest University Adult Lifespan Dataset	494	Cross sectional healthy subjects
Dallas Lifespan Brain Study	350	Healthy
Child Mind Institute Healthy Brain Network	1551	Healthy children and adolescence
Alzheimer Neuroimaging Initiative	200	Healthy and cognitive impairment
Alzheimer Neuroimaging Initiative-2	550	Healthy, Cognitive impairment and Alzheimer's disease
Open Access Series of Imaging Studies	1098	Healthy, Cognitive Impairment and Alzheimer disease
Attention Deficit Hyperactivity Disorder-200	973	Healthy, Deficit Hyperactivity Disorder
Center for Biomedical Research Excellence	147	Healthy, schizophrenia

of data and their representation have the significant challenges. Major neurological disorders related to brain connectivity network includes Anxiety, Schizophrenia, Depression, Attention Deficit Hyperactive Disorder, Alzheimer's disease. Understanding the functional complexity of the brain is a necessary to analyze the neurological disorders. rsfMRI technique provides a greatpotential for the analysis of functional brain networks. rsfMRI images enable us to understand the association between brain connectivity and psychological status.

Compare to traditional datasets, Large Data have unique features. By using these unique features, new statistical methods for data analysis are in development. Big Data are characterized by huge sample size and high dimensionality. With the massive data, hidden patterns associated with image can be analyzed. In large data era, the big sample size enables us to better understand heterogeneity.

6.3.2   Big Data rfMRI Challenges

Data collected for the various database exhibit numerous large data quantities, rfMRI size is not large as other data format. Due to the large size of other dataset, processing speed of the system will get low. When the size of the image is low, preprocessing and analyzing the data is easy and time-consuming. Methods used to analyze the data's have a difficulty with its large size. Variety of data refers to information within single or multiple bit rfMRI datasets [24]. By combining neuroimaging and behavioral data with rsfMRI large variety of data can occur. Human Connectome Project includes variety of imaging modality like rfMRI, dMRI, MEG, tfMRI which help to analyze the image with multiple modalities. Large Veracity refers to noise, inadequate and wrong information data. Although large information is valuable in finding correlations that may be neglected by investigating lesser datasets, researchers find the correlation on bigger dataset. Preprocessing is an important and vital stage in Big Data research. Different preprocessing steps are dynamically turning out to be more acknowledged as standard in the examination of rfMRI data, computational time is increased by using different preprocessing techniques. So, software packages with advanced analytical methods should be developed for preprocessing the datas. The decrease of Information is another vital stage particularly when managing enormous datas with big veracity that is separating important and significant features or extraction strategies from the entire feature which contain noisy information. Software tools along with the web link for neuroimaging is given below [24]:

1. Analysis of Functional NeuroImages (AFNI) - https://afni.nimh.nih.gov/afni/
2. Advanced Normalization Tools (ANTs) - http://stnava.github.io/ANTs/
3. Free Surfer - https://surfer.nmr.mgh.harvard.edu
4. FMRIB Software Library (FSL) - https://fsl.fmrib.ox.ac.uk/fsl/fslwiki
5. Statistical Parametric Mapping (SPM) - www.fil.ion.ucl.ac.uk/spm/

6.3.3   Large rfMRI Data Software Packages

A figure of necessities and features are essential to be accessible by the software which is designed to analyze big scale rfMRI data such as configurable, vigorous, dependable, and extendable and provenance following. Table 6.2 shows the software package software for fMRI preprocessing [24].

Table 6.2 Software packages of fMRI.

S. no.	Software	Web link	Programming Language
1.	Bet A-Series Correlation	www.nitrc.org/projects/basco/	MATLAB
2.	Scalable fMRI Data Analysis	https:/igithub.com/rboubela/biananes	C
3.	Brain Connectivity Toolbox	www.brain-connectivity-oolbox.net/	MATLAB
4.	Brain Net Viewer	www.nitrc.org/projects/bnv/	MATLAB
5.	Brain VISA	http://brainvisa.info/web/index.html	Python/C++
6.	Software for Fast fMRI	https://github.com/wanderine/BROCCOLI/	Open CL/C++

(*Continued*)

Table 6.2 Software packages of fMRI. (*Continued*)

S. no.	Software	Web link	Programming Language
7.	Connectome Computation System	https://github.com/ zuoxinian/CCS	MATLAB/ Python
8.	Configurable Pipeline for Analysis of Connectome	https://fcp-indi.github. io	python
9.	Functional Connectivity Toolbox	www.nitrc.org/projects/ conn/	MATLAB
10.	Correlation psychophysiological interaction	www.nitrc.org/projects/ cppi_toolbox/	MATLAB
11.	A toolbox for data processing and analysis for brain imaging	http://rfmri.org/dpabi	MATLAB
12.	Data processing Assistant for rsfMRI	http://rfmri.org/DPARSF	MATLAB
13.	Graph Analysis tool	www.nitrc.org/projects/ gat/	MATLAB
14.	Group ICA of fMRI toolbox	http://mialab.mrn.org/ software/gift/index. html	MATLAB
15.	Generalized Psychophysiological Interactions	www.nitrc.org/projects/ gppi	MATLAB
16.	Comprehensive graph analyses of functional brain connectivity	www.nitrc.org/projects/ graphvar	MATLAB
17.	Graphical Analysis of Network	www.nitrc.org/projects/ gretna/	MATLAB

(*Continued*)

Table 6.2 Software packages of fMRI. (*Continued*)

S. no.	Software	Web link	Programming Language
18.	Graph Theory MATLAB Toolbox	www.nitrc.org/projects/ metalab_gtg/	MATLAB
19.	Network-Based Statistic	www.nitrc.org/projects/ nbs/	MATLAB
20.	Neuroimaging Analysis Kit	www.nitrc.org/projects/ niak/	MATLAB/ Octave
21.	Machine learning for Neuro-Imaging	https://nilearn.github.io	Python
22.	Neuroimaging: Pipelines and Interface	http://nipy.org/nipype	Python
23.	Pattern Recognition for Neuroimaging Toolbox	www.mlnl.cs.ucl.ac.uk/ pronto/index.html	MATLAB/C++
24.	Pipeline System for Octave and MATLAB	http://psom.simexp-lab.org	MATLAB/ Octave
25.	Multivariate Analysis of pattern in Python	www.pymvpa.org	Python
26.	Resting-State fMRI Data Analysis Toolkit	http://restfmri.net	MATLAB
27.	Statistical Non Parametric Mapping	http://warwick.ac.uk/ snpm	MATLAB
28.	The Decoding Toolbox MATLAB	https://sites. google.com/site/ tdtdecodingtoolbox/	MATLAB

6.4   Informatics Infrastructure and Analytical Analysis

Big data Informatics is an important element for large data distribution and analytical analysis. It is likely to improve collection, analysis integration and interpretation of data, and have a secure sharing/collaboration of the data. The collection and distribution of Human Connectome Project and Connectome DB database, allows data accessing and automated validation for data Quality Control and allows numerous approaches for accessing the data. Secure access of neuroimaging data is available on Extensible Neuroimaging Archive Toolkit software platform which is utilized by some neuroimaging dataset. Various neuro informatics infrastructure was developed for Processing and analysis for Brain Imaging.

Functional neuroimaging analysis have been developed for data processing, classification and pattern discovery. For classifying the abnormal patterns in the brain like schizophrenia, depression, Alzheimer disease, social anxiety, Mild cognitive impairment, Parkinson disease and other neurological diseases various methods are used. Multiple data models were useful to determine the functional pattern of the brain.

It is challenging to establish neuroimaging across different subjects and imaging modalities. The multi-modal architecture provides an accurate areal map of the human brain. Connectivity domain framework provides a space to exemplify rsfMRI data for the data-driven analysis. Large-scale brain map is formed by integrating meta-analysis to functional neuroimaging.

6.5   Need of Resting-State MRI

6.5.1   Cerebral Energetics

Different states of brain are measured by understanding the brain energy metabolism. The human brain at resting state consumes 20% of the energy and 2% of body mass, maximum of which support of neuronal signaling. Increased in neurological metabolism for task related is <5% compare to large energy consumption during resting state. Less than 1% occur in task related changes.

6.5.2   Signal to Noise Ratio (SNR)

SNR of the resting state studies are better than the task related approaches. rsfMRI emphases on instant activity and it is used as a signal rather noise.

Task based activation have a reduced SNR because the signal is lesser relative to the noise. SNR task-based activation is 20% whereas in resting state it is about three times the SNR. Imaging abnormalities in the patients are identified correctly with improved SNR.

6.5.3   Multi-Purpose Data Sets

Multiple cortical systems can be studied using rsMRI data. In task-activation analyses, keen data acquisitions for each function is required. Acquisition of motor and language task is required to identify motor and language system. In rsfMRI, the single data set can be used to inspect both systems, so the data volume get reduced.

6.5.4   Expanded Patient Populations

rsfMRI allows broader patient population for clinical studies. Patients with cognitive dysfunction or physical impairment are unable to perform tasks exactly in the fMRI scanner, whereas in rsfMRI analysis afford an exact result. rsfMRI requires only marginal strains on the patient. Instant action carries only during the patients are asleep and sedated.

6.5.5   Reliability

Reproducibility and intersubject variability are the significant matters to be consider rsfMRI. Resting State Network can be identified consistently through imaging sessions and in dissimilar cases, there may be some changeability among the subjects. Intraclass correlation of >0.60 are obtained using rsfMRI.

6.6   Technical Development

Technical development in medical field plays a major role in the neuroimaging. Signal-to-noise is highly potential over task based studies, for task based analysis number of trails in SNR gets increased. All the neural fluctuation in the cortical system and non- neuronal sources are not BOLD signal, proper identification of the bold signal is a significant task. Noise impact is relatively lesser to neuronal fluctuations. Non-neuronal fluctuations have less SNR compare to neuronal fluctuations. Scan time and clinical applicability is improved by improving SNR. rsfMRI data can be used for analyzing the brain network in resting state and to increase the number of epochs of task related variance.

6.7   rsfMRI Clinical Applications

rsfMRI has remarkable perceptions on Resting State Network in the healthy and unhealthy states [10]. Here, we have described some potential diseases examines using RS-FMRI [12].

6.7.1   Mild Cognitive Impairment (MCI) and Alzheimer's Disease (AD)

AD is neurological disorder that the brain network is changed during the transition from healthy condition to MCI and AD. AD disease shows the correlation and anticorrelations reduction within the DMN and also clustering coefficient with reduced local connectivity. Symptoms of AD are reduced concentration and thinking, lack in decision-making, memory loss, personality change, depression, sleeping disorder, wandering etc. Symptoms of MCI include Amnestic cognitive impairment which affects the memory of the person and nonamnestic cognitive impairment affects the thinking of the person rather than memory.

rsfMRI imaging is used to find the intrinsic brain connectivity which is considered a promising biomarker for AD and MCI diagnosis. Functional connectivity changes within the DMN have been observed in healthy, MCI and a prodromal stage of AD population. In comparison with health controls, there is a decreased connectivity at baseline in posterior default mode areas and increased in frontal region for AD patients. This result shows that within DMN hyper-connectivity leads to hypo-connectivity of a brain region, and it is a sign of early phase of brain dysfunction. Neuropathology of brain with AD is outlined using rsfMRI which affects temporal lobe, posterolateral cortical regions and the frontal cortex [5]. The significant feature of rsfMRI in AD is the acceptance of data gaining in patients with dementia and to measure functional connectivity without the concert of a task. In Figure 6.1 shows resting-state functional brain image where Green color represent the voxel with DMN. Blue color represents the voxels with decreased Functional Connectivity (FC) in MCI and AD [22]. Figure 6.2 represent rsfMRI BOLD signal, which shows the variation of brain signal during AD and MCI condition [25].

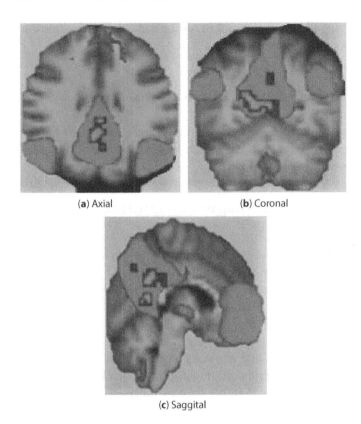

(a) Axial   (b) Coronal

(c) Saggital

Figure 6.1 Resting state functional brain image of MCI and AD.

6.7.2   Fronto-Temporal Dementia (FTD)

FTD is a neurological disorder with the symptoms of behavioral and personal impairment. The common symptoms of FTD are behavioral changes, lack of judgment, impulsive, apathy, decreased confident level, loss of self-awareness, reduced energy level, decreased knowledge level, depending on others, agitation. FTD functional networks implicated as DMN, the networks spread mainly through the left hemisphere. In bvFTD (behavioral variant Frontotemporal dementia), reduced connectivity in all regions such as anterior cingulate, frontal lobe, amygdala, thalamus, insula, and ventral striatum. Figure 6.3 shows the Bold signal variation of rsfMRI image. Decreased connectivity in the network may affect in increased connectivity within the DMN. Figure 6.2 represents the frontal and temporal pattern of FTD [7].

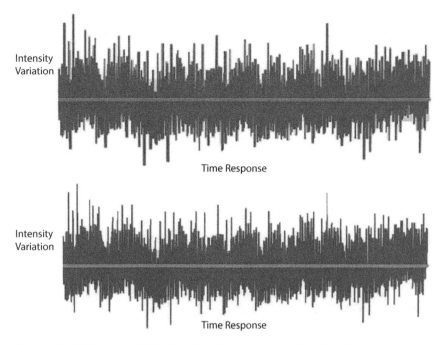

Figure 6.2 BOLD signal of Mild Cognitive Impairment and Alzheimer's Disease.

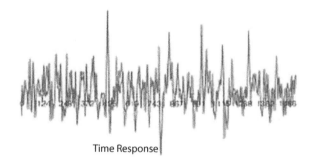

Figure 6.3 BOLD signal of fronto-temporal dementia.

6.7.3   Multiple Sclerosis (MS)

MS is a most common causes of neurological disability, which affects 2.5 million individuals. Symptoms of MS are weakness in one side of the body, loss of vision, dizziness, fatigue, tingling, urinary problem. Connectivity analysis is based on calculation of the temporal correlations among various regions of the brain. The connectivity analysis at resting state, which organizes the multiple neuroanatomic networks. In MS, DMN dysfunction is more noticeable and it is correlated with change in structural connectivity. Anatomical connectivity analysis gives the changes in white matter of MS patient [9].

MS disease leads to the presence of focal lesions and atrophy can complicate functional neuroimaging. Figure 6.4 and Figure 6.5 represents the rsfMRI of normal and multiple sclerosis and Global decreases in brain activity in MS detected. Using the same scale, images from two slice locations in a normal (top row) and a patient with MS (bottom row) displayed. Cerebral glucose metabolism is reduced in the MS patient compared to healthy control. Figure 6.6 shows the Bold signal variation of the rsfMRI image.

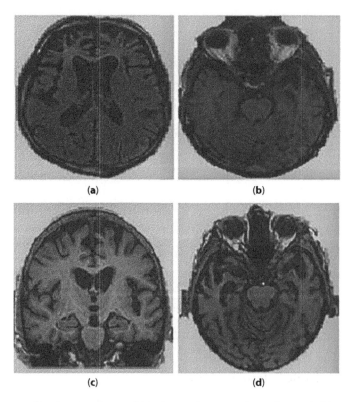

(a)   (b)

(c)   (d)

Figure 6.4 FTD subtypes imaging. (a) Behavioral variant of FTD (bvFTD). (b) Semantic dementia-temporal lobe atrophy. (c) Coronal T1-weighted MR image – non-fluent aphasia and left frontal and superior atrophy. (d) Axial T1-weighted MR image with right temporal atrophy.

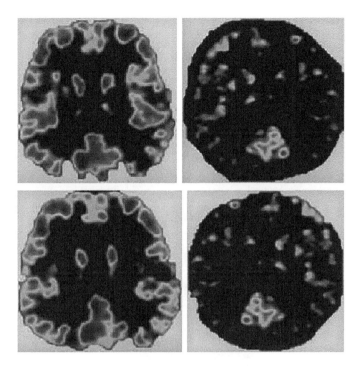

Figure 6.5 rsfMRI of normal and abnormal multiple sclerosis.

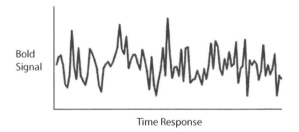

Figure 6.6 rsfMRI Bold signal of multiple sclerosis.

6.7.4 Amyotrophic Lateral Sclerosis (ALS) and Depression

ALS is characterized by downstream muscle weakness, loss of motor neurons in spinal tract and anterior horns, speech problem, uncontrollable crying, laughing, behavioral changes. Dysfunction in ALS is described using rsfMRI. BOLD signal analysis in the rsFMRI benefits from high acquisition times and high-resolution structural protocols. In ALS, there

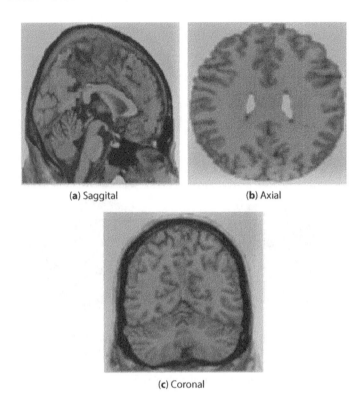

(a) Saggital   (b) Axial

(c) Coronal

Figure 6.7 Resting-state FMRI of depression disorder.

is a decreased connectivity in frontal cortex and decreased connectivity in precuneus [10].

Depression is categorized by mood depression in the patient, lost interest in doing activities, feeling hopeless, depression, losing physical appearance, change in sleep pattern, energy loss, and worthlessness feel. Figure 6.7 shows the resting-state FMRI of depression disorder and Figure 6.8 shows the Bold signal of depression disorder [27]. Functional neuroimaging examines the different cortex region such as Anterior Cingulate, Medial Prefron AFNI tal, Posterior Cingulate, thalamus, and precuneus.

6.7.5   Bipolar

Bipolar disorder is characterized by of mania, decreased sleep, lack of decision-making depression, eating disorder, anxiety disorder and heart problem fMRI uses task-related and resting-state method to analyze the bipolar disorder. Rather than giving information about whole-brain

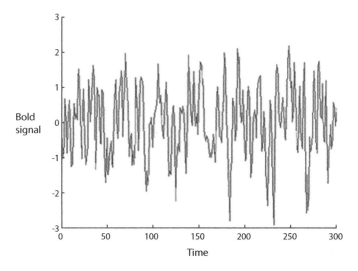

Figure 6.8 rsfMRI bold signal of depression disorder.

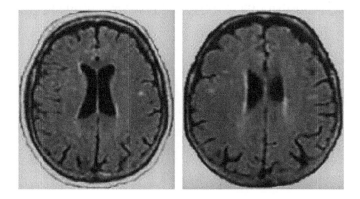

Figure 6.9 rsfMRI bipolar disorder image.

functioning, it gives information about the differences in neuropsychological function and specific task-based brain region. Bipolar disorder activity was spontaneously measured using rsfMRI. Figure 6.9 represents rsfMRI bipolar disorder image.

6.7.6 Schizophrenia

Schizophrenia was a potential disconnection disease characterized by false believe, hallucinations, thinking disorder, sleep disorder, poor hygiene.

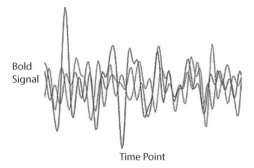

Figure 6.10 rsfMRI Bold signal of schizophrenia.

The underlying symptom of Schizophrenia was functional disconnectivity between brain regions. Schizophrenia have changes in DMN network in frontal and parietal regions shown in the bold signal, Figure 6.10. For schizophrenic patients, the rsfMRI shoes the decreased functional connectivity between medial frontal cortex and precuneus region of the brain. It

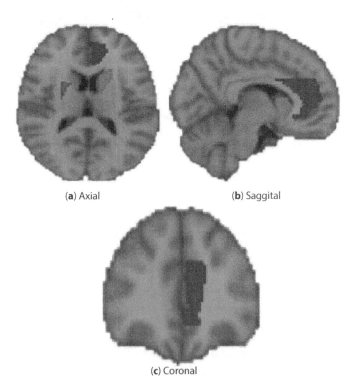

Figure 6.11 rsfMRI of schizophrenia.

is identified that there is a spatial difference in the DMN in schizophrenia patients and the DMN region shows higher frequency variations in early phase of schizophrenia. Figure 6.11 represents the pathological alterations in schizophrenia of rsfMRI Images. Red indicates elevated regional activity and blue represents suppressed regional activity [13, 14].

6.7.7   Attention Deficit Hyperactivity Disorder (ADHD)

ADHD is a neurological disorder and it is characterized by loss of attention, hyperactivity, excessive talking, loss of physical movements and behavioral changes. ADHD patients have the rsfMRI image with low frequency fluctuation and regional homogeneity. ADHD patients have abnormal brain activity of in cerebellar areas. Figure 6.12 shows the rsfMRI image of ADHD. Red color in the image shows the low frequency changes in the brain [8, 17].

6.7.8   Multiple System Atrophy (MSA)

MSA is a neurological disorder characterized by dysfunction, slow movement, cerebellar features and postural variability. Figure 6.13 shows the area of brain affected by MSA.MSA is a rare disease, and resting-state functional connectivity used to analyze the patients with MSA. Overlap of frontal lobe, superior and middle gyri and prefrontal cortex is reported in resting-state connectivity in MSA. There is an increased regional homogeneity in right frontal area and decreased regional homogeneity in left areas. Changes in parietal lobule and posterior cingulate also examined in rsfMRI. Decreased fronto parietal and parieto-cingulate connectivity was associated with MSA [16]. Bold signal variation of Multiple System Atrophy is shown in Figure 6.14.

6.7.9   Epilepsy/Seizures

It is a neurological illness, activity of the brain become aberrant which results in seizer, weakness of nerves and loss of consciousness. Symptoms of epilepsy are anxiety, confusion, jerking of arms and legs and fear. Patient with epilepsy have a seizure symptom frequently. Abnormal activity observed in one region of the brain is called focal seizure. Focal seizures of two types. In one type of seizure patient not loss their consciousness they have symptoms like loss of smell, emotions, feel, sound and also have involuntary movement in the body. On second type of seizure, patient

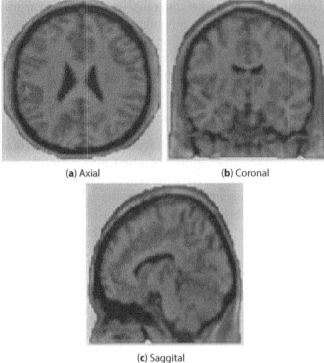

(a) Axial   (b) Coronal

(c) Saggital

Figure 6.12 rsfMRI image of ADHD.

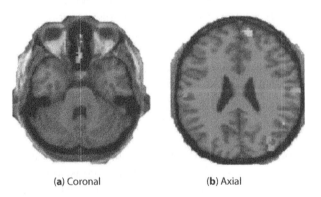

(a) Coronal   (b) Axial

Figure 6.13 rsfMRI image of multiple system atrophy.

loss their consciousness. Epilepsy and seizures occur due to heredity, head injury, change in brain function, brain infection, brain cell death. Figure 6.15 represents the Epilepsy and Seizure rsfMRI image. BOLD signal analysis [26] of the rsfMRI image is shown in the Figure 6.16.

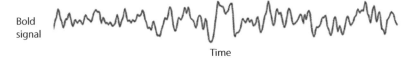

Figure 6.14 Bold signal of multiple system atrophy.

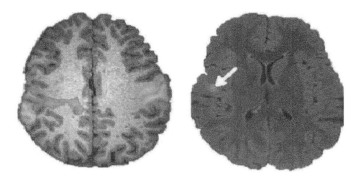

Figure 6.15 rsfMRI image of epilepsy and seizures.

6.7.10   Pediatric Applications

RS-fMRI used to solve multiple pediatric diseases. rsfMRI identify immature forms of Resting state network in infants to determine incorporating
regions identified in older children and adult's longitudinal analysis is
performed during neonatal period for the infants. Resting State Network
difference were recognized between infants and those born prematurely
using rsfMRI. It shows the reduced long-range and improved short-range
correlations in the network. rsfMRI has been used to explore changes in
Resting State Network of pediatric disease [1].

6.8   Resting-State Functional Imaging of Neonatal Brain Image

Infancy brain development is the most important and critical stage in their
life. Infants need sustained development in the functional connectivity of
the brain at rest, it is absorbed using rsfMRI shown in the Figure 6.17.
Functional connectivity used to analyze cognitive process of different brain
region. rsFMRI studies help us find the immature brain development and
different brain injuries of the infants.

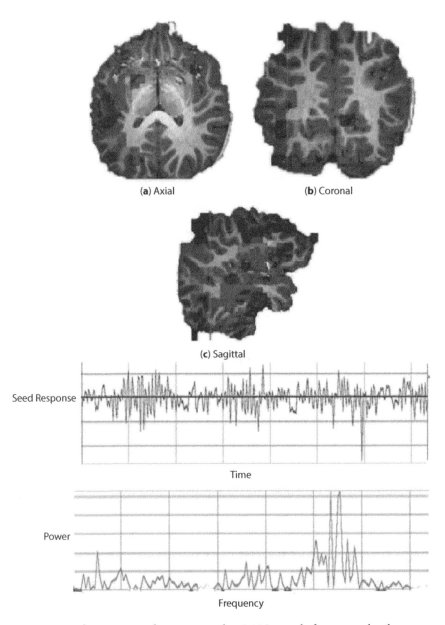

Figure 6.16 rsfMRI image and its corresponding BOLD signal of seizure and epilepsy.

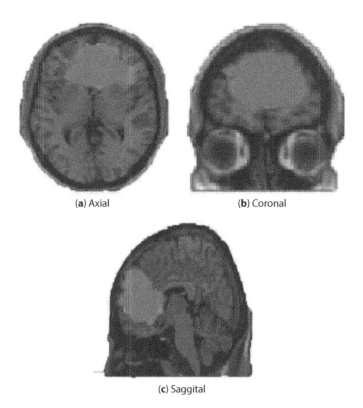

(a) Axial   (b) Coronal

(c) Saggital

Figure 6.17 rsFMRI of infant brain.

6.9   Different Groups in Brain Disease

rsfMRI may be used for various clinical applications, mainly in neurological or psychiatric disorders. Functional abnormalities of different disease states are studied using rsfMRI. Table 6.3 shows the different groups of rsfMRI patterns of brain diseases or conditions [16, 18].

6.10   Learning Algorithms for Analyzing rsfMRI

Machine learning and deep learning techniques play a vital role in analyzing the rsfMRI data. Various supervised and unsupervised learning algorithms analyze the rsfMRI image and identify the different neurological disorders. Unsupervised learning algorithm discover spatial, reproducible pattern and latent factors of resting-state functional MRI images. Supervised learning is used to classify and analyze different brain disorders, hereditary

Table 6.3 Different groups of resting-state MRI patterns of brain diseases or conditions.

Disease	Finding in rsfMRI
Alzheimer	Reduced correlations, anticorrelations in the DMN and reduced local connectivity.
Mild cognitive impairment	Decreased correlations, anticorrelations within the DMN
Fronto-temporal dementia	Salience network- Decreased correlations
Multiple sclerosis	Somatomotor network- Decreased correlations
Amyotrophic Lateral Sclerosis	Decreased connectivity in DMN and somatomotor network
Depression	Reduced corticolimbic connectivity, increased connectivity within the DMN, Reduced connectivity among DMN and caudate
Bipolar	Reduced corticolimbic connectivity
Post-Traumatic Stress Disorder	Reduced connectivity in the DMN
Schizophrenia	Reduced correlations within the DMN. Improved connectivity within the DMN
ADHD	Reduced connectivity and anticorrelations within the DMN
Autism	Reduced connectivity in the DMN
Epilepsy	Reduced connectivity in different networks and Decreased connectivity within the DMN
Blindness	Decreased connectivity in visual cortices, sensory and multimodal regions
Chronic pain	Reduced/improved connectivity in the salience network, Reduced connectivity in attention networks
Coma/vegetative state	Reduced DMN connectivity in impaired consciousness
Generalized anxiety disorder	Improved connectivity between different control network Reduced connectivity in salience network

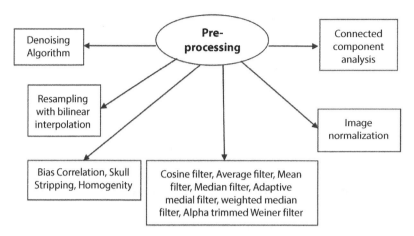

Figure 6.18 Preprocessing methods for rsfMRI analysis.

disorders, psychiatric disorders, brain development etc., Image should be preprocessed before applying the algorithm. Figure 6.18 shows some preprocessing techniques used to process the rsfMRI [28].

Following supervised learning methods are used to analyze the image after preprocessing

1. Linear models
   a. Ridge regression
   b. LASSO regression
   c. Elastic-Net regression
   d. Logistic regression
2. Support vector machine (SVM)
   a. Linear SVM
   b. Kernelized SVM
3. Decision tree
   a. Random forest
   b. Gradient tree
4. Deep learning
   a. Fully connected network
   b. Convolutional network

Unsupervised algorithms used for analyze the image is

1. Clustering
   a. K-means
   b. Spectral

    c. Hierarchical
    d. Gaussian model
  2. Latent models
    a. Decomposition methods
    b. Markov model
  3. Non-linear model
    a. Local linear
    b. Autoencoders

6.11 Conclusion and Future Directions

rsfMRI has delivered novel understandings on the brain network. Synchronous spontaneous BOLD fluctuations of various Resting State Network detects various neurological and Psychiatric disorders. Numerous clinical applications are presently examined and take presurgical planning for different brain disorders. rsfMRI is a non-invasive technique so it does not need patient cooperation. Functional and structural connectivity of brain network is analyzed accurately using different learning algorithms.

The growth of rsfMRI techniques creates an innovative knowledge in the fields of neurology, neuroscience and psychiatry. Enhanced medical applicability moves rsfMRI scanner to multimodal inspections. Impulsive variations of the BOLD signal are correlated with Electroencephalogram, the electron grid records local field and slow cortical potential. Using near infrared spectroscopy spontaneous fluctuations observed using resting-state functional connectivity analyses. Advancement is necessary to analysis different analytical methods and to increase the efficiency in detecting varies brain disease.

References

1. Lee, M.H., Smyser, C.D., Shimony, J.S., Resting-state fMRI: A review of methods and clinical applications. *AJNR Am. J. Neuroradiol.*, 34, 10, 1866–1872, Oct. 2013.
2. Alves, P.N., Foulon, C., Karolis, V. *et al.*, An improved neuroanatomical model of the default-mode network reconciles previous neuroimaging and neuropathological findings. *Commun. Biol.*, 2, 1–14, 2019.
3. de la Iglesia-Vaya, M., Molina-Mateo, J., Escarti-Fabra, M.J., Kanaan, A.S., Marti-Bonmati, L., Brain connections – Resting state fMRI functional

connectivity, novel frontiers of advanced neuroimaging, Jan 9th 2013. Available: https://www.intechopen.com/chapters/41878

4. Li, X., Guo, N., Li, Q., Functional neuroimaging in the new era of big data. *Genom. Proteomic. Bioinform.*, 17, 4, 393–401, 2019.

5. Hohenfeld, C., Werner, C.J., Reetz, K., Resting-state connectivity in neurodegenerative disorders: Is there potential for an imaging biomarker? *NeuroImage Clin.*, 18, 849– 870, Mar.16, 2018.

6. Phinyomark, A., Ibáñez-Marcelo, E., Petri, G., Resting-state fMRI functional connectivity: Big data preprocessing pipelines and topological data analysis. *IEEE Trans. Big Data*, 3, 4, 415–428, Dec. 2017.

7. Gordon, E., Rohrer, J.D., Fox, N.C., Advances in neuroimaging in fronto temporal dementia. *J. Neurochem.*, 138, Suppl 1, 193–210, Aug 2016.

8. Tang, C., Y.Wei, J., Zhao, J.N., Different developmental pattern of brain activities in ADHD: A study of resting-state fMRI. *Dev. Neurosci.*, 40, 3, 246–257, 2018.

9. Proudfoot, M., Bede, P., Turner, M.R., Imaging cerebral activity in amyotrophic lateral sclerosis. *Front. Neurol.*, 9, 1–13, Jan. 2019.

10. Lígia, C., Carlos, S., Elie, C., Diogo, T.-C., Neuroimaging correlates of depression—Implications to clinical practice. *Front. Psychiatry*, 10, 703, 2019.

11. Ramasamy, M.D., Periasamy, K., Krishnasamy, L., Dhanaraj, R.K., Kadry, S., Nam, Y., Multi-disease classification model using Strassen's half of threshold (SHoT) training algorithm in healthcare sector. *IEEE Access*, 9, 112624–112636, 2021.

12. Lee, M.H., Smyser, C.D., Shimony, J.S., Resting-state fMRI: A review of methods and clinical applications. *Am. J. Neuroradiol.*, 34, 10, 1866–1872, Oct 2013.

13. Kalmady, S.V., Towards artificial intelligence in mental health by improving schizophrenia prediction with multiple brain parcellation ensemble-learning. *NPJ Schizophr.*, 5, 1, 1–11, 18 Jan. 2019.

14. Lottman, K.K., Gawne, J.T., Nina. Kraguljac, V., Jeffrey. Killen, F., Meredith. Reid, A., Lahti, C.A., Examining resting-state functional connectivity in first-episode schizophrenia with 7T fMRI and MEG. *NeuroImage Clin.*, 24, 1–10, 2019.

15. Dhanaraj, R.K. *et al.*, Random forest bagging and X-means clustered antipattern detection from SQL query log for accessing secure mobile data. *Wirel. Commun. Mobile Comput.*, 2021, 1–9, 2021.

16. Uddin, L.Q. and Karlsgodt, K.H., Future directions for examination of brain networks in neurodevelopmental disorders, in: *Journal of Clinical Child and Adolescent Psychology: The Official Journal for the Society of Cinical Child and Adolescent Psychology, American Psychological Association, division 53*, vol. 47, 2018.

17. Sudre, G., Choudhuri, S., Szekely, E., Bonner, T., Goduni, E., Sharp, W., Shaw, P., Estimating the heritability of structural and functional brain connectivity

in families affected by attentiondeficit/hyperactivity disorder. *JAMA Psychiatry*, 74, 76–84, 2017.

18. Sripada, C.S., Kessler, D., Angstadt, M., Lag in maturation of the brain's intrinsic functional architecture in attention-deficit/hyperactivity disorder. *Proceedings of the National Academy of Sciences of the United States of America*, vol. 111, pp. 14259–64, 2014.

19. Yan, C.G., Wang, X.D., Zuo, X.N., Zang, Y.F., DPABI: Data processing & analysis for (RestingState) brain imaging. *Neuroinformatics*, 14, 339–351, 2016.

20. Laird, A.R., Eickhoff, S.B., Li, K., Robin, D.A., Glahn, D.C., Fox, P.T., Investigating the functional heterogeneity of the default mode network using coordinate-based meta-analytic modeling, in: *The Journal of Neuroscience: the Official Journal of the Society for Neuroscience*, vol. 29, pp. 14496–505, 2009.

21. Chandraprabha, M. and Dhanaraj, R.K., Machine learning based pedantic analysis of predictive algorithms in crop yield management. *2020 4th International Conference on Electronics, Communication and Aerospace Technology (ICECA). 2020 4th International Conference on Electronics, Communication and Aerospace Technology (ICECA)*, 2020, November 5.

22. Binnewijzend, M.A., Schoonheim, M.M., Sanz-Arigita, E., Wink, A.M., van der Flier, W.M., Tolboom, N., Adriaanse, S.M., Damoiseaux, J.S., Scheltens, P., van Berckel, B.N., Barkhof, F., Resting-state fMRI changes in Alzheimer's disease and mild cognitive impairment. *Neurobiol. Aging*, 33, 9, 2018–28, 2012.

23. Mohammadi-Nejad, A.-R., Mahmoudzadeh, M., Hassanpour, M.S., Otto, F.W., Neonatal brain resting-state functional connectivity imaging modalities. *Photoacoustics*, 10, 1–19, 2018.

24. Phinyomark, A., Ibáñez-Marcelo, E., Petri, G., Resting-state fMRI functional connectivity: Big data preprocessing pipelines and topological data analysis. *IEEE Trans. Big Data*, 3, 4, 415–428, 1 Dec. 2017.

25. Sathish, R. and Kumar, D.R., Proficient algorithms for replication attack detection in wireless sensor networks—A survey, in: *2013 IEEE International Conference ON Emerging Trends in Computing, Communication and Nanotechnology (ICECCN)*, IEEE, pp. 1–7, 2013, March.

26. Boerwinkle, A.L., Vedantam, A., Lam, S., Wilfong, A.A., Curry, D.J., Connectivity changes after laser ablation: Resting-state fMRI. *Epilepsy Res.*, 142, 156–160, 2018.

27. Ries, A., Spectral analysis of resting-state fMRI BOLD signal in healthy subjects and patients suffering from major depressive disorder, 2019.

28. Khosla, M., Jamison, K., Ngo, G.H., Kuceyeski, A., Sabuncu, M.R., Machine learning in resting-state fMRI analysis. *Magn. Reson. Imaging*, 64, 101–121, 2019.

7

Early Prediction of Epileptic Seizure Using Deep Learning Algorithm

T. Jagadesh[1]*, A. Reethika[1], B. Jaishankar[1] and M.S. Kanivarshini[2]

[1]Department of Electronics and Communication Engineering, KPR Institute of Engineering and Technology, Coimbatore, Tamil Nadu, India
[2]HCL Technologies, Chennai, Tamil Nadu, India

Abstract

Epilepsy is one of the most common neurological disorders in the world. Early expectation remains based on approach of seizures affects existence with epileptic patients. A novel patient-explicit seizure is defined in this article, expectation procedure dependent on profound learning and functional to extended haul scalp electroencephalograms (EEG) chronicles is proposed. The main objective is to recognize the preictal mind state besides separate it from predominant at the state of interictal at the correct time as could be expected and make it reasonable for continuous. In this highlights, extraction and characterization measures were consolidated into a solitary computerized framework. Crude EEG signal with no pre-processing is well-thought-out as contribution to the framework, further lessens the calculations. Four profound learning models have been proposed to extricate the most judicial highlights that upgrade the order exactness and expectation time. Our new approach exploits the convolutional neuronic organization in removing the huge spatial highlights from various scalp positions and the repetitive neural organization in expecting the frequency of seizures sooner than the current techniques. A semi-directed methodology dependent on exchange learning strategy is acquainted with enhancement issue. A channel choice calculation is proposed to choose the most pertinent EEG, which makes the projected framework great possibility for continuous use. A powerful test technique is used to guarantee vigor.

Corresponding author: jackshree@gmail.com

M.G. Sumithra, Rajesh Kumar Dhanaraj, Mariofanna Milanova, Balamurugan Balusamy and Chandran Venkatesan (eds.) Brain-Computer Interface: Using Deep Learning Applications, (157–178) © 2023 Scrivener Publishing LLC

Keywords: Epileptic seizure, deep learning, EEG signal

7.1 Introduction

Seizures are a symptom of a primary brain disorder that might short-term or long-term. These arise by chemical changes in nerve cells causing an aberrant burst of electrical commotion in the brain. In most cases, excitant and repressive brain cells are in equilibrium. Former encourages action, whereas latter discourages. When this equilibrium is disturbed and there is either too much or too little activity, seizures (as shown in Figure 7.1) can develop.

Reasons for Seizure Disorders
Seizures consist of many factors:

- Hypoxic-ischemic encephalopathy (HIE)
- Birth injury/trauma

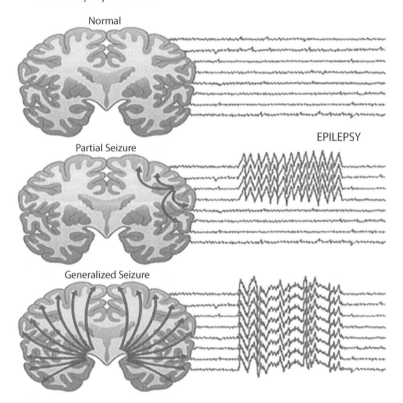

Figure 7.1 Seizure identification.

- Infection
- Genetic factors
- Metabolic/chemical imbalances
- Medication side effects
- Brain tumors

Twitching, spasms, and loss of consciousness are all symptoms of seizures. Changes in feelings and behavior are also possible. It's crucial to understand that seizures can be mild and don't always include the spectacular convulsions that most people associate with them. If a parent or guardian suspects their kid is experiencing a seizure, they should seek medical help immediately.

Seizure disorder diagnostic, such as:

- Electroencephalogram (EEG)
- Bloodwork
- Computed tomography scan (CT or CAT scan)
- Magnetic resonance imaging (MRI)
- Lumbar puncture (spinal tap)

Epilepsy is formed by gathering of nervous problems portrayed by intermittent epileptic seizures [10, 11], scenes can be changed from ephemeral and almost imperceptible stages of extensive stretches to enthusiastic trembling because of unusual electrical movement in the brain [1]. These scenes can bring about actual wounds, either straight-forwardly like broken bones or through causing accidents [1]. In epilepsy, seizures tend to repeat and have no prompt basic reason [10]. Isolated seizures triggered by a specific cause, such as harming, are not thought to be epilepsy [12]. People affected by epilepsy can treated in various method and feel vary degrees of social shame as a result of their diagnosis [1]. Extreme and strange synaptic action in the cortex of the brain is the secret weapon of epileptic seizures [12]. The cause of epilepsy remains unexplained much of the time [1] a few results (Figure 7.2 shows all the types of results) of brain damage, cerebrum cancers, cerebrum defects, or birth deserts in an epileptogenic period [1–3]. Known hereditary transformations are straightforwardly connected to a little extent of cases [4, 13]. The analysis includes precluding different conditions that may cause comparable indications, for example, swooning, and deciding whether another reason for seizures is available, like liquor taking away or electrolyte problems [4]. This might be a part of the way done by the imaging mind and blood tests.

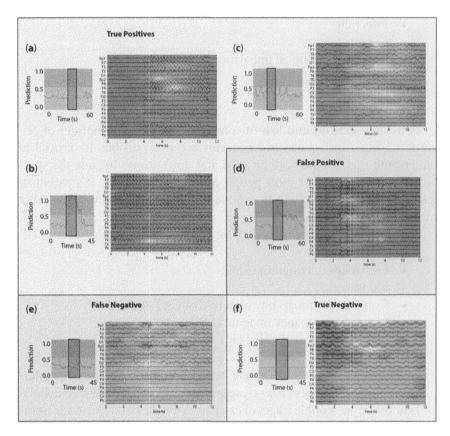

Figure 7.2 Seizure detection simulation results.

Epilepsy that happens because of different issues might curable [1]. Controllable with prescription in the range of 70% cases [7]; cheap enemy of seizure drugs are regularly available [1]. In those whose seizures don't react to medicine, medical procedure, dietary changes may be considered [5, 6]. It is not considered in all instances of deep rooted epilepsy, numerous individuals to point therapy [1].

The most widely recognized sort (60%) of seizures is convulsive which include compulsory muscle contractions [23]; 33% start as summed up seizures from the beginning, influencing the two sides of the equator of the mind and impeding consciousness [23]; 66% start as central seizures (which influence one half of the globe of the cerebrum) advance to summed up [23]. The excess 40% of seizures are non-convulsive. An illustration of sort is the nonattendance seizure, which presents as a diminished degree of cognizance and ordinarily keeps going around 10 seconds [24].

Central seizures are frequently gone before by specific encounters, known as auras. Seizures incorporate tactile (visual, hearing, or smell), clairvoyant, autonomic and engine wonders relying upon what portion of the cerebrum is involved [2]. Muscle jerks may begin in a particular muscle gathering and spread to encompassing bunches, it is known as a Jacksonian march. Automatisms may happen, which are non-deliberately created exercises, for the most part basic dull developments like resembling the lips or more mind boggling exercises, for example, endeavors to get something.

There are six primary kinds of summed up seizures: tonic-clonic, tonic, myoclonic, nonappearance, and unaccented seizures. They all include loss of cognizance and ordinarily occur abruptly.

Tonic-clonic happens in constriction of appendages tracked by their expansion alongside angling of the back which keeps going 10–30 seconds (tonic stage). An exclamation cry might hear because of the constriction of chest muscles, trailed by a shuddering of the appendages as one (clonic stage). Tonic seizures yield consistent compressions of muscles. An individual regularly becomes blue as conscious is halted. In clonic seizures, there is shaking of appendages as one. After the shuddering, halted might require 10–30 minutes for an individual to get back to the business as usual; this is known as "postictal state". Damage inside or bladder control might happen during seizure. Society encountering a seizure stay quiet, either the tip or on the sides; tonic-clonic seizure, chomps sides are added common. Tongue nibbles additionally moderately basic psychogenic non-epileptic seizures.

Myoclonic seizures include fleeting fits of muscles in a couple of regions or all over. Occasionally, it causes the individual to fall, which may get injury. Absence of seizures can be unpretentious with a slight turn of the head or eye squinting with weakened mindfulness [2]; regularly, individual doesn't drop over and gets back to its ordinary at it ends [2]. Atonic seizures includes the deficiency of muscle movement for more than 1 second, normally happening at the two sides of body. Scarcer seizure can cause compulsory abnormal snickering crying, or further perplexing encounters, for example, déjà vu.

About 6% of epilepsy have seizures were regularly set off by explicit occasions known as reflex seizures. With reflex epilepsy are just set off by explicit stimuli. Communal triggers incorporate blazing illuminations and unexpected sounds. In particular sorts of epilepsy frequently during sleep, and in different kinds it happens practically just while sleeping.

Assuming seizures emerge from a particular space of the cerebrum, the underlying indications of the seizure regularly mirror the elements of that space. The correct portion of the mind control the left half of our body, and the left 50% of the cerebrum control the correct side of our body. For instance, if a seizure begins from the correct side of the cerebrum in the space that controls development in the thumb, at that point the seizure may start with jolting of the left thumb or hand.

Seizures differ such that a lot of epilepsy experts habitually rename seizure types. Commonly, seizures have a place in one of two fundamental classifications: essential summed up and incomplete seizures. The contrast can be analyzed between the sorts of the way start. Essential summed up seizures start with a far-reaching electrical release that includes the two sides of the cerebrum immediately. Halfway seizures start with an electrical release in one restricted space of the cerebrum.

Epilepsy in which the seizures start from the two sides of the mind simultaneously is called essential summed up epilepsy. Innate elements are significant in fractional summed up epilepsy, which is bound to include hereditary variables than incomplete epilepsy – a condition where the seizures emerge from a restricted space of the mind.

Some fractional seizures are identified with head injury, mind contamination, stroke or tumor be that as it may, much of the time, the reason is obscure. One inquiry that is utilized to additionally order incomplete seizures is whether awareness (the capacity to react and recall) is hindered or protected. The distinction may appear glaringly evident, yet there are numerous levels of cognizance impedance or conservation.

Epilepsy might be treated with antiepileptic drugs (AEDs), diet treatment, and medical procedure. Prescriptions are the underlying treatment decision for practically all patients with different seizures. A few patients who just have a solitary seizure and whose tests don't show a high probability of seizure repeat may not need drugs. The meds treat the manifestations of epilepsy (the seizures), instead of relieving the fundamental condition. They are exceptionally successful and totally control seizures in the dominant part (roughly 70%) of patients. The medications keep seizures from beginning by lessening the inclination of synapses to convey unreasonable and confounded electrical messages.

Profound learning has been generally utilized for computerized EEG preparing in various settings, for example, mind PC interfaces [7–10], programmed rest scoring [11–14] and epileptic seizure prediction [15–17], and detection [18–22], due to its ability to take in rich portrayals from crude data [23] and its fruitful presentation on visual acknowledgment undertakings, particularly on common images [24]. Specifically, for the programmed seizure identification issue, late methodologies are summed up in Table 7.1. In this table, the initial two sections allude to the technique, the third to

Table 7.1 Classifiers with mean error and standard deviation.

S. no.	Classifiers	Mean error	Standard deviation
1.	LDC	0.17	0.043
2.	QDC	0.15	0.051
3.	UDC	0.30	0.044
4.	TREEC	0.20	0.046
5.	LOGLC	0.18	0.041
6.	SVC	0.15	0.037
7.	PARZENC	0.13	0.043

the data set utilized for the assessment, and the last ones to the detailed measurements, when accessible, for assessing the calculation: grouping and affectability in the reach [0, 100], dormancy right away, and bogus positive rate each hour (FPR/h). In the accompanying sections, we depict more in detail a portion of these examinations. Late commitments to the utilization of profound learning techniques for seizure identification have been created on the dataset given by the University of Bonn26. This data set permits the investigation of an assortment of errands since it includes intracranial EEG signs of interictal and ictal scenes from epileptic patients, just as would be expected scalp accounts of solid subjects. Specifically, in [22], a solitary Recurrent Neural Network (RNN) was proposed to abuse the worldly conditions in EEG signals, which was assessed in a paired (ordinary EEG versus ictal) and a multi-class characterization (ordinary versus interictal versus ictal) plan. In a 13-layer of Convolutional Neural Network (CNN) is assessed on a variation of the multi-class issue, which straightforwardly incorporated the pre-ictal classification. In the paired undertaking, the creators of [21] characterized an increase conspire with covering windows to ease the meager few accessible information to prepare profound learning models. Also, they presented a pyramidal one-dimensional CNN that use nearby data to create a last expectation. Albeit the past strategies effectively distinguished seizures portions, they require extra acclimations to measure multi-channel information, and all the more significantly, they should be approved on long haul EEG signals since the exceptionally brief length of accounts in this data set (23.6s) forestalls an assessment of their power and speculation abilities.

In this work, we address the seizure location issue following a profound taking in procedure got from hearty techniques for object acknowledgment errands in the PC vision field. We will likely copy the visual examination performed by clinical experts when perusing EEG chronicles. For this, we propose a procedure to produce picture portrayals of crude EEG flags that we use as contributions to our seizure identification calculations. We tried our procedures in two diverse datasets, one with just scalp cathodes and the other with consolidated scalp and intracranial chronicles. Our lightweight model with just 314 thousand boundaries and insignificant pre-preparing steps arrived at high seizure location execution, practically identical or in any event, improving past examinations in which signal changes are required for its execution.

Regardless of the advances inside the most recent 20 years, In the EEG seizure identification besides expectation arena, summed up location methods continue moderately deprived. Particularly genuine after contrasted with patient-explicit examinations as talked about. Given this helpless achievement, it very well might be simpler to use an observational in reverse looking, "information mining", or "animal power" approach. This goes against a forward-thinking, rational paradigm approach to finding the right epilepsy highlights. The main examinations in EEG investigation are to distinguish patient-explicit central seizures and general seizures in a much larger population. A seizure EEG design is explicit to a single patient, as Shoeb [5] clarifies. The principle is at the central seizures consists in any part of the mind and as a result in the EEG on explicit channels.

7.2   Methodology

To determine their ability to detect seizers, researchers focused on relationship measurement and the largest Lyapunov type. The research revealed that neither test by itself was useful for the task, but when used together, they performed better. The additionally noticed that connection measurement was simply valuable when extended recurrence sub bands (theta, delta, alpha, gamma and beta), rather than whole 0–60 Hertz spectrum recurrence investigated. The creators inferred those adjustments of elements are not fanned out across the whole range however are restricted to certain recurrence groups. In a near report, investigated the utilization of connection measurement, alongside Hurst type, biggest Lyapunov example, and entropy to recognize typical EEG of seizures. The outcomes description of a general precision is 90%. In the meantime, utilization of the relationship measurement with contends is just mirrors the change in and was little defense of utilization is easier in direct proportional difference.

Despite the fact that numerous methods for seizure detection (Figure 7.3) have recently been proposed, the sub pattern relation between EEG signals

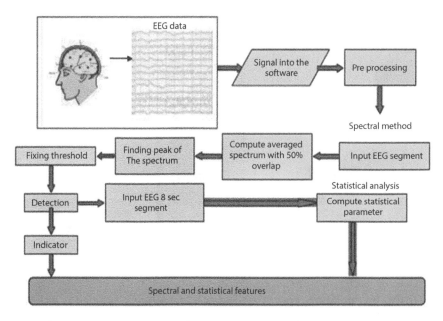

Figure 7.3 Design of block diagram for seizure detection algorithm.

has not been thoroughly examined. The partnership between sub pattern sets is an important role for capturing instructional highlights in neighboring sets that is recorded in an EEG signal has a unique example. For signal classification, SpPCA and SubXPCA used to abstract the secreted instances. Before now, the success of sub pattern-based component decreases methods in EEG signals for seizure analysis had not been studied.

The issue of characterizing the sign as being from an epileptic source is planned to grouping RPS pictures (Figure 7.4 shows the abnormal electrical brain activity due to seizures) of epileptic/non-epileptic subjects utilizing profound learning. Preparing profound learning models requires an enormous dataset of pictures and various emphases for convergence. As getting a huge dataset is testing, we embrace move learning for the task. Move learning plans to utilize the information gained from the source area to the objective spaces. It empowers us to make exact models without preparing a whole organization without any preparation even with a deficient dataset. Instead of gaining without any preparation, we start with designs realized when taking care of an alternate issue. Accordingly, we acquire information (highlights and loads) from recently educated models to prepare new models and try not to continue from scratch. Pre-prepared CNN models like LeNet, AlexNet, VGGNet, GoogLeNet, ResNet, and so on, can be utilized for the assignment.

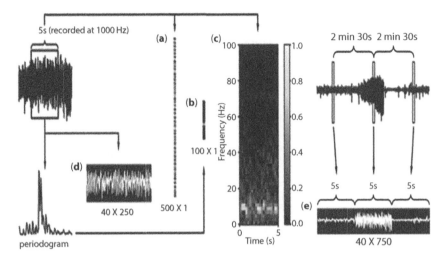

Figure 7.4 Epileptic seizure.

In this investigation, a pre-prepared AlexNet model is utilized as it shows better execution in ordering epileptic seizure sets when contrasted with another best in class of CNN models to be specific LeNet and GoogLeNet. AlexNet changed every one of the records of prior non-profound learning-based strategies. AlexNet contains five convolution (Conv) layers and 3 completely associated (FC) layers. Every convolution layer comprises of 96–384 channels and the size of the channels goes from 3×3 to 11×11 with the element guide of 3–256 channels each. In each layer, a non-direct ReLU (Rectified Linear Unit) enactment work is utilized. ReLU is a significant component of AlexNet rather than the tanh or sigmoid actuation work used to prepare a model for a neural organization. The essential purposes behind utilizing ReLU in Convolution layers are quicker union attributable to the absence of disappearing slope issue and inciting sparsity in the highlights. 3×3 Max pooling is applied to the yields of layer 1, 2 and 5. In the main layer, a step of 4 is utilized to lessen the calculation.

For preparing the proposed model, 90% of epileptic and non-epileptic RPS pictures of the dataset (segment 5.1) are used (75% preparing and 15% approval); 10% of the information is saved for testing. To enhance the presentation defined 10-crease cross approval (CV) is performed. The 10-overlay CV parts the information at irregular into 10-disjoint sub-sets called folds. The defined folds keep up the mean reaction esteem in all folds, which is roughly equivalent. Each crease holds similar extents of the two kinds of class names, in particular epileptic (Set E) and non-epileptic (Sets A, B, C, and D) classes.

Preparing AlexNet model requires weight (Kernels) to be gained from the information. We use back-propagation with cross entropy as the misfortune work alongside the stochastic angle drop for improvement to get familiar with these boundaries. The model is prepared for picture characterization utilizing the Caffe structure. This model is prepared for 200 ages with learning rate (0.01), clump size (128), weight rot (0.0001), gamma (0.1), and force (0.9) as hyper-boundaries. The result is that the model's profundity is huge for its high productivity, which is computationally costly yet made conceivable utilizing designs handling units (GPUs). A few other convoluted CNNs can perform adequately on quicker GPUs, even on enormous datasets. Utilizing K80 GPU machine, this progression takes around 45 minutes for one run of preparing for calculation on UoB datasets.

In view of data from magnetoencephalogram, electromyogram, electrooculogram, electrocardiogram, and EEG, nonlinear unique procedures are successfully utilized in biomedical applications [2–8]. This examination centers around displaying the nonlinear elements of the cerebrum. As generally acknowledged, the mind is viewed as a tumultuous powerful framework, and it produces EEG flags that are typically chaotic [9]. In another sense, an EEG signal as shown in Figure 7.5 is turbulent, as its sufficiency changes haphazardly after some time. These turbulent signs are described by long haul capriciousness, which makes traditional sign preparing strategies less accommodating. Demonstrating the elements is a test when utilizing regular highlights/models.

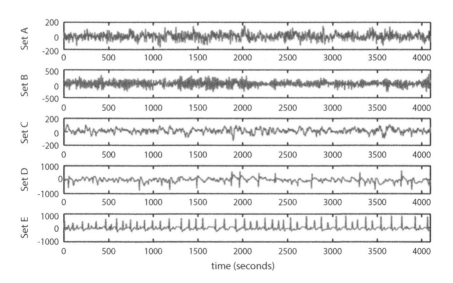

Figure 7.5 Seizure detection.

The AUC results for a couple of classifiers with mean error (as shown in Table 7.1) also showed improvements, with the KNNC classifier achieving 93%. An example for seizure classifier is given in the Figure 7.6. Given that sensitivities are more essential than specificities in this study, this is empowering. The underlying necessity is to gather the dataset of cerebrum signals. Table 7.2 shows the known seizure detection types and their acronyms. For this, diverse observing apparatuses are utilized. EEG and ECoG are the most often used

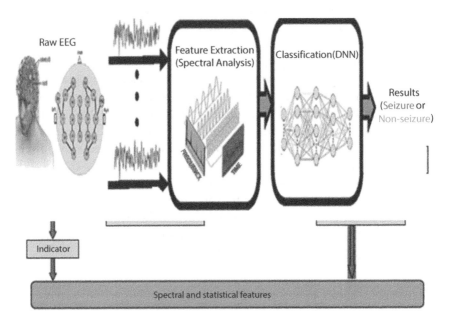

Figure 7.6 DNN-based seizure classifier.

Table 7.2 Acronym of seizure detection.

S. no.	Acronym	Type of detection	Explanation
1.	TP	True positive	Seizure detected
2.	TN	True negative	Non-seizure (no disorder) detected
3.	FP	False positive	Wrong detection of normal patient as seizure
4.	FN	False negative	Inaccurately detecting seizure patient as normal

devices since in channels or anodes were embedded to stick on the outside of scalp accordingly at range of 10–20 Global frameworks in various flaps. Every one of them has a wire association with the EEG gadget, giving convenient data about the varieties in voltage, alongside worldly and spatial data.

There are three parameters for measuring seizure. They are precision, recall, and F-Measure. The ration of true positive to overall positives observed is known as precision. The percentage of true positive events is referred to as recall. The choral precision and recalls the estimated using the F-measure. For information researchers and scientists, a collection of data utilized to significant designed for assessing the presentation of others proposed models. We ought to capture cerebrum signals in epileptic seizure detection. EEG monitoring the most common way intended observing for brain activity. These accounts play a key in AI classifiers that look at novel seizure detection techniques several ways, as early capture diagnosis, quick seizure venue, enduring confiscation exploration, and annexation limitation. Value of publicity is available in the datasets of a baseline to compare and contrast results. Well-known collections of data are widely used in epilepsy will be depicted in the adjacent region.

It is discovered that contrasted with seizure identification, seizure confinement hasn't seen much use of AI classifiers. However, there is some writing on the topic. In these instances, detailed work, creators didn't specify the level of the influenced locale of the mind by a seizure and they couldn't distinguish the specific area at the flaps like occipital, front facing, parietal left and parietal right. Despite the fact that, it isn't our essential goal in this survey paper, while examining the connected distributed exploration, we tracked down some fascinating signs for seizure restriction.

7.3   Experimental Results

The critical factual highlights were extricated by various sorts of change procedures; Discrete Wavelet Changes (DWT), Consistent Wavelet Change (CWT), Fourier change (FT), Discrete Cosine Change (DCT), Solitary Worth Disintegration (SWD), Characteristic Mode Work (IMF), and time–recurrence space in EEG channel. These highlights guarantee to appropriate for capture recognition and in cerebrum linked applications like PC interface (BCI). Asserted exhibition stood assessed utilizing the accompanying measurements like affectability, explicitness, F-score, collector working attributes (ROC) bend, and percentile bootstrap measures.

This dataset involved EEG accounts got from five pharmacoresistant worldly flap patients with 3750 central and non-central bi-variant EEG records. Three affected roles were without seizure, with two patients just taking atmospheres yet no different seizures following a medical procedure. An intracranial strip and profundity cathodes were used to capture the multiple channel EEG signals as shown in Figure 7.7. The terminals were implanted in 10–20 positioning. Depending on if the EEG signals were registered with more than 64 channels, they were measured at 512 or 1024 Hz.

Utilizing the CNN structure, RMSprop (5) calculation and EEG signal, the learning of the weight boundaries of CNN was performed. Keras, an incredible profound learning library that sudden spikes in demand for top of TensorFlow, was used for displaying. During preparing, the cluster size for the information was chosen as 100, and this was used for every one of the preparation refreshes. Since the info information is a one-dimensional cerebrum signal, the CNN model is intended to acknowledge one-dimensional information of size 4096. Z-score standardization was applied for the scaling of each info signal and the upgrade of model speculation was figured it out. Subsequent to getting the info information, the first convolutional activity was applied to the info information and afterward the second convolutional activity was applied to the consequence of the first convolutional activity. Subsequently, the pooling was applied to the yields of the convolutional layer. Pooling diminishes the elements of the information.

Expanding the quantity of convolutional layers will permit us to acquire all the more profound highlights; however, this likewise builds the

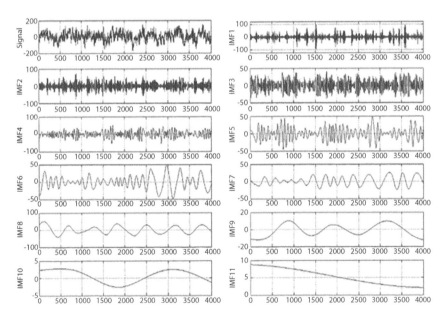

Figure 7.7 Simulated EEG signals with epilepsy.

computational time. The completely associated network with three layers is applied for grouping purposes.

We performed weight regularization to improve the learning of the CNN. This permitted us to decrease over-fitting prompting quicker advancement of the CNN model. We likewise rearranged the information previously parting it into the preparation and testing sets. Around there, the classes were similarly disseminated over the preparing and testing sets. Then, we applied the dropout activity. A profound neural organization needs to get familiar with countless boundaries, which on account of a little dataset is probably going to cause over-fitting. This issue is addressed by planning dropout innovation to forestall include locators from co-adapting. The vital idea of dropout is to drop units haphazardly from the neural organization during preparing, with a predefined likelihood (alongside their associations). Dropout strategy significantly takes out over-fitting and gives significant benefits over different types of regularization. We presented the dropout layer in the proposed model after the last ReLU actuation work. The built model incorporates include extraction and characterization modules, which improves the design of the epilepsy ID model. By including more convolutional layers or utilizing other non-direct capacities, we can expand the exhibition qualities and furthermore the precision of

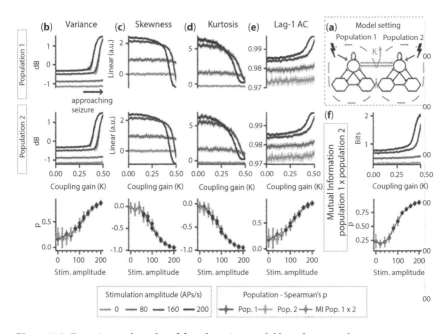

Figure 7.8 Experimental results of deep learning model based seizure detection.

the model. Be that as it may, this will prompt complexity of the design and learning interaction of the model. Subsequently, diminishing the quantity of layers prompts an abatement in the precision pace of CNN.

Some measurable highlights were separated from EEG signals and these highlights were used as contribution to a strategic model tree (LMT) for epileptic seizure ID. The introduced technique was tried utilizing benchmark EEG dataset. The detection results are given in Figure 7.8. The papers referenced above portray various philosophies utilized for extraction of highlights and grouping purposes. The correctness's of these planned models are significant execution attributes of the planned frameworks. In the paper [21] that utilized discrete wavelet change (DWT), the EEG signals were divided into recurrence sub-groups prompting the extraction of factual highlights. The PCA, free segments examination (ICA) and straight discriminant investigation (LDA) were used for information size decrease.

7.4   Taking Care of Children with Seizure Disorders

Managing a seizure condition in a kid relies on a variety of circumstances, including the age, overall health and type of seizure that occurs. Seizures in children can be treated.

Seizure medications: For children with seizure disorders, a wide range of medicines can be administered. Doctors do tests such as blood work, urinalysis, and EEGs to check how patients are reacting for a particular drug and if required, modify the type of medication.

7.5   Ketogenic Diet

A low-carbohydrate, high-protein, high-fat diet and induce the body to generate ketones, energy when carbohydrate intake is insufficient. The generation of ketones is critical to the effectiveness of this diet in terms of seizure management. The ketogenic diet should only be tried under the supervision of a physician.

7.6   Vagus Nerve Stimulation (VNS)

Process that involves surgically implanting a tiny battery into the chest and connecting it to the vague nerve using thin cables (located in the neck). When a kid detects the onset of a seizure, a magnet is placed over the battery, will stop the seizure.

7.7   Brain Surgeries

Brain surgery may be a possibility if a child's seizures are uncontrollable by conventional means. This entails either eliminating the portion of the brain that is generating the seizures or blocking the propagation of seizure-inducing electric currents. While considering the brain surgery for seizures, a vital to think about how the removal of seizure-causing ports could influence other processes.

Consult experienced medical specialists to identify the best treatment choices for your kid. Individual symptoms will determine a safe and effective seizure therapy choice.

Some want to have a seizure dog in addition to medical assistance. These animals are taught to notify family members and shield the kid from danger during uncontrollable movements, or activate an alarm system in the event of a seizure. They can even predict seizures before they happen in some situations.

7.8   Conclusion

With the expansion of epilepsy, its precise identification turns out to be progressively significant. A significant test is to recognize seizures accurately from an enormous dimension of information. Due to intricacy of EEG signals in several datasets, AI classifiers suitable for precise detection of seizure. Regardless, picking out the suitable classifiers and highlights is, critical. Thus, this paper has exhaustively checked on AI approaches for seizure discovery. Accordingly, we presume that 'non-discovery' classifiers— choice woodland (outfit of choice trees) is best. This is on the grounds that it can deliver numerous reasonable, illustrative logic rules for forecasting with high accuracy. Further, it may also assist in the discovery of relevant information such as seizure restriction and seizure forms. Actually, 'discovery' classifiers can't produce rationale rules, despite the fact that they can accomplish high prescient precision. Concerning choosing appropriate highlights, we should choose those that can give consistent outcomes. All the patients have been tested and were encountered up to 2–5 seizures, and a dataset consists of chronicles of 87 seizures from 21 patients. In the view of data collections, 6 contacts has been chosen for better understanding through visual review in the iEEG information by knowledgeable epileptologists: three close to the epileptic center (epileptogenic zone) and other three were in far off areas associated with annexation spread and proliferation. The subject went in age from the range of 10–50 years and infused with 13 ladies and eight men. Three distinctive type of seizure was addressed mid of the subjects, with basic incomplete (SP), complex halfway (CP), summed up tonic-clonic (GTC), and all subjects obligated encountered in any event two sorts. The epileptic center was situated in neocortical mind edifices with eleven patients, then hippocampus in eight patients, and two patients in two areas. The annexation begins occasionally and epileptic form exercises were commented by the ensured epileptologists at the Epilepsy Centre.

The characterization of interictal, ictal and preictal signals, just in precision of each tolerant was introduced; normal exactness of grouping among 21 patients was 92.3%. Patients were correctness's order for nine patients with >95%, which has been viewed as an incredible outcome, and the characterization exactness was useful for eight patients, with values going somewhere in the range of 90% and 95%. The precision of sign grouping for the other four patients was <90%.

Seizure expectation is characterized as the programmed acknowledgment of forthcoming seizures where the forecast window can be up to a few minutes [18]. Achievement in foreseeing epileptic seizures would do horde advantages such as evasion of wounds, calming nervousness, crisis help and early mediation (for example early drug, electric incitement of vague nerve, profound cerebrum incitement). Four key stages are basic to investigation of seizure expectation. They are: 1) "interictal", demonstrating the "ordinary" cerebrum state which is a long way from seizures; 2) "preictal "alluding to the time stretch preceding the seizure; 3) "ictal", as time-frame in which seizure0happens; 4) "postictal stage", relating to the period following a seizure and before an "ordinary" mind state. The preictal period, described by powerful development of EEG signals preceding seizures is the examination center for the seizure expectation. Because of the powerful idea of preictal EEG, it is accounted for that the hypothesis of turbulent elements exhibits preferred unsurprising capacity over direct estimations [13]. The benefits of bi-variate and multivariate gauges over uni-variate (for example ghastly force) have been demonstrated [14].

Finding the essential epileptogenic zone is troublesome, since electric movement of seizure may upheaval unexpectedly and all the while proliferating over a wide scope of cortical zones. Signs gathered by intracranial cathodes with high goal are viewed as the ideal to research the SOZ. Among them, high recurrence swaying (HFO) conveys data distinction from low-recurrence releases, which is featured as SOZ corresponded biomarkers in epilepsy. In the past examinations, a few basic highlights or segments (quick movement, signal leveling, moderate expected shift, and so forth) have been investigated utilizing intracranial anodes (counting stereotactically-embedded intracranial EEG [SEEG], subdural electrocorticography [ECoG], and so forth) Given seizure beginning is a perplexing marvel which is created by different spatio-worldly components, focusing on single element can't be assessed in disconnection. Consequently, we construed ML procedures could address those worries. Grinenko *et al.* built up a SVM-based learning model to find a "unique mark", which adequately separated time-recurrence examples of the SOZ from spaces of engendering [24].

ML as an arising method renders principled, programmed and target calculations for high-dimensioned furthermore, convoluted information, which shows its benefit in EEG signal investigation contrasted with conventional techniques. Regardless of the benefits of ML (for example little biasness and high affectability to designs acknowledgment), solid classifiers, explicit component extraction, very much chose information and calculation cost should all be thought about. For instance, channel choice on specific conditions can decrease calculation stacking of both element extraction and example acknowledgment, which is attainable for the on-line calculation particularly for some wearable or implantable gadgets in genuine application. Another likely option is to exploit distributed computing connected by 5G innovation to acknowledge constant trade of EEG recording. As for ML techniques, profound learning as a hot procedure in picture preparing, yet it is simply beginning to arise in EEG handling, which show its predominance in EEG design acknowledgment

References

1. Tzimourta, K.D., Tzallas, A.T., Giannakeas, N., Astrakas, L.G., Tsalikakis, D.G., Angelidis, P., Tsipouras, M.G., A robust methodology for classification of epileptic seizures in eeg signals. *Health Technol.*, 9, 2, 135–142, 2019.
2. Alickovic, E., Kevric, J., Subasi, A., Performance evaluation of empirical mode decomposition, discrete wavelet transform, and wavelet packed decomposition for automated epileptic seizure detection and prediction. *Biomed. Sign Process. Contr.*, 39, 94–102, 2018.
3. Shimizu, M., Iiya, M., Fujii, H., Kimura, S., Suzuki, M., Nishizaki, M., Left ventricular end-systolic contractile entropy can predict cardiac prognosis in patients with complete left bundle branch block. *J. Nucl. Cardiol.*, 3, 1–10, 2019.
4. Altunay, S., Telatar, Z., Erogul, O., Epileptic EEG detection using the linear prediction error energy. *Exp. Syst. Appl.*, 37, 8, 5661–5665, 2010.
5. Lee, S.-H., Lim, J.S., Kim, J.-K., Yang, J., Lee, Y., Classification of normal and epileptic seizure eeg signals using wavelet transform, phase-space

reconstruction, and Euclidean distance. *Comput. Methods Progr. Biomed.*, 116, 1, 10–25, 2014.

6. Chandaka, S., Chatterjee, A., Munshi, S., Cross-correlation aided support vector machine classifier for classification of EEG signals. *Exp. Syst. Appl.*, 36, 2, 1329–1336, 2009.

7. Moslem, B., Karlsson, B., Diab, M.O., Khalil, M., Marque, C., Classification performance of the frequency-related parameters derived from uterine EMG signals, in: *Proceedings of the International Conference of the IEEE Engineering in Medicine and Biology Society*, Massachusetts, USA, Boston, pp. 3371–3374, 2011.

8. Hassan, M., Terrien, J., Marque, C., Karlsson, B., Comparison between approximate entropy, correntropy and time reversibility: Application to uterine electromyogram signals. *Med. Eng. Phys.*, 33, 8, 980–986, 2011.

9. Wang, C.-M., Zhang, C.-M., Zou, J.-Z., Zhang, J., Performance evaluation for epileptic electroencephalogram (EEG) detection by using Neyman–Pearson criteria and a support vector machine. *Physica A: Stat. Mech. Appl.*, 391, 4, 1602–1609, 2012.

10. Patnaik, L.M. and Manyam, O.K., Epileptic EEG detection using neural networks and post-classification. *Comput. Method. Prog. Biomed.*, 91, 2, 100–109, 2008.

11. Srinivasan, V., Eswaran, C., Sriraam, N., Approximate entropy-based epileptic EEG detection using artificial neural networks. *IEEE Trans. Inform. Technol. Biomed.*, 11, 3, 288–295, 2007.

12. Panda, R., Khobragade, P.S., Jambhule, P.D., Jengthe, S.N., Pal, P.R., Ghandhi, T.K., Classification of EEG signal using wavelet transform and support vector machine for epileptic seizure diction, in: *Proceedings of the International Conference on Systems in Medicine and Biology*, Kharagpur, India, pp. 405–408, December 2010.

13. Nasehi, S. and Pourghassem, H., Patient-specific epileptic seizure onset detection algorithm based on spectral features and IPSONN classifier, in: *Proceedings of the 3rd International Conference on Communication Systems and Network Technologies (CSNT '13)*, Gwalior, India, IEEE, pp. 186–190, 2013.

14. Williamson, J.R., Bliss, D.W., Browne, D.W., Epileptic seizure prediction using the spatiotemporal correlation structure of intracranial EEG, in: *Proceedings of the IEEE International Conference on Acoustics, Speech, and Signal Processing (ICASSP '11)*, Prague, Czech Republic, IEEE, pp. 665–668, May 2011.

15. Taft, L.M., Evans, R.S., Shyu, C.R. *et al.*, Countering imbalanced datasets to improve adverse drug event predictive models in labor and delivery. *J. Biomed. Inform.*, 42, 2, 356–364, 2009.

16. Chandaka, S., Chatterjee, A., Munshi, S., Cross-correlation aided support vector machine classifier for classification of EEG signals. *Exp. Syst. Appl.*, 36, 2, 1329–1336, 2009.

17. Polat, K. and Gunes, S., A novel data reduction method: Distance based data reduction and its application to classification of epileptiform EEG signals. *Appl. Math. Comput.*, 200, 1, 10–27, 2008.

18. Khan, Y.U., Rafiuddin, N., Farooq, O., Automated seizure detection in scalp EEG using multiple wavelet scales, in: *Proceedings of the IEEE International Conference on Signal Processing, Computing and Control (ISPCC '12)*, IEEE, Waknaghat, India, pp. 1–5, March 2012.

19. Chandaka, S., Chatterjee, A., Munshi, S., Cross-correlation aided support vector machine classifier for classification of EEG signals. *Exp. Syst. Appl.*, 36, 2, 1329–1336, 2009.

20. Wang, Y., Simon, M., Bonde, P. *et al.*, Prognosis of right ventricular failure in patients with left ventricular assist device based on decision tree with SMOTE. *IEEE Trans. Inform. Technol. Biomed.*, 16, 3, 383– 390, 2012.

21. Acir, N. and Guzelis, C., Automatic spike detection in EEG by a two-stage procedure based on support vector machines. *Comput. Biol. Med.*, 34, 7, 561–575, 2004.

22. Leman, H., Marque, C., Gondry, J., Use of the electro-hysterogram signal for characterization of contractions during pregnancy. *IEEE Trans. Biomed. Eng.*, 46, 10, 1222–1229, 1999.

23. LeVan, P., Urrestarazu, E., Gotman, J., A system for automatic artifact removal in ictal scalp EEG based on independent component analysis and Bayesian classification. *Clin. Neurophysiol.*, 117, 4, 912–927, 2006.

24. Blanco, S., Kochen, S., Rosso, O.A., Salgado, P., Applying time-frequency analysis to seizure EEG activity. *IEEE Eng. Med. Biol. Mag.*, 16, 1, 64–71, 1997.

8

Brain–Computer Interface-Based Real-Time Movement of Upper Limb Prostheses Topic: Improving the Quality of the Elderly with Brain-Computer Interface

S. Vairaprakash[1]* and S. Rajagopal[2]

[1]*Department of Electronics and Communication Engineering, Ramco Institute of Technology, Rajapalayam, Tamil Nadu, India*
[2]*Department of Information Technology, National Engineering College, Kovilpatti, Tamil Nadu, India*

Abstract

The early development of Human-Computer Interaction (HCI) was limited to a couple of external computer interfaces, like the keyboard, mouse, or graphical user interface, to enable users to communicate easily with the computer. Modern HCI includes input interfaces, including a joystick, bio-sensors, and power-input devices, for example, steering wheel, and electromechanical actuators, biomechanical, and optical/optoelectronic equipment. The BCI interfaces usually bypass the natural neuro-muscular controls and aim to serve as an alternative means of communication/control in the event of a neuronal/motor failure. The chapter covers BCI on cognition, sensors, machine learning, neurophysiology, psychology, signal detection and processing, source localization, pattern recognition, clustering, and classification of the signals. The components of an EEG-BCI are (i) preprocessing, (ii) extraction of the feature, (iii) selection of features, and (iv) classification. In the pre-processing stage, preliminary processing like the filtering of EEG signals takes place. The EEG signals are subsequently processed using one or more extraction methods after pre-processing. This step is designed to extract relevant special signals that match the various mental state of the user. The selection of functionality in a BCI system is an optional step, which mainly seeks to

Corresponding author: vairamp123@gmail.com

M.G. Sumithra, Rajesh Kumar Dhanaraj, Mariofanna Milanova, Balamurugan Balusamy and Chandran Venkatesan (eds.) Brain-Computer Interface: Using Deep Learning Applications, (179–204) © 2023 Scrivener Publishing LLC

select from the original feature vector (received as a result of the extraction process) the most important differentiable features and to delete redundant features. Only those features that have high discrimination in different mental states are thus retained after this step. A BCI system's main task is to correctly identify the user's different mental conditions from the incoming EEG by using a classifier. The feature selection, as well as the classification algorithm designed for that purpose, must therefore take into account two important issues: (i) unstable (ii) uncertain nature of EEG. The objective of an ideal BCI system is to produce a recognition rate of 100% in the real world, taking both issues into account. Secondly, different BCI strategies for real-time control of a robot arm have been designed using brain signals such as motor imagery, error-related signals, and P300.

Keywords: BCI interface, EEG, signal processing, classification, machine learning, error-related signal, P300, preprocessing

8.1   Introduction

Interaction between human and computer systems is intended to refine non-muscular communication between humans (users) and computers (or machine). Brain Computer (BCI) is the most prevalent kind of HCI which aims at translating ideas into signals needed to run a computer or move a robot (in brain signals). Researchers are now researching on the BCI technologies for use in industrial and military applications in the areas of refurbishment, gaming, communication, and hands-free robot control. The present work provides an overview of the benefits of electroencephalography (EEG) in BCI for rehabilitation purposes. This proposed work also addresses the various kinds of EEG signals acquired during various cognitive activities. Different strategies of extraction, feature selection, and classification carried out by researchers worldwide in recent years are particularly noted. Main attention in this work is placed on diverse control systems for artificial instruments, such as wheelchair, upper limb prothesis and the BCI technology cursor and keyboard controls.

BCI technologies are intended to decode brain signals to detect the cognitive tasks done by a user. The visually evocative (SDV) potential, SCP, P300, ERD/ERS and error-related potential, is a few well-known signals of the brain (depending on the cognitive tasks performed). The EEG-BCI analysis relies on the individual's cognitive task for choosing brain signals (or the modality of signals). The results of ERD/ERS have been encouraging for the identification of visually inspired errors – whether it be motor planning, imagination or performance (also known as motor image signal); These signals are therefore significant in our current inquiry. Early research at BCI employed a single signal mode in P300, SSVEP and ERD control applications.

Recent research, however, have highlighted the efficacy of the hybrid BCI (i.e. detection of at least two blood states simultaneously or sequentially) in control applications. For example, a motor-image-based switch was employed by [1] to change ON/OFF into a BCI-based SSVEP. [2] employed engine and P300 signal imaging for continuous 2D cursor control as well as for wheelchair direction and speed correspondingly. In addition, the BCI control system is prone to mistakes when recognizing the object, as is any other communication modality based on physiologically based signals and bodily channels (e.g. muscle activity, talk and gesticulation). So it is not enough to use simply MI signals in the actual world for controlling an external device. To increase the performance of a control system, it is required to have another signal modality in place of MI signals to discover mistakes. In addition, if the error occurs by the person, the brain generates a unique sort of EEG. The BCI control system may be equated with this sort of EEG, called Error Related Potential (ErRP), as an error feedback feature.

Most ErRP studies are conventional tasks for reacting with a stimulus when participants reply and if the subject does an improper action, ErRP takes place. Other investigations include employing ErRP as a feedback that shows inaccurate interface replies and not the subjects themselves any longer. An example of this is when a person is trying to move a robot arm to a target, but the system might either not reach the goal or totally crossed the target. Error-related negativity (ERN) and error-related positivity (Pe) are distinguished by the existence of ErRP. Early following the error during different choices, the ERN component is noticed even when the participant is unaware of the error. The ERN is characterized by a strong negative signal that begins in the same way as any wrong response and normally peaks 80–150 milliseconds after the misrepresentation.

8.1.1   Motor Imagery Signal Decoding

Engine imagery is one of BCI's most often investigated brain signals. In [3] present a way of classifying between left and right images using a self-organizing flush neural network-based time series predictor. For each electrode, a separate fuzzy neural network is employed to extract its related functions over time. Features are built by a sliding window from the average squared error of the forecasts. There are several inputs and just one output in the design of the two-organized fuzzy neural networks.

The reason for the use of an automated, fumigated neural network was that they can acclimate themselves with very little information of the subject or the parameter selection to the EEG signals of each individual. The system is designed to work in real time, where the dynamic of the EEG of each individual is continual learning and continual adjustment. In 300 trials of two participants the algorithm was evaluated. In around 3–4 seconds, more than 75% accuracy was reached. Another research reported in [4] offered the extraction process using the Approximate Entropy statistic approach (ApEn). ApEn assesses the predictability of oscillations in a time series so that complicated issues may be categorized. ApEn has the benefit of being robust or artifacts-free. Initially, ApEn was created for handling short and noisy data from series times, and it could identify changes in the underlying episode which otherwise would not be reflected in peak events or amplitudes. The more complicated the data sequence, the greater the ApEn value. In [5] used two standard datasets as the basis for extraction of features and used the classification of linear discrimination. For all participants in both data sets, a precision of greater than 90% was obtained. Compared to quick Fourier transformations as another extractor, ApEn delivered a superior outcome with 10 % more precision for all topics.

8.2   Literature Survey

In [6] developed a wavelet independent packet-based component analysis (WPICA), which was used to remove the ERD/ERS patterns from various frequency bands in a complicated low limb motion picture. No imaginary portion that negates the impact of frequency permutation emerges in WPICA processing. The original signal is also converted into a sparse distribution that stresses the non-Gaussian character of the signal detected. Due to the three complicated imaging motions, which integrate standing and right/hand movement and homolateral motions, EEG data have been acquired in this investigation. Then each characteristic frequency band extracts its independent components from the WPICA and the main ones which carry the greatest ERD/ERS information are redirected to its respective electrode time frequency domain. The approach provided was evaluated with 10 participants. The precision of WPICA, higher than the conventional ICA (72.3%) and not spatial filter conditions was attained in about 80% (68.34%). This approach is an excellent strategy for recognizing ERD/ERS designs and increases the performance of complicated mental tasks in pattern categorization. Genetic algorithms were used as a feature selection approach by [7] for classifying motor imaging data between two groups. The study uses a mixture of spectral characteristics and continual transformation of the wavelet utilizing the Mother Wavelet Morlet, discrete transformation of the wavelet, autoregressive models, and a matching μ rhythm filter. The best appropriate set is chosen with Genetic Algorithm from this wide range of attributes. The methodology presented was applied to the BCI competition IV dataset IIb and produced a coefficient of 0.613 kappa. CSP is highly adapted to discriminating ERD/ERS patterns in mind. common spatial patterns are highly suited. For the removal of discriminatory patterns from EEG, many variations of the CSP have been developed. Time delay was used in one approach [8] to extend the CSP method to state space. In classification precision and in its generalization capacity, this kind of CSP was considered to exceed traditional CSP. Another technique employs the CSP adaptive methods of learning [9], that extracts the first CSP component and an online deflation process estimates minor components. Compared to the retraining of all data, this technique has reduced calculation costs and is better fit for developing the BCI online system. A fixed filter bank of Chebyshev Type 2 IIR filter is used for the CSP subband (SBCS P), and a CSP extractor for each frequency band (CSP) is followed by the extraction of CSP functions [10]. A proposal was made to Filter Bank CSP (FBCSP) to find the optimal frequency bands by computing the reciprocal information with a class label between the CSP characteristics [11]. The FCSP (DFBCSP) discriminative was suggested on the basis of analyzing the fishery relationship of the EEG-filtered signal of channels C3 or C4 [12] for attaining a particular discriminatory topic FB. The CSP (SWDCSP) sliding window filters the raw EEG data in a series of overlapped frequency bands using a sliding window, and then selects a discriminatory function set using an unattended technique called Affinity Propagation (AP) [13]. In [14] developed an Artificial Neural Evolutionary Network (EANN) for the categorization of motor imagery data. The ANN design was developed by the application of Genetic Algorithms (GA) and Particle Swarm Optimization (PSO) to tune its parameters in this study. The CSP is picked as a feature vector and the PSO-based technique exhibited an impaired execution time of 28%, and the average accuracy of 78% was compared to the classical technique and was similar to the best result. In [15], Khushaba *et al.* suggested an FS methodology based on differential evolution (DE), which exceeded the FS methodology of GA and PSO. DEFS has also experienced a reduction in the memory need and the cost of computing. The EEG information generated from parietal brain in the work of [16] was obtained as subject-specific characteristics of the time and frequencies. A sliding window was utilized to improve latency and frequency, and a low-pass filter was utilized in order to remove the frequency components. The standardized amplitudes for each window were then selected. The feature vector is linked to an SVM classification using RBF as the kernel. The outcome was 80.25% categorization. The accuracy of classifications in a research also varied from 90.5% to 99.7% with an average of 96%, with a linear support vector machine as a classification [17]. The Linear Vector Quantization (LVQ) was employed for online categorization in a research conducted by [18]. The characteristics chosen for the classification have been derived from two channels from a 1 second epoch, 4 band power estimations, each of 250 milliseconds, per EEG channel and range. The LVQ classifier produces a classification plus a measure on the basis of these 16 features by trial that defines the certainty of the classification. The online rating results were from 10% to 38.12% mistake, with average of 21.9%±6.40 inaccuracy. In [19] used two HMM's, one for left motor imaging and the other for right motor imagery. During their respective motor images, they were instructed utilizing trials. As a feature-vector set in this example, Hjorth Parameters were employed. Two categorization approaches were explored in another paper by [20]: (1) PCA+HMM+SVM (HMM1), and (2) (HMM2). The accuracy of HMM1 using PCA is measured at 75.70%, whereas 60,63% of raw data accuracy is derived. There was a comparable rise in HMM2 although it was also more precise in HMM1. Hybrid classifiers for the categorization of motor images are therefore also conceivable.

8.3   Methodology of Proposed Work

Current research in neuro-prosthetics is targeted at creating numerous rehabilitative assistance computational models and methodologies. In this chapter we are aiming for classification of finger, elbow and shoulder movement alongside left and right movement, so that a simulated robot arm may be navigated in 3D to a given place. The key contribution of this chapter is the development of an energy optimum trajectory planner based on differential developments that may determine the ideal route towards the goal by means of the classification output for the robot arm. A trajectory planner is engaged by the classification result for each individual movement package. As elements of this study, the distribution of the likelihood of Hurst coefficients, which is derived after a multi-fractal declined fluctuation analysis of the inbound EEG data, is employed. While neural-network-based classifiers such as Adaptive Neural Fuzzy Inference System (ANFIS) are effective at dealing with EEG signals, the type-2 interval fuzzy system was proposed for improvement of its unsafe management. In addition, a classifier must identify more than two mental states in real-time settings. Thus, in this chapter is introduced a multi-class discriminating algorithm based on the merger of interval type 2 and ANFIS. Two variations have been created of this approach using One-vs.-All and One-vs.-One techniques, which are utilized to generate the final hyperplan from each ANFIS contradiction. The control and classification scheme were evaluated in experiments to plan trajectory of the simulated robot arm and the accuracy of the classification achieved above 88%, and the success rate of the robot arm to reach the goal exceeds 85% of the classifier. The result demonstrates the efficiency of our classification method in the field of uncertain and uncertain signal classifying above other conventional ones.

8.3.1   Proposed Control Scheme

Figure 8.1 summarizes the fundamental approach for controlling a limb of a robot utilizing engine execution signals as control commands. The research volunteers need to maneuver the virtual robot arm to a predetermined final location in its start position. To do this assignment, the subject decides the current movement of the robot according to the present robot location in respect to the known target (or goal) location. The controlling signals would be generated using the following execution commands: Left Finger (RF), Right Elbow (RE), and Right Shoulder (RS) are recorded in the form of an EEG Sign from the subject's scalp, and Left Elbow (LE) and RS are also recorded in the form of an EEG sign. Table 8.1 shows the list of execution controls for the robot arm subject and his related control signals.

The recorded EEG is then first filtered on the two channels, and then multi-factor, trend-strength fluctuation analysis extracts characteristics related to the motor execution signals. The characteristics should then be sent to the proposed ANT2FIS multiclass classificatory for determining engine execution outputs.

The output of the classifier is then supplied into the local trajectory planner as control signals (i.e. trajectory planners for every control signal), simulating robot-arm movement based on the energy-efficient method for the trajectory planner. Based on the performance of chasseurs, the trajectory planner plans the most energy-efficient way and offers comments on this topic. The topic would pick the next move on the basis of comments and continue till the objective is achieved. Furthermore, for each state the local trajectory planner would interpolate the location of every robot arm link (w.r.t. target location), thereby minimizing the energy usage.

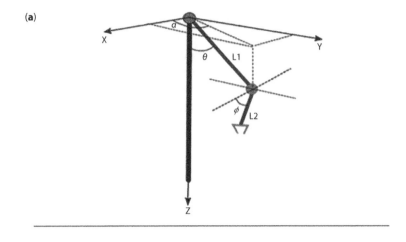

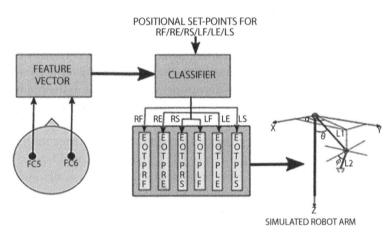

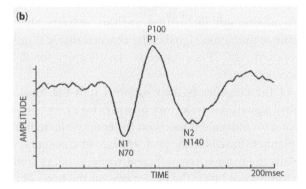

Figure 8.1 (a) The proposed robot arm management approach employing the energy optimized trajectory planner (EOTP). (b) Waveform of related potential.

Table 8.1 Mental tasks and their respective Scheme 1 control instructions.

Motor execution commands	Encoding	Motion
Right Shoulder Right Elbow Right Finger Left Shoulder Left Elbow Left Finger No motion	1–100 1–200 1–300 2–100 2–200 3–300 1–000/2–000	$\alpha sp = \alpha sp + 10°$ $\alpha sp = \theta sp + 10°$ Release object α $sp = \alpha sp - 10 circ$ θ $sp = \theta sp - 10 circ$ Grasp object no motion

8.3.2 One Versus All Adaptive Neural Type-2 Fuzzy Inference System (OVAANT2FIS)

N binary ANFIS classifiers are required in accordance with the OVA technique to differentiate between each class and the appropriate (N - 1) classes. Here, the hyperplane fi is built by the i_{th} classifier, with N such fi to yield the last output combination.

The distance from its respective hyperplane fi for all known classes of a certain collection of vectors for each binary classifier output is calculated in OVA-ANT2FIS. If the data-point distance x is positive or zero from f1, x is class 1 x. Instead, x will not belong to class 1, if the distance is negative. The classificatory corresponding to that class shall, in the ideal circumstance, give a positive or zero distance for a given class, say class 1. The other classifier shall provide a negative distance. However, more than one classifier can achieve a positive or zero distance in practice. The distances between each such classificatory are compared and the classifier is selected for the final output class to which the data point belongs with the highest distance from its respective hyperplane connector. The basis of this step is the idea that, as the distance is increasingly positive, the chance of x belonging to class I increases and is independent of the differences introduced by previous classifiers (N-1).

8.3.3 Position Control of Robot Arm Using Hybrid BCI for Rehabilitation Purpose

The trials were conducted in five normal right-hand individuals aged between 22 and 28 years. The brain signals are recorded during the studies with a neuron (made by NASAN) EEG 19 Electrodes EEG (Figure 4.1).

Motor imaging indications were found in the prior literature [21] to come from the cortical motor regions (primary motor cortex, sensor area, and pre-motor cortex) and to create significant P300 signals in the cingulated cortex region. Data are processed in accordance with C3 and C4 sites for motor imaging (MI), Fz error detection signal (ErRP) and Pz signal for P300 detection The test session is equivalent to a training session with an additional 2 second feedback time after each exam. Again, an additional feedback time of 2 seconds is provided after a statement in the online test stimulus (b). The test stimuli comprise of 20 error-responding studies and 80 correct answers investigations.

The ErRP classification concept and test are similar to those for P300 detection. In Schema 1 and 2, if the ErRP detector produces y = 1 output, the system moves the robot's arm farther and if y = 0. The robot's arm continues to travel. The main difference between Scheme 1 and Scheme 2 is observed after error detection: In Scheme 1, the detector registers the preceding system status. After the MI detector is activated prior to ErRP (directional error), the robot arm is stopped and returned to the former location of the detector. When a P300 detector is enabled before the ErRP detector is active (positional error occurrence), the system re-aligns the robot arm with an offset toward the target position. In system 2, the detector pauses the robot arm movement and offsets the robot arm to the target point. Figure 8.2 gives the electrode distribution in the proposed work.

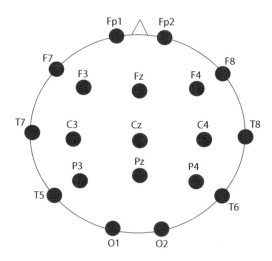

Figure 8.2 Ten to 20 electrode sites on the 19 channels selected.

8.3.4   Jaco Robot Arm

Built in by Kinova, Jaco Robot Arm is a six-axis, three-fingered hand robotic manipulator. With a maximum range of 90 cm radius and a maximums range of 30 cm/sec the arm has entire flexibility of six degrees. It consists of three sensors: strength, location, and speed.

This arm can be fitted to a wheelchair for someone with an upper arm impairment. The robot's top arm consists of three bonds which resemble the human body's top extremity. The manufacturer provides an API which provides additional user control flexibility.

8.3.5   Scheme 1: Random Order Positional Control

The fundamental scheme block diagram is shown in Figure 8.3. The suggested controlling technique allows the three links of the robot arm to move in any random sequence (translation/rotation), as the user wanted. Three detectors for the identification of MI, P300 and ErRP signal are used in the control scheme. The directional motion of the Robot arm is controlled by MI detectors. Once the robot arm is reached, the P300 detector stops moving.

The ErRP detector identifies the existence of a directional (because of a MI detector) or positional error (because of a P300 detector) error in the inbound signal. The driver that regulates the movement of the robot appropriately supplies the outputs of each detector.

The robot arm here may spin its Link1 in the direction of clock and clock and translate its Link2 and Link3 to the direction of the forward one. In order to comprehend the motor the user intended to move the robot arm, the obtained C3 and C4 signals are decoded.

The job, i.e. move right, move left, go forward, or not go forward. In Table 8.2 these outputs form the robot commands. If the user intended, for example, to reverse the robot, he thought he would kinastically shift his hand to the left.

The user observes the robot arm's progress and recognizes the inaccuracy visually as the robot moves to the target point. The robot would return to his spot and if he wanders in a direction not intended by this topic the subject would have to repeat the instructions again (direction mistake). When a visually achieved or crossed target is identified, the final robot arm effector is generated by a P300 Waveform that stops moving the robot arm. After an ErRP has been identified, it means you cross the connection end for your robot arm (positional error).

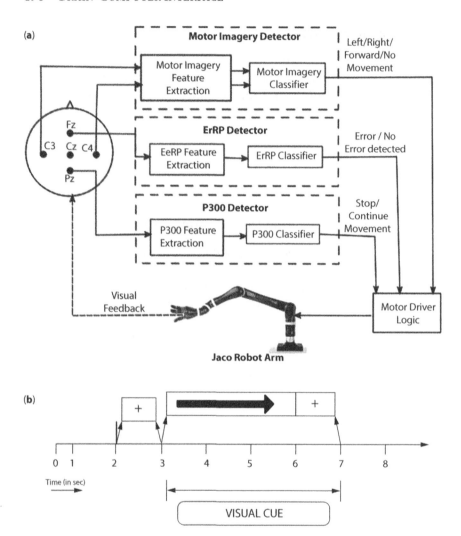

Figure 8.3 (a) The suggested scheme block diagram 1. (b) Timing diagram of proposed model.

In this scenario, the controller would try to re-align the link end with an offset (experimental). The visual error detection is processed by the EEG at Fz and by an electrode at Pz the P300 signal is identified. The scheme must show that when you activate the P300 or ErRP detector, no outputs are given.

We have a different engine intent classifier for every single connection, as shown in Figure 8.4, and in one particular case, only one of the three classifiers operates. The topic begins with an imagining of turning Link1 in

Table 8.2 Scheme 1 mental tasks and their respective control instructions.

Mental task	Control commands
Left-hand responsibility metaphors	Interchange Link1 Counter-Circular
Right movement metaphors	Interchange Link1 Circular
Onward movement metaphors	Interchange Link2 and Link3 Onward
No Measure	Break in proceedings at present place and wait for succeeding command
Concentration on mark spot (P300)	Rest Robot Movement
Recognition of ErRP	Make required improvement

the first slot, therefore in this instance the engine purpose classification for Link1 is active. If the error signal for connection is detected1, all the engine imagining classifiers except for Link2 will be automatically disconnected. While the actuator for connection1 strives to align Link1 with the target position, the engine imagination classification for connection2 is ready to accept information from the selection unit. When the error signal happens for Link2 and Link3, a similar situation happens. The above-mentioned ErRP motor intention classification switch is not included, but is added for clarity and simplicity.

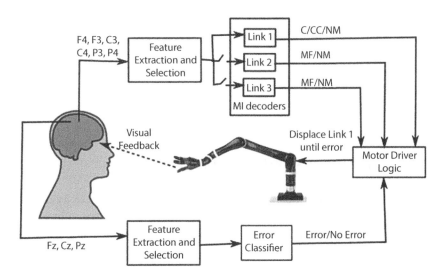

Figure 8.4 Schematic diagram of proposed model.

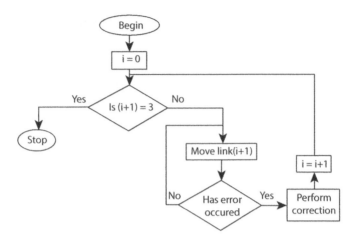

Figure 8.5 Logic of motor driver.

The logic on the motor driver in Figure 8.5 is employed when the decoded motor movement command of a particular limb has been received. The motor is also activated to halt and turn in the back direction, attached to a particular connection. The Boolean function that follows motor driver logic is forward (TFi) and stops and reverses (STBi).

$$TFi = MICi$$
$$STBi = ErRPi \qquad (8.1)$$

where $MICi$ = true indicates that motor intention classifier i has classified the motor imagination

The error-related potential for Link1 shows, in favor of linking 1 and ErRPi = true, that for link1 a position mistake has occurred. This scheme uses the same settings as prior robot control methods.

8.4   Experiments and Data Processing

In EEG sensors (electrodes) from the user's scalp, neuronal activity during motor imagery, error detection, or detection tasks of P300 are collected. A noteworthy component of this work is thus the decoding of motor intents and identification of P300 and ErRP signals by EEG analyses. EEG is a non-Gaussian and non-stationary signal and it is not easy to recognize mental processes directly from the raw signal. Experimentally, EEG signals produce a special signature in the treatment of the signal for various motor imagery tasks, and these distinct signatures are referred to as 'features'. Due to the non-linearity and characteristics of the signal, the various mental states of users have to be detected by classifiers. Once the user has recognized his motor intents using the classifiers, the outputs are created as commands for doing the work the subject wants to do. This section describes experiments to activate the subject's motor images, P300 and ErRP signals. It outlines the various strategies used to provide control signals for signal processing and classification in this study. The design of the controller for the real-time application is covered towards the conclusion of this section.

The guidance of a robot arm is controlled by the left, right and front (or foot) motor signals, as discussed before in the preceding section reveals that the ERD/ERS occur in the contralateral area of the brain (respecting the moving hand), as well as in the case of imagined foot movements in the frequency range of 8–12 Hz (mu-rhythm) and 16–24 Hz between the two hemispheric (central). A four-class classifier is used for generating directional output based on the control mechanisms for Scheme 1: left, right, forward and no motion. Like the scheme 2, the Link1 decoder is used to decode left- and right-hand motion instances, while binary gradations are used when Link2 and Link3 are activated to decode between foot motor imagery and no movement.

A visual stimulus was first intended to guide users through the stimulation, to carry out the required engine imagining activities. The user is thereby trained to recognize the stimuli's signature. The participant is instructed in seven sessions in this study. The motor imagining stimulus. It can be seen from Figure 8.6 that the stimulus is composed of three components, each in a defined order over a specific period of time: 1 second fastening cross, 4 seconds motor activation followed by 2 seconds of a blank line. The fixing cross is meant to warn the individual to prepare for a future engine imagination. This activity relates to one of the three categories of motor imagination: i) predefined direction translation, ii) defined orientation rotation, and iii) halt movement simply. Figures 8.6 A & B shows simulation results of motor imagining stimulus over a specific period of time. These results related to prefined, defined and halt movement of the motor imagination.

(A)

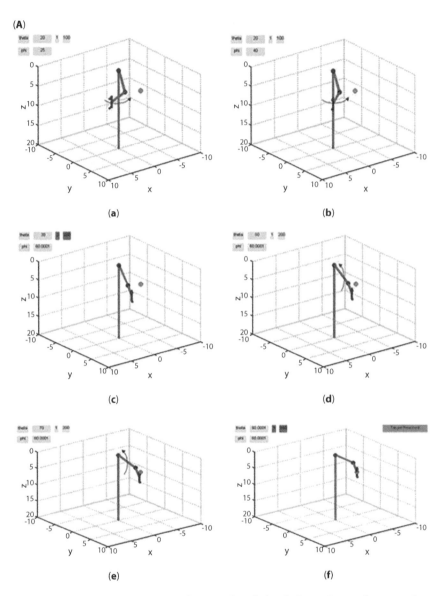

Figure 8.6A Trajectory movement of proposed work (a - f) shows the simulation results of arm controlled by the movement of motor in different directions.

Figure 8.6 B (a,b) shows the number of coefficients obtained by the path followed by a projectile flying or an object (arm) moving under the action

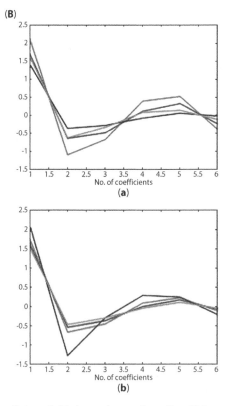

Figure 8.6B ARR co-efficient. (a,b) shows the number of coefficients obtained by the path followed by a projectile flying or an object (arm) moving under the action.

8.4.1 Feature Extraction

Incoming EEG signals are first filtered spatially by means of common average references, and an 8–24 Hz elliptical band-pass filter of the 6th order is applied. The advantage of the choice of an elliptical filter is the good features of its frequency domain by its sharp rolling off and the good attenuating effect of the ribbon and stop-band. Next, the EEG data from sites C3 and C4 is spatially filtered by the Laplacian method with the purpose of eliminating the impact of the adjacent electrodes. A self-retrieving adaptive p, AAR(p) model is described as

$$x(k) = \Sigma_{(i=1)}^{p}\, a_i(k)x(k-i) + \eta(k) \tag{8.2}$$

with

$$\eta(k) = N\left\{0, \sigma_{(\eta,i)}(k)^2\right\} \tag{8.3}$$

Where x(k) is the observation k^th sample, α(k) is the zero-mean gay noise, μ n(k)^2, and a i(k) are the time coefficients of AR changing. As indicated in (8.3), former samples and the new information supplied in the route prexlect a current sample. So the innovation process is sometimes referred to as β(k). The AAR coefficients are measured using different techniques such as the Lower Mean-square (LMS), the recursive-least-square technique (RLS), the recursive AR (RAR) technique and Kalman filtering.

In this study, Kalman filter has been employed as the estimation algorithm, which is summarized as where, e_k is the one-step prediction error, $\vec{k}_k$ is the Kalman gain vector, $\vec{I}$ is the identity matrix, $\vec{X}_k = \left[x_{k-1}, x_{k-2}, \ldots, x_{k-p} \right]^T$ is a vector of the values of the past samples, $\vec{a}_k = \left[\hat{a}_{1,k}, \hat{a}_{2,k}, \ldots, \hat{a}_{p,k} \right]^T$ is a vector of the AAR parameters, and $[x]^T$ is vector transpose.

Details on AAR as an estimator using Kalman filter are discussed. Experiments conducted here demonstrate that an AAR order 6 model and a coefficient of update = 0.0085 adequately differentiate the MI tasks. The vector range [-1,1] is also available. AAR coefficient are the ultimate dimensions of the dataset (for all sessions). An example of the C3 and C4 AAR features. The figure illustrates the coefficients for various engine imaging jobs.

Classification Accuracy (CA): the ratio of the properly recognized number of examples to the total number of occurrences.
True Positive Rate (TPR): is the percent of the accurately detected positive cases.
False Positive Rate (FPR): It is the fraction that is wrongly determined to be positive in negative circumstances.
CT: The time the trained classifier takes to achieve the target performance.
Transfer rate of information (ITR): ITR (Bt)[48] is the method bit rate (in bits/min) that is indicated as

$$Bt = (\log2\ N + P \log2\ P + (1 - P) \log2\ ) \times 2 \qquad (8.4)$$

where N denotes the number of potential states and P is the accuracy of the categorization from 0–1. T is the time needed to transfer every action to the same categorized output inside the second/symbol, i.e. the time interval from a command issue. The control unit performance on the robot arm Jaco is checked by three metrics: I a success rate, (ii) stable-state error, (iii) an overhead peak and (iv) an adjustment time. The parameters for ready reference are specified below.

Percentage Success (percentage SR) rate: The number of times the subject reaches the target place for a particular Z attempt within 1%.

Error (ess) in steady state: The difference between a certain set-up point and the plant's time-response after a vast (theoretically infinite) time interval after start-up of the plants in a loop-closed system feedback system.

Peak overflow (MP): The largest departure from its steady-state value, often a unit step function, by the time-response of a plant divided by the steady-state value. MP is called percentage MP and calculated when presented in percentage.

Time of settlement: time taken to attain and remain within 1% of its steady-state value by an installation's reaction.

This section highlights the findings gathered by individual detectors during offline training and online testing. An overview of the results of the project gained during real time control of the Jaco robot arm is provided.

8.4.2   Performance Analysis of the Detectors

Scheme 1

CA, TPR, FPR, and ITR are summarized in Table 8.3 in the course of training and on-line testing of detectors MI, P300, and ErRP. The best outcome of this training is provided by the motor imagery classifier for subject 3, as stated in Table 8.3. Table 8.3 shows that the P300 subject 2 and 3 classifications produce the highest results in training and their training performance during the test subject 3. Table 8.3 shows the best results for training and testing in the ErRP project. These results illustrate that the performance of each individual changes with the same amount of experiments. The reason is that each participant interprets the experiment differently and hence requires a distinct training period. In the training stage, it is also found that the subject is doing well.

In the CA, TPR, FPR and ITR grades, identical to Scheme 1, is shown in Table 8.4 in the Link1 motor image classifier Link2, Link3 engine image classifiers and ErRP graders. Because the Link2 and Link3 classifiers offer the same kind of output, the two links are trained in parallel.

The switch is dependent on the engine driver logic outputs. The results of experiments in Table 8.4 reveal that the training accuracy of all classifiers exceeds 90% for all detectors. For Scheme 1 this is also stated in Table 8.4.

A separate training result is produced by each classifier for each subject. As demonstrated in Table 8.4, the strongest qualifying classifiers are

Table 8.3 Precision of classification (C.A. in percent) and transfer rate of information (ITR in percentage/min) for five motor imaging training and online testing (MI), P300, and ErRP sensors.

Detectors	Subject ID	Training	Online testing			
		C.A.	TPR	FPR	C.A.	ITR
MI	1	96.00	0.96	0.00	75.00	15.88
	2	91.00	0.91	0.06	78.00	11.11
	3	100.00	1.00	0.00	81.00	19.51
	4	96.00	0.91	0.08	80.00	11.75
	5	97.00	1.00	0.05	80.00	11.75
Average		96.20	0.96	0.05	79.10	11.11
P300	1	88.00	0.85	0.11	80.00	11.57
	2	100.00	1.00	0.00	77.50	11.97
	3	100.00	1.00	0.00	85.00	15.51
	4	96.00	0.91	0.01	85.00	15.18
	5	91.00	0.81	0.06	81.00	11.91
Average		95.20	0.91	0.05	81.50	11.81

the Link1, Class 2 and Link3, Subject 4 and the ErRP, Class5. The greater accuracy is also apparent in the results of online training for the same categorization group.

8.4.3   Performance of the Real Time Robot Arm Controllers

For five participants across 20 experimental instances the percentage SR, ess, Mp, and ts are averaged to achieve the ultimate results for Scheme 1 and Scheme 2 controllers in Table 8.5. Furthermore, only the motor-image detector findings of another controller are contained in the comparative table. The insertion of ErRP and P300 as control instructions increase the overall performance of the controller with a more than 30% improvement in SR, 3.4% in ess, and 1% in Mp, as seen in Table 8.5. As other detectors are involved in the two systems, they both take a little longer to settle.

When comparing our two proposed systems, Scheme 2 has a higher target success rate than Scheme 1. Both techniques achieve a static error and a

Table 8.4 Accuracy of classification (C.A. in percent) and the information transfer rate of five individuals Link 1-engine imaging, Link 2 and 3-engine imaging and ErRP-detectors for online education and testing.

Detectors	Subject ID	Training	Online testing			
		C.A.	TPR	FPR	C.A.	ITR
Link1	1	97.33	0.88	0.20	76.00	27.53
class2–7	2	100.00	1.00	0.00	88.00	15.46
	3	88.67	0.95	0.25	80.00	22.67
	4	95.50	0.98	0.06	78.00	25.35
	5	92.67	0.90	0.11	82.50	17.23
	Average	94.83	0.94	0.12	80.90	21.65
Link2 and	1	97.50	0.95	0.00	86.67	16.50
3	2	98.67	1.00	0.05	88.50	15.54
	3	95.00	0.92	0.10	87.50	16.00
	4	100.00	1.00	0.00	91.50	11.10
	5	96.33	0.95	0.04	88.50	15.54
Average	97.50	0.96	0.04	88.53	14.94	
ErRP	1	96.67	0.96	0.00	84.50	20.56
	2	97.50	1.00	0.00	82.00	22.37
	3	93.33	0.97	0.09	79.50	25.74
	4	92.67	0.91	0.06	79.50	25.74
	5	98.00	0.95	0.03	85.00	18.83
Average	95.63	0.96	0.04	82.10	22.65	

maximum overflow with an insignificant variance which may be attributed to the occurrence of several experimental circumstances. As Table 8.5 shows, although Scheme 2 succeeds more than Scheme 1 in achieving the objective, it takes longer to attain its ultimate position. Due to the sequential technique and the delays incorporated into Scheme 2, the robot arm is controlled whereas Scheme 1 uses a random strategy for a similar control.

The classifiers provided by McNemar's test were also statistically similar. In order to accomplish the real time control, the proportion of successful hits, the percentage departure from the target and the average calculation time required are defined. For the OVA-ANT2FIS and OVO-ANT2FIS algorithms, the average success rate achieved from the 12 participants is 85% and 90%.

Table 8.5 Average of the controller performance for five subjects.

Parameters	Controller	
	Scheme 1	Scheme 2
Regular achievement amount (in %)	95.00	65.00
Steady-state fault (in %)	1.45	4.8
Peak Exceed (in %)	2.8	4.8
Subsiding period (in sec)	50	48
Balance	4 cm	-

For the OVA-ANT2FIS and OVO-ANT2FIS, the average deviation of more than 20 is 4.75%, for 11 subjects 3.75%. This finding indicated an effective way to handle unstationary and unpredictable signal data categorization, such as EEG, under the suggested ANT2FIS methodology to multiclass detection. The OVO strategy has also been more successful in attaining the goal than the OVA technique. The OVA technique would be preferable for online application if the balance between success rate and calculation time was maintained.

8.5 Discussion

In this section, two independent control systems, employing the components MI, P300, and ErRP from an EEG signal, were developed effectively to control the movement of a robot arm. In the one scheme, the user manages the movement of the entire robot arm without thinking of activating individual connections while in the other the position of each individual link to control the movement of the robot arm. The first method controls the robot arm's position. The first strategy uses MI components in direct transmission or rotation of the robot arm, P300 in order to halt the motion of the robot arm and ErRP in order to detect if the MI decoder is installed Incoming input signals were misclassified, or the robot link-end passed the target point before the P300 decoder was activated. Once the ErRP signal has been detected, either the robot arm is sent to their former location or the robot arm is re-alignable to the desired target position. The first technology is difficult, but it requires just minor switching effort.

The second strategy is significantly simpler than the first scheme, as a fixed order connection monitoring procedure is followed by a position control of the connections in a (predefined) set order and only needs a MI and ErRP signal. However, between activation of two linkages this approach involves a large change effort. Of course in Scheme 2 the engine imagination should be decoded at a predetermined time interval to make single link motions, where the ith interval corresponds to the motor imagination decoding for the robot's connection. The other schema relating to control of fixed order links demands that the (i+1)th categorizer be automatically selected when the engine imagination has automatically finished its ith work (for ith link). This is achieved by measuring the decoded error signal offset for the third time slot in the proposed system. There is, then, two objectives for the error signal decoded in the ith-time slot. To accurately modify the link position (by a slight offset angle to turn it back), the error sensor is first utilized to regulate the position controller.

The results in the preceding section indicate that both methods provide similar outcomes throughout training and online testing. However, it should be emphasized that the precisions of training and online testing vary widely. Such changes in the accuracy might be due to the non-static nature of EEG signals and, in this instance, the mental state of the individual. The classifier Offline training and online testing is conducted by means of two separate data sets that are obtained throughout several experimental sessions. This raises the chances that our results will show a misclassification.

An ideal feature classifier combination must thus be developed, so that these challenges may be dealt with.

A feature selection or reduction phase can even be included between the extraction of the feature and its categorization in the same way. This component of this study is accessible for researchers to choose from. Both systems also have a similar controller performance. The controller of Scheme 1 is more advanced than that of Scheme 2. The success probability of Scheme 2 therefore exceeds Scheme 1. However, because of the fixed scheme 2 consumes time over scheme 1.

Order method and delays between switches followed by the system. The advantages and disadvantages of both schemes are observed, therefore, and the choice of schemes is entirely allowed to be applied. If the robot arm requires an application to move all its associations to complete a job, Scheme 2 is the best solution. If a robot arm is only to be moved regardless of the positioning of the linkages, Scheme 1 is the best solution. Finally, both techniques, indicating the purpose to manage the robotics system position of the subject's own limbs, have direct applications in smart control of prothesis limbs.

8.6 Conclusion and Future Research Directions

While innovative and self-sufficient, the efforts detailed in this thesis offer up new paths in the BCI area. In order to enhance the control systems, further research relating to the functioning of the brain are required. In future investigations, studies will be conducted in conjunction with the movement of the upper limb. Studies on several movement features, such speed, location, will be carried out in order to manage the prosthetic device more precisely.

As to the suggested algorithms for selection of features, more work will be carried out in terms of accuracy and calculation time to improve its performance and to allow it to be operational in real time. More study will also be undertaken in the future to increase the performance of our suggested ANT2FIS classification. In addition, we would approach strategies based on statistical approaches and probabilistic models to satisfy our real-time monitoring requirements. Further efforts will be taken to build an optimum mix of extraction selection features for real-time control.

The BCI System based on EEG may also be employed to enhance the functioning of other physiological parameters, such as electromyography (EMG) galvanic skin resistance (GSR) and other non-invasive biopotential signal. Studies based on the connection of the EMG and EEG data might give additional information to assist us build better prosthetic limb control strategies. In order to bring it closer to real-time monitoring, initiatives to minimize the computing time of the BCI system must also be made. Finally, we intend to incorporate the optimum control system in an embedded platform to address rehabilitation challenges with real-world solutions. The control programmed would be further refined on topics with clinical problems.

References

1. Dornhege, G., del R. Millan, J., Hinterberger, T., McFarland, D.J., Muller, K.-R., *Towards Brain Computer Interfacing*, MIT Press, MA, 2007.
2. Tan, D.S. and Nijholt, A., *Brain-computer interfaces: Applying our mind to human-computer interaction*, London: Springer, 2010.
3. Wolpaw, J. and Wolpaw, E.W., *Brain-computer interfaces: Principles and practice*, London: Oxford University Press, 2012.
4. Hwang, H.-J., Kim, S., Choi, S., Im, C.-H., EEG-based brain-computer interfaces: A thorough literature survey. *Int. J. Hum. Comput. Interact.*, Taylor & Francis, 29, 12, 814–826, 2013.
5. Rao, R.P.N. and Scherer, R., Brain-computer interfacing [In the Spotlight]. *IEEE Signal Process. Mag.*, 27, 4, 150–152, 2010.
6. Kubler, A. and Muller, K.R., An introduction to brain-computer interfacing, in: *Toward brain-computer interfacing*, G. Dornhege, J.R. Millan, T. Hinterberger, D.J. McFarland, K.R. Muller (Eds.), pp. 1–25, MIT Press, MA, 2007.
7. Dhanaraj, R.K., Krishnasamy, L., Geman, O., Izdrui, D.R., Black hole and sink hole attack detection in wireless body area networks. *Comput. Mater. Continua*, Tech Science Press, US, 68, 2, 1949–1965, 2021.
8. Kassubek, J., Unrath, A., Huppertz, H.J., Lule, D., Ethofer, T., Sperfeld, A.D., Ludolph, A.C., Global brain atrophy and corticospinal tract alterations in ALS, as investigated by voxel-based morphometry of 3-D MRI. *Amyotroph. Lateral Scler. Motor Neuron Dis.*, Springer, 6, 4, 213–220, 2005.
9. Hanagasi, H.A., Gurvit, I.H., Ermutlu, N., Kaptanoglu, G., Karamursel, S., Idrisoglu, H.A., Emre, M., Demiralp, T., Cognitive impairment in amyotrophic lateral sclerosis: evidence from neuropsychological investigation and event-related potentials. *Cogn. Brain Res.*, Elsevier, 14, 2, 234–244, 2002.
10. Jurkiewicz, M.T., Crawley, A.P., Verrier, M.C., Fehlings, M.G., Milkulis, D.J., Somatosensory cortical atrophy after the spinal cord injury: A voxel-based morphometry study. *Neurology*, American Academy of Neurology, 66, 5, 762–764, 2006.
11. Hochberg, L.R., Serruya, M.D., Friehs, G.M., Mukand, J.A., Saleh, M., Caplan, A.H., Branner, A., Chen, D., Penn, R.D., Donoghue, J.P., Neuronal ensemble control of prosthetic devices by a human with tetraplegia. *Nature*, London, 442, 7099, 164–171, 2006.
12. Huber, H., The use of virtual realities in psychological treatment. *Psychol. Osterreich*, 25, 1, 13–200, 2005.
13. Oum, K., Ayaz, H., Shewokis, P.A., Diefenbach, P., MindTactics: A brain computer interface gaming platform, in: *2010 International IEEE Consumer Electronics Society's Games Innovations Conference (ICE-GIC)*, pp. 1–5, 2010.
14. Angeloni, C., Salter, D., Corbit, V., Lorence, T., Yu, Y.-C., Gabel, L.A., P300-based brain-computer interface memory game to improve motivation and

performance, in: *2012 38th Annual Northeast Bioengineering Conference (NEBEC)*, pp. 35–36, 2012.

15. Parafita, R., Pires, G., Nunes, U., Castelo-Branco, M., A spacecraft game controlled with a brain computer interface using SSVEP with phase tagging. *2013 IEEE 2nd International Conference on Serious Games and Applications for Health (SeGAH)*, pp. 1–6, 2013.

16. Brumberg, J.S., Lorenz, S.D., Galbraith, B.V., Guenther, F.H., The unlock project: A python-based framework for practical brain-computer interface communication "app" development, in: *2012 Annual International Conference of the IEEE Engineering in Medicine and Biology Society (EMBC)*, pp. 2505–2508, 2012.

17. Ebrahimi, T., Vesin, J., Garcia, G., Brain-computer interface in multimedia communication. *IEEE Signal Process. Mag.*, 20, 1, 14–24, 2003.

18. Biao, Z., Wang, J., Fuhlbrigge, T., A review of the commercial brain-computer interface technology from perspective of industrial robotics, in: *2010 IEEE International Conference on Automation and Logistics (ICAL)*, pp. 379–384, 2010.

19. Garcia, A.P., Schjolberg, I., Gale, S., EEG control of an industrial robot manipulator, in: *2013 IEEE 4th International Conference on Cognitive Infocommunications (CogInfoCom)*, pp. 39–44, 2013.

20. Al-Sagban, M., El-Halawani, O., Lulu, T., Al-Nashash, H., Al-assaf, Y., Brain computer interface as a forensic tool, in: *5th International Symposium on Mechatronics and Its Applications (ISMA 2008)*, pp. 1–5, 2008.

21. Zhang, S.-M., Zhan, Q.-C., Du, H.-M., Research on the human computer interaction of E-learning, in: *2010 International Conference on Artificial Intelligence and Education (ICAIE)*, pp. 5–8, 2010.

9

Brain–Computer Interface-Assisted Automated Wheelchair Control Management–Cerebro: A BCI Application

Sudhendra Kambhamettu[1], Meenalosini Vimal Cruz[2], Anitha S.[1], Sibi Chakkaravarthy S.[1]* and K. Nandeesh Kumar[1]

[1]Center of Excellence, Artificial Intelligence and Robotics (AIR) and School of Computer Science and Engineering, VIT-AP University, Andhra Pradesh, India
[2]Georgia Southern University, Georgia, United States

Abstract

Technology today serves millions of people suffering from mobility impairments across the globe in numerous ways. Although advancements in medicine and healthcare systems improve the life expectancy of the general population, sophisticated engineering techniques and computing processes have long facilitated the patient in the recovery process. People struggling with mobility impairments and especially spine injuries which also leads to loss of speech, often have a narrow group of devices to aid them move from place-to-place and they are often limited to just movement functionality. BCI (Brain Computer Interface) powered wheelchairs leverage the power of the brain, i.e. translating the thoughts/neural activity into real-world movement providing automated motion without any third party intervention. Many BCI powered wheelchairs in the market are cumbersome to operate and provide only singular functionality of movement. To address this problem and improve the state of BCI products, Cerebro introduces the first ever go-to market product utilizing Artificial Intelligence to facilitate mobility features with built-in speech functionality via blink detection. Further sections of the Chapter take an in-depth look into each layer of the Cerebro system.

Keywords: BCI, cerebro, motor imagery, EEG, deep learning, artifact, support vector machine, Raspberry Pi3

Corresponding author: sb.sibi@gmail.com

M.G. Sumithra, Rajesh Kumar Dhanaraj, Mariofanna Milanova, Balamurugan Balusamy and Chandran Venkatesan (eds.) Brain-Computer Interface: Using Deep Learning Applications, (205–230) © 2023 Scrivener Publishing LLC

9.1   Introduction

According to the WHO disability report, 15% of the world's population is living with some sort of disability, about 2–4% of them experience significant difficulties in functioning. Also, every year about 250,000–500,000 people suffer a spinal cord injury (SCI) which leads to mobility impairment in these patients. Although their brain activity is intact, their fundamental functional abilities like walking, running and also in serious cases, talking are debilitated. While the cause for these injuries could be prevented, the ones suffering need a viable product in order to help them communicate better and avail spatial movement.

There have been numerous attempts at developing a non-invasive style BCI controlled wheelchair in the past decade itself. BCI presents itself as an interesting application, when the discussion is on products/concepts to aid the disabled, thanks to the rigid structure of human anatomy keeping the brain from most of the damage. Brain is one of the most integral parts of the human anatomy as it is the source of all control, behavior, thought and movement. Neural pathways are wide spread to reach every organ and every part of the body tallying up to, about 7 trillion nerves in an average human body.

The primal mode of communication through the neural pathways are the brain signals originated from the brain, which are triggered upon the intent for a specific action. These brain signals are small electrical impulses which can be detected by the right equipment. After further processing of these signals, they can be converted into readable and control transferable signals which can then be mapped to enable external actions i.e. motor movements, key-taps, playing a sound etc. Several brainwave reading strategies such as SSVEP, EEG – Motor Imagery, etc., which we will be discussing further in the chapter, were implemented to achieve the control of the wheelchair from imagination of the perceived movement. For example, this study by Doron Friedman *et al.* in 2007 explores the possibility of BCI based wheelchair control for a tetraplegic in a VR environment via translation of imagined motion of paralyzed legs [4].

Another study in 2013, developed a hybrid BCI system combining P300 and steady-state visual evoked potential (SSVEP) strategy for a wheelchair offering control via flickering buttons set on a graphical user interface [5]. The conventional methods and design of a BCI controlled wheelchair is standard and addresses just the mobility issue. However a novel device, Cerebro is introduced which takes it a step further by offering two distinct modes of control and communication. One for the spatial mobility of the wheelchair through imagined motion by classifying Motor Imagery using Deep Learning methods and the other, availing faculties for patients with speech impediments, offering text to speech control via BCI. In depth look into these systems will be followed further in the chapter (In the Section "Control System"). Let's take a look at what BCI is and understand its basic fundamentals.

9.1.1 What is a BCI?

The first ever BCI (Brain–Computer Interface) was introduced in 1964, in an experiment to observe the correlation between the action performed and the recorded brain wave activity. Dr. Grey Walter, who performed this experiment on a patient who was connected with electrodes, had to introduce a delay from detection of brain wave activity until the task prescribed was done, as he observed the intent of performing the task in the brain-wave activity, prior to the patient actually performing it. Voila! This was the conclusive proof for the existence of control without muscular movements, a true BCI [1].

Alright, so how do we describe a BCI? Informally, A device which can read brain signals and convert them into control and communication signals. Natural forms of communication or control require peripheral nerves and muscles to act together by which means, signals from the brain are transmitted to achieve the imagined action. This flow is called the Efferent pathway/Efferent communication. [Efferent pathway - motor control, Afferent pathway - Sensory control]. And more formally, BCI is an artificial system acting as an alternative to the natural efferent pathways i.e. the neuromuscular output channels of the body [2], offering control and communication by the translation of brainwave activity into control signals after various processes such as signal processing and pattern recognition. Essentially, BCI is a device which accepts voluntary commands directly from the brain without requiring physical movements [3].

9.2 How Do BCI's Work?

BCI essentially records brain activity and converts them into control signals as we already know. To understand it better, knowledge on how the brain activity is measured is of key importance.

9.2.1   Measuring Brain Activity

Broadly, brain activity can be measured in two distinct processes. With surgery and without surgery. While most BCI's rely on electrical measures of brain activity, some methods also have been developed to measure brain activity via magnetic measures, since neural signal transference produces both electrical and magnetic activity.

9.2.1.1   Without Surgery

The orthodox method of gathering brain activity relies upon placing electrodes/ sensors on the subjects' head. A popular method, Electroencephalography (EEG) is used to record electrical activity from the scalp with electrodes. It is a reputed and clinically well tested method and has been in use since decades. While EEG provides a good temporal resolution i.e. ability to detect changes in brainwave activity within a short interval of time, the spatial resolution and the frequency range is limited. EEG is also highly susceptible to artifacts (Corruption in EEG data caused by other electrical activities in the body caused by eye movements, blink: EOG (electrooculography) and muscular: EMG (electromyography) close to the recording sites). EEG is highly advantageous in terms of its cost and portability while its application procedure is clumsy and inconvenient. EEG procedures are often done by two methods, wet electrodes and dry electrodes. Wet electrodes involve electrodes sticking to the scalp requiring a gel like substance for improved receptibility of brainwave activity. Although, there have been many improvements since and portable products with dry electrodes are gaining popularity among researchers as they offer a significant improvement in EEG recording and they are convenient in comparison to the traditional wet electrodes. EEG caps are designed using the International 10–20 system which is used to accurately place electrodes to obtain recordings from specific regions of the brain [6]. Figure 9.1 depicts the international 10–20 system.

Other non-surgical procedures involve MEG (Magnetoencephalography) which records magnetic fields associated with brain activity, fMRI (Functional magnetic resonance imaging) which measures minute changes in the blood oxygenation level-dependent (BOLD) signals which are associated with the cortical activation.

9.2.1.2   With Surgery

A surgical procedure named craniotomy is involved with cutting the membranes that cover the brain to implant the necessary sensors in order

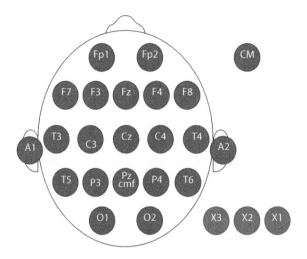

Figure 9.1 Placement of electrodes according to the international 10/20 system.

to record brain activity. ECoG and Intra cortical reading techniques are used to read the brainwave data. While such procedures yield much better results which are less prone to artifacts, it is not widely adopted unless it's absolutely necessary.

9.2.2 Mental Strategies

BCI is often misinterpreted to read thoughts, which isn't the case at all. BCI can merely classify patterns generated by the electrical activity in the brain associated with a task performed by the subject and then translate them into control signals which can be mapped onto desired actions. Thus, just obtaining the brainwave activity does not decode what was thought/imagined by the patient. As such, mental strategies are developed which help associate a particular pattern corresponding to a neural activity, to an interpretation, i.e., a mental strategy is what a patient/subject must perform in order to produce these patterns. These mental strategies are constrained by the hardware and software capabilities of the systems available. There are multiple mental strategies that could be used and depending on the chosen mental strategy, certain actions must be performed by the subject to generate the desired patterns. Subjects must be trained for a certain period of time to replicate specific actions in order to generate the desired patterns. The training time is highly dependent on the mental strategy chosen. Selective attention and Motor imagery are the most common types of strategies incorporated [7, 8]. Motor imagery has been adopted for generating necessary data in case of Cerebro. Let's briefly take a look at two most popular and widely used mental strategies viz. SSVEP (steady-state visual evoked potentials) and Neural Motor Imagery.

9.2.2.1   SSVEP

Steady state visual evoked potentials is a part of the broader classification, Selective attention. The primary principle of selective attention is to focus the subjects' attention on a selected stimulus (visual, audio etc.) which is associated with a particular command that controls the BCI application. For example, let's say the musical note "A" is associated with a pattern generated by looking at a visual source pointing left and "B" is associated with a pattern generated by looking at a visual source pointing right. In order to play the note "A", the subject must selectively focus their attention on the light source which points to the right.

SSVEP is a pattern generated by following the mental strategy which is based on visual stimulus. Wherein a constant source of multiple flickering visual stimuli is displayed, each with a varying frequency and each of which corresponds to a particular action. Selective attention to a particular flicker will evoke an SSVEP in the visual cortex with the exact same frequency as the target flicker. For example, if the target visual stimulus flickers at 5 Hz, the elicited resultant SSVEP will also flicker at 5 Hz. Thus by looking at the SSVEP stimuli from the visual cortex BCI can determine the target flicker which can be mapped to the corresponding command associated with the flicker. This strategy, although effective, wasn't chosen to implement for Cerebro, as SSVEP might require the subject to shift gaze. And completely locked-in patients however cannot do that.

9.2.2.2   Neural Motor Imagery

The brain activity in the cortex is not only susceptible to the tiniest movements of any muscle in the body but also the imagination of the movements causes neural activity. The resultant activity from imagination of movements can be recorded through SMR's (Sensorimotor rhythms). These oscillations are typically categorized into 4 distinct categories each with a specified frequency band, i.e. delta: <4 Hz, theta: 4–7 Hz, alpha/mu: 8–12 Hz, beta: 12–30 Hz, gamma: >30 Hz. Mu and beta bands hold the most significance in the resultant EEG data for observing the motor movements. ERS and ERD respectively are changes observed as increasing and decreasing in oscillatory activity of specific frequencies. These changes in the EEG data depict the motor imagination activity. For them to be

Table 9.1 Depicting the corresponding electrode location (according to the International 10/20 system of EEG electrode arrangement) for ERD/ERS activity produced as a resultant of movement of these body parts.

Movement	Electrode location
Right hand	C3
Left hand	C4
Feet	Cz

sufficiently prominent (stand out amidst the background EEG noise), the cortical areas which are targeted need to be large enough, which in general are observed to be the hand, foot, and the tongue areas. This is the reason why NMI is recorded by imagining the movement of Left hand, Right hand, feet and tongue [23].

It is important to note that ERD/ERS patterns, as observed, evoke only specific locations in the EEG headset (see Table 9.1).

Cerebro utilizes this method of EEG data collection for further classification by a deep learning model. The following section will explain the data collection process and the preprocessing steps taken in depth.

9.3   Data Collection

As discussed in the previous section of the chapter, Motor imagery was used to collect data to be trained for a classification model. Let's take a look at collection methodologies and pre-processing techniques used to prepare the data.

9.3.1   Overview of the Data

Motor images collected were categorized into 5 distinct classes. Left, Right, Front, Back left and Back right. Totally 10 healthy subjects aged 22–42 years (7 males, 3 females) were recruited to participate in this study. EEG data corresponding to each channel is recorded in their respective channels. Thus 10 recordings pertaining to each class. Each class contains 25 columns (1 Time column and 24 EEG channels) and each column contains roughly ~36000 data points i.e. rows. Here's a quick descriptive statistics of a generic data sheet (see Table 9.2). Note that, the below data depicts a rough statistical summary of a single class pertaining to a single subject.

Table 9.2 Describes the standard statistical measures of the EEG data procured across 24 channels.

	Time	ch_1	ch_2	ch_3	ch_4	ch_5	ch_6	ch_7	ch_8	ch_9	ch_10	ch_11
count	8	8	8	8	8	8	8	8	8	8	8	8
mean	4636.906	4588.046	4591.133	4592.245	4591.757	4590.241	4590.241	4588.015	4587.557	4597.169	4586.457	4597.667
std	12952.67	12972.37	12971.17	12970.94	12971.01	12971.51	12971.51	12972.38	12972.58	12970.74	12973.08	12970.79
min	0.0033	-25.8	-58	-144.6	-102.6	-46.4	-46.4	-24.7	-41.9	-414.7	-90.8	-437.8
25%	34.12625	-0.875	-1.45	-2.875	-2.45	-1.6	-1.6	-0.825	-1.3	-10.375	-1.47258	-4.4
50%	61.15668	2.068967	3.257354	4.923022	3.995419	3.248853	3.248853	1.978758	2.741079	14.59839	3.5	4.996145
75%	99.37748	12.14556	28.51237	57.7087	44.59733	42.37522	23.72302	11.62059	16.45572	157.3678	27.66596	159.659
max	36693	36693	36693	36693	36693	36693	36693	36693	36693	36693	36693	36693

	ch_12	ch_13	ch_14	ch_15	ch_16	ch_17	ch_18	ch_19	ch_20	ch_21	ch_22	ch_23	ch_24
count	8	8	8	8	8	8	8	8	8	8	8	8	8
mean	4594.69	4596.286	4587.578	4588.148	4587.5	4586.629	4586.641	4604.432	4616.494	4586.641	4587.387	4588.746	4589.68
std	12971.15	12969.2	12972.58	12972.34	12972.6	12972.6	12972.93	12967.12	12961.55	12972.93	12972.75	12972.1	12971.84
min	-353.6	-95.6	-53.2	-39	-38.6	-0.6	-0.5	-295.5	-127.5	-0.5	-108.2	-40.7	-108.9
25%	-5.05	-3.55917	-1.6	-1.36057	-1.1	-0.02509	-0.02528	-2.775	-4.225	-0.02531	-1.82382	-1.75	-3.1609
50%	4.517862	8.3	2.836611	2.6	2.502446	0.05	0.05	4.318794	3.603381	0.05	3.5	3.383113	6.35
75%	131.8147	54.42378	19.71269	16.84735	15.09376	0.225053	0.221253	126.7628	109.5571	0.22303	34.89816	19.5768	42.89329
max	36693	36693	36693	36693	36693	36693	36693	36693	36693	36693	36693	36693	36693

Before data collection, it was verified that none of them reported a clinical history of psychiatric and neurological conditions or brain diseases. All the human subjects are right-handed, had either normal or corrected to normal vision. All subjects were instructed about the experimental procedures, aim, and scope of the study and completed the consent form and a brief questionnaire before data collection. This study was approved and carried out in accordance with the recommendations of the Institutional IRB committee.

9.3.2   EEG Headset

In order to successfully implement the BCI for the automated wheelchair task, the EEG headset must be portable and convenient. For better convenience of the human subjects, a dry electrode EEG headset is preferable (see Figure 9.2). Hence to meet the above two needs, the EEG data were recorded from 23 electrode channels via the wearable sensing dry electrode EEG headset.

The dry electrode is made with silver/silver chloride tips (see Figure 9.3) to resist the noise signals, and there is a hybrid resistive and capacitive amplifier behind each electrode. Both the electrode and amplifier are protected in a faraday cage to get the high-quality signal with low noise. The signal gets

Figure 9.2 Wearable sensing EEG dry electrode headset.

Figure 9.3 Electrode placements in BCI headset.

amplified immediately, which helps to get the clean signals without electrical artifacts. There is a spring attached to each electrode that regulates downward pressure and stabilizes the sensor during any movement to avoid mechanical artifacts. Within the sensor itself, another spring can absorb shock in both the vertical and horizontal planes. The second spring also ensures that the outer ring is always flush with the inner ring during recording, enabling the faraday cage to enclose the inner electrodes completely.

A combination of active sensors (sensors right at the electrode tip), with ultra-high impedance amplifiers and proprietary circuitry, and optimized Ag/AgCl electrode tips help record signal quality comparable to that obtained with wet electrode systems. Furthermore, the DSI streamer software that comes with the headset has the capability for continuous impedance monitoring to ensure good signal quality during recording.

The channels of the headset were arranged primarily over the motor and parietal cortical areas according to the international 10/20 system. The channel reference positions are FP1, FP2, FZ, F3, F3, F7, F8, CZ, C3, C4, T3, T4, T5, T6, P3, P4, O1, O2, A1, A2. The reference electrode was placed on Pzcmf.

9.3.3 EEG Signal Collection

The study aims to design a model to classify the EEG signal to control the wheelchair using four possible commands: Turn left, Turn right, Move forward, and Move backward. The EEG headset is placed on the subject's head and adjusted to sit in the correct position, as shown in Figure 9.3. Through the DSI steamer software, the placement of the electrodes and the impedance level were monitored. The participants were instructed about the basics of EEG recording, such as blinking, and jaw clenching should be avoided during data collection.

Following the EEG headset placement, subjects were seated in a comfortable chair placed in a quite soundproofed room. Before each recording segment, subjects were instructed to assume a comfortable position in a chair. Other brain activities might suppress the desired signal. In order to obtain the alpha signal before the experimental task, subjects were instructed to close their eyes and to relax but to stay awake for a few seconds, and then the subjects were instructed to open their eyes to fixate on a multicolor subject at 1 m distance and to relax.

Data acquisition was divided into five parts, subjects were asked to imagine looking on the right side, the signal was collected for 120 seconds. Then after a few minutes of break, the same process was repeated for imaging looking on the left side, the signal was collected for 120 seconds, then in the third section, the subjects were asked to imagine moving straight for 120 seconds, and the signal was collected. Then to model the backward driving of the wheelchair, the subjects were asked to imagine moving backward on the left side, and the signal was collected for 60 seconds, and then the subjects were asked to imagine moving backward on the right side, and the signal was collected for 60 seconds.

There were around 36,000 rows of information collected for 2 minutes of reading from all 21 channels for each direction. So, totally around 3,024,000 data points were collected from each subject to implement the classification model.

9.4   Data Pre-Processing

Pre-processing is an essential step to prepare data and make it ready for training. Pre-processing of data is usually done for two main reasons: (i) identify the problems with the data and (ii) preparation for data analysis [9]. Common methods like outlier detection and removal, cleaning data, maintaining coherence are employed to identify the gaps in the data. One of the major problems with EEG data is the interference of artifacts. As mentioned earlier in section 9.2.1.1, EEG data is extremely prone to artifacts i.e. pollution by EOG and EMG data as shown in the Figure 9.4. The other issue that persists is the extremely high dimensional nature of the collected data. Due to this, the size and learnability of the

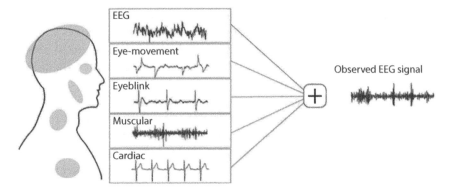

Figure 9.4 Contamination of target EEG signals by the biological artifacts [21].

existing patterns by the Machine Learning algorithms increases drastically. Thus dimensionality reduction helps in extracting more relevant information from big collections of data aimed at improving the performance of a pattern recognition system drastically [10]. Similarly reducing the complexity of the data while keeping the crux patterns intact by signal processing techniques, reduces the computational strain that is experienced to train the model. Let's take a look at each of the pre-processing techniques.

9.4.1   Artifact Removal

The lack of dealing with artifacts significantly reduces the performance of the BCI system in practical applications [11]. Thus, it's important to recognize them and remove them. Many automated systems have been developed for rejection or removal of artifacts [20]. The general method for doing so, is to discard the severely distributed EEG segments. As such, this method has also been implemented for the Cerebro BCI system as an early pre-processing step. Since this rudimentary method doesn't ensure the removal of artifacts in sparsely distributed EEG segments, methods such as CSP and Riemannian geometric techniques are also employed. Section 9.5.3. Elaborates the discussion on the same, further in the chapter. Several other novel methods have also been introduced where artifacts are considered as missing values and BTF (Bayesian-tensor factorization) methods are used to fill the gaps to complete the EEG segment [12]. Although, BTF method isn't employed for the Cerebro system.

9.4.2   Signal Processing and Dimensionality Reduction

The recorded EEG data inherently is polluted with noise of various types generated by environmental, instrumental causes or even by the signal source. The presence of noise masks the target signal diminishing the relevant characteristics of the patterns associated with the EEG signal. Depending on the stage one's in on the Data pipeline, filters are chosen to clip the noise [14]. In the pre-processing step, signals are filtered through a low-pass filter to extract the lower dimensional features. These features contain a more distinct representation of the underlying patterns. Butterworth low-pass filter is being implemented for Cerebro as it is tested positively across many BCI and EEG related literatures [13, 14]. Butterworth filter is essentially designed to obtain a flat frequency response in the passband. The above step also acts as a dimensionality reduction step. The changes in the EEG signal before and after are observed in the Figure 9.5. It is also to be noted that there are a few more methods such as SWT (stationary wavelet transform) which also work exceptionally well with EEG data [15].

9.4.3   Feature Extraction

The key question persists, what are the important features of the obtained EEG data that discriminate between any two given classes. This is important because, the higher the difference between the classes of motor imagery, the better the classification. As such, CSP (Common Spatial Pattern)

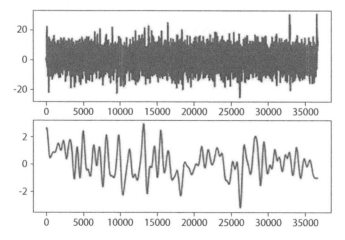

Figure 9.5 Before and after applying Butterworth low-pass filter to an EEG signal corresponding to the class – "Right".

feature extraction is used to find projections that maximize the discrimination between different classes [16] and a classification technique which exploits the structure of tangent space features drawn from the Riemannian geometry framework are employed [17].

The CSP method involves finding an optimal number of spatial filters from the given input data, to compute the features whose variances are optimal for discriminating between two classes of EEG recordings [19]. That is achieved by using the concept of diagonalization of the covariance matrix for both groups (any two given classes) simultaneously [18]. These covariances are generated using the pyriemann package which are then fitted on the data to produce the features. The following is the code which depicts the functions to perform the above tasks.

```
X, labels = load_data()
covariances = pyriemann.estimation.Covariances()
features = covariances.fit_transform(X)
```

Covariance matrices computed through spatial filters as discussed above are largely used in NMI (Neural Motor Imagery) based BCI systems. Cerebro also employs it to yield improved results and efficiency of the classifier. These covariance matrices lie in SPD spaces (Symmetric Positives-Definite), which are a subset of the Riemannian Geometrical domain of computations [21]. As such tangent space features drawn from the Riemannian geometry framework that is shared among the training data of multiple subjects are exploited [18] to increase the classification efficiency and aid in removal of artifacts [22]. These are also generated using the pyriemann package as shown below.

```
tangent_spaces = pyriemann.tangentspace.TangentSpace()
```

9.5　Classification

Classification is an integral part of the Cerebro BCI system as it actively recognizes and classifies what movement has been imagined by the subject. While the end result of a trained model is deployed on a micro-computer, it is essential to understand the DL and the training process. A deep learning model trains over the EEG data obtained and finally when input a new EEG data, the model classifies the input by mapping it to corresponding class. The overview of the process is represented below (see Figure 9.6).

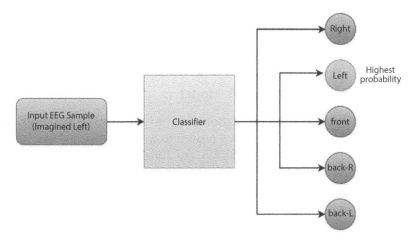

Figure 9.6 System level overview of the classification process.

Figure 9.7 Typical pipeline for classification models.

The typical pipeline for the classification process involves a few prior steps which we have covered in previous sections. Check Figure 9.7 for a complete overview of the pipeline.

9.5.1 Deep Learning (DL) Model Pipeline

To test the performance of the cerebro system, two pipelines were constructed and tested accordingly, on the collected data. The motive for testing multiple DL pipelines was to compare the performance and efficiency of the system to be able to deploy on an end product. Each pipeline contains three specific stages. Preprocessing, Training and Cross Validation. To design BCI's based on the CSP algorithm, the common preprocessing step involves extracting the covariance matrices of the EEG signal for each class (left, right, back etc.). This step also facilitates better handling of dimensionality. Common training paradigm used in all three pipelines includes a Support Vector Machine (SVM) as was found to be the best in several pre-established BCI related literatures. Although, variants of SVM kernels were used for each CSP method and the Riemannian geometry method. Finally, for the validation step, K-fold cross-validation (with five splits) was implemented for estimating the performance of the trained models, as was found to deliver results that are generally less biased in estimating the models' skill, by several earlier literatures.

9.5.2 Architecture of the DL Model

As mentioned in the previous section, Cerebro leverages SVM's for training on EEG data as they have been proven to work the best for BCI based multi-class classification [24]. SVM's are fundamentally different from ANN's (Artificial Neural Networks), as its core mechanisms are based on statistical and geometrical approaches as opposed to ANN's which try to emulate the neural system of the human brain. SVM's are used to perform both binary and multi-class classification tasks. While a linear binary SVM classification includes calculation of the optimal hyperplane decision boundary that separates one class from another, multi-class classification breaks down the problem into multiple sets of binary classifications for computing the decision boundaries [25]. In general two approaches i.e. (i) pairwise and (ii) one-versus-all classification paradigms are used for a multi-class problem. Figure 9.8 shows the mapping of input-space into a

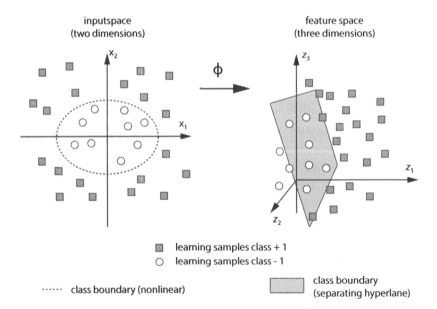

Figure 9.8 Non-linear-mapping from two-dimensional input space with non-linear class boundaries into a three-dimensional feature space with linear separation by a hyperplane. Courtesy of SVM article on http://www.neural-forecasting.com.

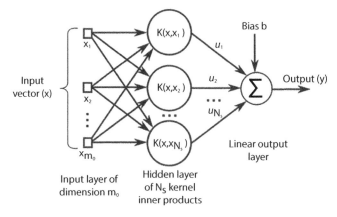

Figure 9.9 SVM classifier architecture [25].

feature space with a division of binary classes by a linear hyperplane. Figure 9.9 depicts the resultant decision function of the SVM architecture after the computations of weights and support vectors have been completed in the training stage. For in depth understanding of SVM please refer to [26].

Two kernels, linear and rbf (radial basis function) are offered for each CSP and Riemannian approaches of classification. Hyperparameters of each are shown in Table 9.3.

9.5.3   Output Metrics of the Classifier

The custom trained SVM with tuned hyper-parameters yields an average accuracy score of 0.7477175231044293 ~75% with the Riemannian Geometry technique and a 0.7382235458425794 ~74% with the CSP technique. This result is yielded over an average training period of 91.88 sec, 117.45 sec for CSP and Riemannian techniques respectively over 1000 epochs. It essentially means that the model predicts correctly what direction the subject (user) is thinking seven to eight times out of 10 on an average. The average precision and recall for each on average is 80%, 85% respectively for each technique. It is expected that given more training data collected from a diversified group of individuals and trained over a longer period of time, accuracy and precision score can potentially be improved significantly.

9.5.4   Deployment of DL Model

The trained model is finally deployed on the Raspberry Pi3 microcomputer. The EEG data read from the user will be served as input to this

Table 9.3 Depicting the hyperparameter values of the different SVM kernels. Note that these are parameters of the SVM methods offered by the sklearn.svm package.

Hyperparameter	C	Loss	max_iter	Multi_class	Penalty	Random_state	Gamma	Tol	Degree
Linear SVM	0.1	'hinge'	1000	'ovr'	l2	1	default	0.00001	default
RBF SVM	20	default	-1	'ovr'	default	default	auto	0.001	10

deployed model, which then predicts the imagined motion and takes necessary actions. The next section elaborates on the entire control system of Cerebro.

9.5.5   Control System

The Control system forms the topmost layer of the Cerebro system. The output from the Classification layer is transmitted to the Control system which maps the received signal to its respective control operation. This is the final stage of the BCI system where the natural efferent pathways are bypassed to achieve the desired action (control and communication). A Raspberry Pi3 Micro-computer is the central unit of the control system and responsible for collection and re-directing of all input signals. Detailed architecture of the entire Cerebro system will be elaborated in the next section. The control system offers two modes of operation, each for a specific application.

9.5.6   Control Flow Overview

A flip switch is fitted to shift from one mode to another. It must be noted that while operating Cerebro in one mode, the other cannot be accessed. This lock ensures the safety of the patient/user from any system mishap.

9.6   Control Modes

9.6.1   Speech Mode

In this mode, the user can essentially type out the words he/she intends to speak and then convert them into speech. This involves a two-step process. One where the patient is prompted to input text of interest and the other, converting the text into speech. Since the user is a disabled individual and can only leverage the power of the brain, Cerebro integrates the speech module (see Figure 9.10) with the main BCI system via blink recognition. The following sections take a detailed look into each of these systems.

9.6.2   Blink Stimulus Mapping

It is a known fact pre-established by several literatures that BCI's are able to detect intentional eye blinks of a person based on their blink strength. This feature is utilized to map each intentional/pressured blink with the

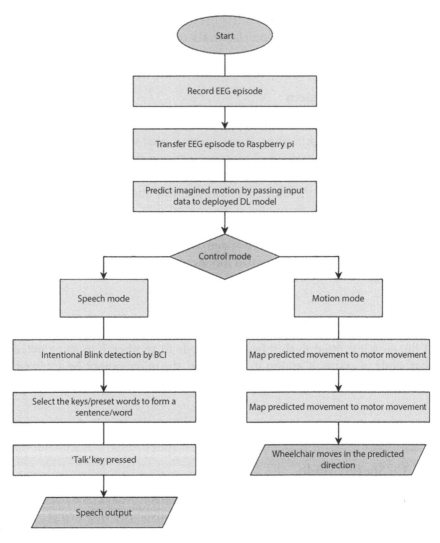

Figure 9.10 Complete system level overview of Cerebro.

selection of a key on the automated keyboard. For example, in speech mode if the user intentionally blinks with a little pressure, the key with the cursor on it will be selected. This way, the disabled individual can type out entire words and sentences. Intentional Blink stimulus from the BCI is sent to the Raspberry Pi3 module which triggers the selection of key whenever the BCI sends a blink signal.

9.6.3   Text Interface

An LCD interface is fitted onto the Raspberry Pi3 micro-computer which runs an automated python GUI keyboard interface. The cursor of the keyboard interface moves across the screen iterating over every key in a loop until one is selected by blinking. The layout of the keyboard can be observed in Figure 9.11. Preset sentences like "hey", "how are you?", "I am hungry", "I am happy" and emergency sentences like, "Help me" are set to facilitate ease of access for the patient. A "talk" key is displayed on the keyboard interface, upon selection it converts the typed out text into voice using the python package gTTS API. And finally the speakers attached to the Cerebro Wheelchair present the speech output.

9.6.4   Motion Mode

In this mode of operation, the user is only able to control the wheelchairs' movement and not the speech functionality. Motors attached to the wheelchair for its mobility are controlled by the motor driver which receives signals from the Raspberry Pi3.

9.6.5   Motor Arrangement

The arrangement of the motors is designed in such a way that the rear rotors (tires) are driven by the motors while the front is fitted with a castor wheel for ease of movement. The rotation axis and direction of the rear motors control the direction of movement of the Cerebro wheelchair. These motors are connected to the motor driver (L293D) which dictates

DISPLAY									
Q	W	E	R	T	Y	U	I	O	P
Hi	A	S	D	F	G	H	J	K	L
I'm fine	Z	X	C	V	B	N	M	Thank You	I'm Happy
How are you?	Help me	I'm not okay	Restroom	I need to sleep	I'm lost	medicines	I'm hungry	Goodbye	< clear
		Talk				Space			

Figure 9.11 The automated cursor movement keyboard GUI displayed on the LCD operated by the Raspberry Pi.

the direction and the speed of the wheelchair. The motor driver in turn is connected to the raspberry pi which maps the prediction of imagined direction by the user to actual rotation of the motors to execute the imagined movement.

9.6.6   Imagined Motion Mapping

The classifier in the Cerebro system predicts and categorizes what is imagined by the user into its respective class (left, right etc.). These predictions need to be executed in order for the wheelchair to move. The central system monitored and operated by the Raspberry Pi3 module receives the prediction results from the classifier by Bluetooth communication channel and based on the predicted class, certain commands are signaled to the motor driver which then executes them accordingly. Thus moving the motors to achieve the imagined motion.

9.7   Compilation of All Systems

The complete architecture of Cerebro is shown in Figure 9.11. The EEG records the brain waves and sends it to the raspberry pi where the deployed dl model predicts the imagined motion. If the Cerebro system is in Motion mode, this output is then transferred to the motor unit where a motor driver converts this data into a communication signal for the rear rotors to move in the predicted direction. In the case of Speech Mode, an automated keyboard GUI with preset sentences is displayed on the LCD panel where the user can select letters and form sentences by intentionally blinking. The BCI in this mode instead of capturing EEG records for movement, detects intentional blinks and sends the signal to the micro-computer where this signal is processed into a communication signal for the cursor to select the key when blinked. After forming a sentence, the user must select the "Talk" key from the keyboard to convert the typed out text into speech through a mounted speaker.

9.8   Conclusion

Cerebro proposes a novel coalition of DL based BCI technology and automated systems with speech facilities offering an all-round functionality for the disabled. Additional testing with more data is expected to improve its performance in recognizing the brain patterns with greater accuracy. With advancements and sincere effort by the researchers in this field day-by-day, better devices and products are to be expected, which can also potentially improve the overall design of the end product. To my knowledge as of today, cerebro marks the first effort to build a complete BCI go-to market product with speech support features aiding the unfortunate.

References

1. Block, N., The Journal of Philosophy. *JSTOR*, 90, 4, 181–193, 1993. www.jstor.org/stable/2940970.
2. Wolpaw, R., Birbaumer, N., McFarland, D.J., Pfurtscheller, G., Vaughan, T.M., Brain computer interfaces for communication and control. *Clin. Neurophysiol.*, 113, 767–791, 2002.
3. Levine, S.P., Huggins, J.E., BeMent, S.L., Kushwaha, R.K., Schuh, L.A., Passaro, E.A., Rohde, M.M., Ross, D.A., Identification of electrocorticogram patterns as the basis for a direct brain interface. *J. Clin. Neurophysiol.*, 16, 5, 439, September 1999.
4. Leeb, R., Friedman, D., Müller-Putz, G.R., Scherer, R., Slater, M., Pfurtscheller, G., Self-paced (Asynchronous) BCI control of a wheelchair in virtual environments: A case study with a tetraplegic. *Comput. Intell. Neurosci.*, Article ID 079642, 8, 2007.
5. Li Y, Pan J, Wang F, Yu Z. A hybrid BCI system combining P300 and SSVEP and its application to wheelchair control. *IEEE Trans Biomed Eng.*, 60, 11, 3156–3166, 2013 Nov. Epub 2013 Jun 20. PMID: 23799679.
6. Schomer, D. and Silva, F., *Niedermeyer's electroencephalography: Basic principles, clinical applications, and related fields*, Wolters Kluwer Health, Lippincott Williams & Wilkins, Philadelphia, USA, 2012.
7. McFarland, D. and Wolpaw, J., Brain-computer interfaces for communication and control. *Commun. ACM*, 54, 5, 60–66, 2011.
8. Allison, B.Z., McFarland, D.J., Schalk, G., Dong Zheng, S., Jackson, M.M., Wolpaw, J.R., Towards an independent brain–computer interface using steady state visual evoked potentials. *Clin. Neurophysiol.*, 119, 2, 399–408, 2008.
9. Famili, A., *et al.* Data preprocessing and intelligent data analysis. *Intelligent data analysis.*, 1.1, 3-23, 1997.
10. ESANN 2014 proceedings. *European Symposium on Artificial Neural Networks, Computational Intelligence and Machine Learning*, Bruges, Belgium, pp. 23–25, April 2014, i6doc.com publ., http://www.i6doc.com/fr/livre/?GCOI=28001100432440.
11. Wagner, J.M., Dromerick, A.W., Sahrmann, S.A., Lang, C.E., Upper extremity muscle activation during recovery of reaching in subjects with

post-stroke hemiparesis. *Clin. Neurophysiol.*, 118, 1, 164–176, 2007, https://doi.org/10.1016/j.clinph.2006.09.022.

12. Zhang, Y., Zhao, Q., Zhou, G., Jin, J., Wang, X., Cichocki, A., Removal of EEG artifacts for BCI applications using fully Bayesian tensor completion. *2016 IEEE International Conference on Acoustics, Speech and Signal Processing (ICASSP)*, pp. 819–823, 2016.

13. Deo, A., Pandey, S.K., Joshi, A., Sharma, S.K., Shrimali, H., Design of a third order butterworth Gm-C filter for EEG signal detection application. *2018 25th International Conference "Mixed Design of Integrated Circuits and System" (MIXDES)*, pp. 361–365, 2018.

14. Shakshi, R.J., Brain wave classification and feature extraction of EEG signal by using FFT on lab view. *Int. Res. J. Eng. Technol.*, 3, 1208–1212, 2016.

15. Butterworth Bandpass and Stationary Wavelet Transform Filter Comparison for Electroencephalography Signal S. S. Daud, R. Sudirman Department of Electronic and Computer Engineering Faculty of Electrical Engineering. *6th International Conference on Intelligent Systems, Modelling and Simulation*, UTM 81310 UTM Johor Bahru, 2015.

16. Belhadj, S.A., Benmoussat, N., Della Krachai, M., CSP features extraction and FLDA classification of EEG-based motor imagery for brain-computer interaction. *2015 4th International Conference on Electrical Engineering (ICEE)*, pp. 1–6, 2015.

17. Gaur, P., Tangent space features-based transfer learning classification model for two-class motor imagery brain–computer interface. *Int. J. Neural Syst.*, 29, 10, 1950025, 2019.

18. Afrakhteh, S. and Mosavi, M.R., Chapter 2 - Applying an efficient evolutionary algorithm for EEG signal feature selection and classification in decision-based systems, in: *Energy efficiency of medical devices and healthcare applications*, A. Mohamed (Ed.), pp. 25–52, Academic Press, London, United Kingdom, 2020, https://doi.org/10.1016/B978-0-12-819045-6.00002-9.

19. Lisi, G. and Morimoto, J., Chapter Seven - Noninvasive brain machine interfaces for assistive and rehabilitation robotics: A review, in: *Human modelling for bio-inspired robotics*, J. Ueda and Y. Kurita (Eds.), pp. 187–216, Academic Press, London, United Kingdom, 2017, https://doi.org/10.1016/B978-0-12-803137-7.00006-9.

20. Kanoga, S. and Mitsukura, Y., Review of artifact rejection methods for electroencephalographic systems. *Electroencephalography*, 69, 69–89, 2017.

21. Barachant, C., Riemannian geometry applied to BCI classification, in: *Latent variable analysis and signal separation*, pp. 629–636, Springer, Berlin Heidelberg, 2010.

22. Xu, J., Grosse-Wentrup, M., Jayaram, V., Tangent space spatial filters for interpretable and efficient Riemannian classification. *J. Neural Eng.*, 17, 2, 026043, 2020.

23. Rajesh Kumar, D., Vinothsaravanan, R., Poongodi, M., Krishnasamy, L., Hamdi, M., Kotecha, K., Vijayakumar, V., Random forest bagging and

x-means clustered antipattern detection from SQL query log for accessing secure mobile data, *Wireless Communications and Mobile Computing*, 2021, Article ID 2730246, 9 pages, 2021. https://doi.org/10.1155/2021/2730246

24. Schlögl, A. *et al.*, Characterization of four-class motor imagery EEG data for the BCI-competition 2005. *J. Neural Eng.*, 2, 4, L14, 2005.

25. Ruiz-Gonzalez, R., Gomez-Gil, J., Gomez-Gil, F.J., Martínez-Martínez, V., An SVM-based classifier for estimating the state of various rotating components in agro-industrial machinery with a vibration signal acquired from a single point on the machine chassis. *Sensors.*, 14, 11, 20713–20735, 2014.

26. Joachims, T., Making large-scale SVM learning practical. EconStor: Making large-scale SVM learning practical, *Practical Advances in Kernel Methods-Support Vector Learning*, 1999, USA: MIT Press, Cambridge, MA, 1998. http://hdl.handle.net/10419/77178.

10

Identification of Imagined Bengali Vowels from EEG Signals Using Activity Map and Convolutional Neural Network

Rajdeep Ghosh[1*], Nidul Sinha[2] and Souvik Phadikar[2]

[1]*School of Computing Science and Engineering, VIT Bhopal University, Kotri Kalan, Madhya Pradesh, India*
[2]*Department of E.E., NIT Silchar, Silchar, Assam, India*

Abstract

Classification of electroencephalogram (EEG) signals is challenging due to its non-stationary nature and poor spectral resolution w.r.t. time. This chapter presents a novel feature representation termed as activity map (AM) for the classification of imagined vowels from EEG. The proposed AM provides a visualization of the temporal and spectral information of the EEG data. The AM is created for each of the EEG recorded from 22 subjects imagining five Bengali vowels /আ/, /ই/, /উ/, /এ/, and /ও/ using 64 channels. The AM is generated by extracting the band power in delta, theta, alpha, beta, and gamma bands for each second of the EEG and subsequently stacking them to form a matrix. The matrix is then converted into a heat map of 100×200 pixels called AM. The AM thus obtained, is classified using a convolutional neural network (CNN), achieving an average accuracy of 68.9% in classifying the imagined vowels. The CNN demonstrates superior performance in comparison to other methods reported in the literature using various features such as common spatial pattern (CSP), discrete wavelet transform (DWT), etc. and with different classifiers such as kNN (k nearest neighbor), support vector machine (SVM), linear discriminant analysis (LDA), and multilayer perceptron neural network (MLPNN).

Keywords: Activity map, band power, brain-computer interface (BCI), convolutional neural network (CNN), electroencephalogram (EEG), imagined speech, silent speech (SS)

Corresponding author: rajdeep.publication@gmail.com

M.G. Sumithra, Rajesh Kumar Dhanaraj, Mariofanna Milanova, Balamurugan Balusamy and Chandran Venkatesan (eds.) Brain-Computer Interface: Using Deep Learning Applications, (231–254) © 2023 Scrivener Publishing LLC

10.1   Introduction

The brain is a complex organ generating electrical and chemical responses. The electrical activity of the human brain was first measured by a German psychiatrist named Hans Berger in the year 1929 [16]. The works of Hans Berger have inspired many and the domain has developed since then, especially in the last decade. The potential for the application of the brain signals has generated quite a lot of interest in researchers and has paved the way for the development of a research area known as a brain-computer interface (BCI) which utilizes EEG signals for controlling devices. Besides, EEG signal processing is also being used extensively to analyze various neurological disorders like epilepsy, sleep study, etc.

The brain-computer interface (BCI) is an intermediate arrangement that allows the communication between the brain of an individual and an external output device. It first measures the brain activity of an individual relating to a particular task, after which it extracts features about that activity, and converts those features to generate a suitable output or control signals for an external device. BCIs are developed to improve or enhance certain functions in disabled individuals who have lost their muscular coordination due to diseases like paralysis, locked-in syndrome, injuries, etc. but have a functional brain. BCI serves as an alternative form of communication for such individuals. The measurement of the brain activity can again be carried out in multiple paradigms:

i) **Invasive:** In the invasive method, a chip is implanted inside the head directly on the Gray matter of the brain, and as such produces a high-quality electrical signal capturing the electrical activity of the brain. But the major problem is that to implant a chip, neurological surgery is needed and has a very high risk of building-up of scar tissue in the operated part. Example: Local field potential (LFP) [17].

ii) **Partially Invasive:** In this method, the electrodes are placed to record the electrical activity inside the skull, but on the surface of the membrane that protects the brain. The signal quality is lower than the invasive method, but the risk of forming scar tissue is lower, but is not free from scar tissue formation. Example: Electrocorticography (ECoG) [17].

iii) **Non-invasive:** It is the most popular approach for recording brain signals. It is the safest way to record brain signals as the recording is done externally on the scalp. The electrodes or sensors are placed on the surface of the scalp. It produces a poor signal and low spatial resolution. Example EEG, functional magnetic resonance imaging (fMRI) [18].

10.1.1   Electroencephalography (EEG)

The neurons inside the brain communicate with each other with the help of electrical signals. These electrical signals can be measured with the help of electrodes placed at various locations on the scalp of an individual. EEG signals have been extensively used by neurologists to identify and treat different diseases such as epilepsy, Alzheimer's disease, etc. associated with the brain. Besides, EEG can also be used for evaluating the sleep pattern of an individual, understand learning or attention disorders. Commonly Ag-AgCl electrodes are used as electrodes. The signal values obtained are in the range of 0.5–100 µV. EEG measures the voltage difference between the two electrodes [19].

EEG is one of the widely used devices in BCI for recording the excitation of the brain due to its non-invasive recording methodology, low cost, high temporal resolution, and ease of use. BCIs have been used in various applications like prosthetics, classifying emotions, etc. An important application of BCI has focused on the development of a communication interface for enabling paralyzed individuals to communicate with the external world [12, 15, 29]. The necessity for such an interface has led to the concept of recognition of speech from the human brain. The focus of this chapter is to describe an application of a well-known deep learning model known as the convolutional neural network (CNN) to classify imagined vowels from the EEG recordings of individuals.

10.1.2   Imagined Speech or Silent Speech

An interpretation of silent speech or imagined speech can be referred to as the words heard or conceived by an individual in his head without any vocalization to the environment. To understand imagined speech it is very essential to understand the stages of speech communication carried out by an individual. The first stage is the conceptualization and formulation of the speech which occurs in the brain. In this process, the communication intentions are converted into messages known as the surface structure following the grammatical rules of the language in which verbal communication is to be made. In the next step, the surface structure is converted to the phonetic plan, where a sequence of phonemes that form the speech is fed

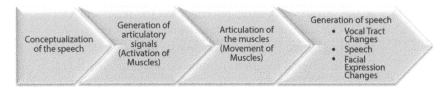

Figure 10.1 Speech production process by an individual.

to the articulators. After which, electrical impulses are given to the articulators to start the articulation process. The final stage produces the acoustic speech signal as a result of the consequent effects from the previous phases. Hence, silent speech can be defined as speech originating inside the human brain which has not been vocalized by the individual [20]. Figure 10.1 represents the speech production process in an individual.

The focus of the present study deals with identifying silent/imagined speech by measuring the electrical activity of the brain. The present chapter is concerned with the recognition of only five imagined Bengali vowels /আ/, /ই/, /উ/, /এ/, and /ও/ from the EEG recordings of an individual.

10.2   Literature Survey

The earliest efforts in this respect were made by Birbaumer *et al.* [1], who developed the thought translation device for locked-in patients using slow cortical potentials (SCP), which permits the users to select a particular letter in the English language for communication. Wester [2] classified mumbled, unspoken, silent, whispered, and normal speech, from EEG recordings by using linear discriminant analysis (LDA) as a classifier. He cited the importance of Wernicke's area and Broca's area in the brain for speech communication. DaSalla *et al.* [3] classified three imagined states: a state of no action, the imagination of the English vowel /a/, and the English vowel /u/ from three subjects by using a non-linear support vector machine (SVM). Brigham *et al.* [11] considered the recognition of two syllables /ba/ and /ku/ from the EEG recorded from seven subjects. In their work, the EEG data were pre-processed to reduce the effects of artifacts and noise using independent component analysis (ICA). After the removal of artifacts from the EEG, autoregressive (AR) coefficients were evaluated for the classification of imagined syllables using a kNN classifier. They obtained an average classification accuracy of 61% in classifying the syllables, which suggests that it was possible to identify imagined speech syllables from the EEG.

Calliess [21] further extended the works carried out by Wester [2] and placed electrodes primarily in the orofacial motor cortex with a different cap arrangement to capture the EEG data more efficiently. In this work, it was further established that the successful recognition rate in [2] was due to the temporal correlation among the EEG data created during the collection of the data. It was further reported that the repeated imagination of a word created a high recognition rate. However, the accuracy dropped if the EEG data for the words were recorded in random order.

Mesgarani *et al.* [22] measured the electrical activity from the primary auditory cortex in response to sentences from the Texas Instruments (TI) and Massachusetts Institute of Technology (TIMIT) database. They examined the effect of various phonemes on the different subsets of auditory neurons. Their study reflected that the neurons with different spectro-temporal tuning responded differently in response to specific auditory stimuli, which could be represented explicitly in a multidimensional articulatory feature representation, which is independent of the speaker and the context. Galgano and Froud [23] established the existence of voice-related cortical potentials (VRCP) in their study. They used a 43 channel EEG instrument to record the neuronal activity of the subjects who were instructed to hum in response to a stimulus and found a slow, negative cortical potential before 250 msec from the start of phonation by the subjects.

Efforts have also been made by D'Zmura *et al.* [24] for recognizing imagined syllables from the EEG recordings. They considered two syllables /ba/ and /ku/ for recognition. 20 EEG trials were recorded from four subjects under six experimental conditions where the syllables were presented in a randomized order of the subjects. Analysis of the EEG was carried out w.r.t. the three bands theta, alpha, and beta bands showing the presence of information. Envelopes were created using Hilbert transformation to compute matched filters corresponding to the particular imagined syllable to yield the degree of similarity in the respective EEG bands. The classification accuracy achieved was around 60%. However, the removal of electrodes containing the artifacts resulted in the loss of neural information for the recognition of the syllables in their work.

Santana [25] in his work classified two English vowels /a/ and /u/ from the EEG recordings of three subjects. Spatial filters were evaluated using CSP and then classified. The performance of classification was analyzed for 10 classifiers. He concluded that simple classifiers like Gaussian naive Bayes classifier outperformed the SVM classifier. He further added that different classifiers exploit different mental mechanisms and subjects could be grouped based on the underlying mental mechanisms. Matsumoto [26] investigated the classification of two imagined vowels in Japanese similar to /a/ and /u/ obtained from 4 subjects who were imagining the vocalization of those vowels using 63 EEG channels. An adaptive collection (AC) was used for classification. The obtained accuracy of classification was in the range of 73–92%. Kamalakkannan et al. [27] tried to classify imagined English vowels /a/, /e/, /i/, /o/, and /u/ in their work. EEG data were recorded from 13 subjects using 20 electrodes. They extracted the following features from the EEG recordings: standard deviation, mean, variance, and average power, which were classified using a bipolar neural network. Maximum accuracy of 44% was obtained in their work. Their results showed that some distinctive information was present in the EEG relating to imagined vowels. They also found that the increase in relaxation time increased the classification accuracy. They also suggested that the classification could be extended to major 36 alphanumeric characters.

Salama et al. [28] classified two imagined words, namely, 'yes' and 'no' from the electroencephalographic signals recorded using only a single electrode EEG device. The single electrode setup was adopted in their work due to the following advantages: ease of setup, adjustment, and light weight. Data were recorded from 7 subjects who were imagining the words in response to specific questions. Wavelet packet decomposition was applied to extract features from the EEG and was classified using 4 classifiers: support vector machine (SVM), self-organizing map (SOM), discriminant analysis (DA), feed-forward network (FFN), and ensemble network (EN). The average online classification rate was 57% and the offline recognition rate was 59%.

Nguyen et al. [10] used a covariance matrix descriptor from the Riemannian manifold as features to classify EEG recordings relating to the imagined pronunciation of long words, short words, and vowels collected from a total of 15 subjects, which were subsequently classified using relevance vector machines (RVM) classifier. They achieved an accuracy of 70% in classifying the words from the EEG recordings and concluded that certain aspects such as word complexity, meaning, and sound may affect the classification of the imagined speech from the EEG signals.

Wang et al. [30] classified between motor imagery and speech imagery signals collected from 10 subjects and achieved an accuracy of 74.3% for classification of mental tasks in speech imagery, 71.4% in imagining left-hand movement, and 69.8% in imagining right-hand movement. Time-frequency characteristics were estimated from the EEG signals by using event-related spectral perturbation (ERSP) diagrams which provide a good time-frequency visualization. EEG signals recorded for different imageries have different energy changes which can be extracted using CSP. Moreover, it was observed that the synchronization in the cerebral cortex was different for speech imagery and motor imagery. Recently, Bakshali *et al.* [4] classified EEG data relating to the imagination of words and syllables from the "Kara One" database by using the Riemannian distance evaluated from the correntropy spectral density (CSD) matrices and achieved a significant classification accuracy of 90.25%. The CSD matrix does not contain any frequency information about the channels, but it does contains some similar information regarding the channels. However, an appropriate pre-processing method is essential for achieving a good classification accuracy.

Sereshkeh *et al.* [13] recorded the EEG from 12 participants who were performing the mental imagination of two words "yes" and "no". The EEG was recorded in two sessions for multiple iterations. The individual duration of the EEG recording was 10 seconds. Discrete wavelet transform (DWT) based features were evaluated from the EEG data which were classified using a multilayer perceptron neural network (MLPNN). Average accuracy of 75.7% was achieved in their case. Chi *et al.* [14] classified five types of imagined phonemes that differ in their vocal articulation (jaw, tongue, nasal, lips, and fricative) during speech production. Spectrogram data were directly used for classifying the EEG data. LDA and Naive Bayes (NB) classification methods were used to classify the EEG signals. The classification accuracy varied from 66.4% to 76% on the data collected in multiple sessions. Their results showed that the signals generated during the imagination of phonemes could be differentiated from the EEG generated during periods when there was no imagination by the subjects.

EEG signals are non-stationary and hence present a challenge in their classification. The primary issue remains in identifying suitable features to discriminate between the EEG signals. A variety of methods have been used in the literature to classify silent speech phonemes, syllables from EEG. The methods available in the literature focus on extracting spatial, temporal, and spectral features from the EEG signals to classify imagined speech. Temporal features of the EEG like energy, power, etc. have been used for classifying the imagined speech. Common spatial pattern (CSP) and their variants have been widely used in the literature to classify imagined speech. Besides, ICA has also been used in the literature to process the EEG related to the imagined speech. The usefulness of ICA lies in its ability to separate independent components from the EEG. Various methodologies based on Fourier transform (FT), wavelet transform (WT) have also been used to extract spectral features from the EEG relating to imagined speech. Besides, statistical features like mean, variance, standard deviation, etc. have also been used for the classification of imagined speech. However, selecting features reflecting only temporal or spectral information does not allow an efficient recognition of imagined speech from EEG. It is essential to consider features that reflect different properties of the EEG signal. Hence, the proposed work presents a novel activity map (AM), to represent the changes in various frequency bands w.r.t time.

Deep learning-based methodologies like CNN, autoencoder, etc. have been used to solve a wide variety of problems in recent times. Deep learning methodologies have also been applied for processing EEG signals [5]. The benefit of using deep learning is its ability to learn complex representations from the data. The novel AM generated in the present work is classified using CNN. CNN's have proved their efficiency to classify images and hence have been selected for classification of the AM relating to the respective EEG of the imagined speech. Although various methodologies are available for classifying silent speech from EEG, yet they fail to classify them effectively. Hence, a novel methodology has been developed to classify the imagined speech from EEG.

10.3 Theoretical Background

The work presented in this chapter is focused on the identification of the imagined Bengali vowels from EEG and utilizes the concept of the convolutional neural network to classify the activity maps (AMs) representing the different imagined Bengali vowels. The description of the various concepts is described in this section.

10.3.1 Convolutional Neural Network

Convolutional neural networks originate from the works of Fukushima in 1980 [7] but have seen rapid development recently and have been applied to a variety of applications related to image processing, video processing, drug discovery, etc. A CNN comprises of an input layer, multiple hidden layers, and an output layer. The hidden layers are comprised of numerous convolution layers, pooling layers, flattening layers, followed by a fully connected layer. A typical CNN includes the following layers: convolutional layer, activation layer, pooling layer, flattening layer, a fully connected/dense layer, and a classification layer. The convolutional layer convolves the input image with a set of R filters and adds the respective bias value, which is then forwarded to a nonlinear activation function to generate feature maps:

$$F = g\left(\sum_{i \in m,n,c} \theta(i) * X_r + b_r\right) \tag{10.1}$$

Where $\theta(i)$ represents an $m \times n$ image with c channels, X_r represents the r-th convolution filter or a kernel with dimension $s \times s$, * denotes the convolution operation, and b_r represents the bias term for the r-th filter, R represents the total number of filters, and $g()$ represents the activation function [8]. Different activation functions can be applied in the activation layer. Rectified linear unit (ReLU) function is one of the most commonly used activation functions in CNN and can be described as:

$$R(x) = \begin{cases} 0, x < 0 \\ x, x \geq 0 \end{cases} \tag{10.2}$$

The pooling layer downsamples the feature matrix to lower dimensions. The pooling operation reduces the number of computations and also removes the redundant information while training the CNN. Max-pooling and average-pooling are the two of the most used techniques. The former method selects the maximum pixel value as the representation of a small pooling region, while the latter uses the average value of this region as the representation. The pooling layer is succeeded by a flattening layer, which converts the two-dimensional vector to a one-dimensional vector. The flattening layer is succeeded by a fully connected/dense layer which in turn is connected to the classification layer.

The classification layer has nodes equal to the number of classes in the problem for which the CNN is trained. The softmax activation function is generally used for classification as it provides the output in terms of probability ranges. The layer provides output values between 0 and 1 and the sum of probabilities of the data belonging to a particular class is equal to one. Mathematically the output probability of a node can be expressed as:

$$P_j = \frac{e^{z_j}}{\sum_{j=1}^{N} e^{z_j}} \tag{10.3}$$

z denotes the output value of the node in the softmax layer and N denotes the number of classes.

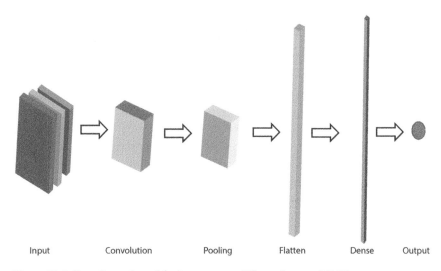

| Input | Convolution | Pooling | Flatten | Dense | Output |

Figure 10.2 Transformation of the image across different layers of CNN.

Figure 10.2 represents the transformation of an image in a CNN. Initially, RGB images can be given as input to the CNN, which is gradually transformed into a 2-dimensional matrix after convolution and pooling. The 2-dimensional matrix is then transformed to a 1-dimensional vector after which an output class label is finally generated. CNN's can be organized in various dimensions and can be utilized for different applications.

10.3.2   Activity Map

The present work describes the creation of a novel activity map (AM), which represents the tempo-spectral information of all the EEG channels which is subsequently converted into an image. EEG signals are categorized into five primary frequency bands delta (f<4 Hz), theta (4≤f<7 Hz), alpha (8≤f<13 Hz), beta (13≤f<30 Hz), and gamma (30 Hz<f) bands based on the nature of the different states in the brain like relaxed, active, etc. Hence, it is essential to capture the activity of a particular band, and band power serves as a useful metric for obtaining the information in a specific frequency band. Band power specifies the average power in a respective frequency band and represents the activity in an individual frequency band. Band power reflects the average power in a particular frequency band. The average power of the signal $x[t]$ within a window of size w can be represented as:

$$P_f = \frac{1}{w} \sum_{k=0}^{w} p[n-k] \qquad (10.4)$$

This means the power is averaged over window w over which the frequency is estimated. $p[n]$ represents the power spectral density of a particular frequency. The procedure to generate the AM is as follows: Let us consider an EEG signal of 5 seconds with 64 channels. The EEG signal for all the channels is split into segments of one second each. From the one-second segment, the band power is evaluated in the respective frequency bands: delta, theta, alpha, beta, and gamma bands. The band power thus obtained is placed sequentially one after the other giving a total of 25 values (5 sec. × 5 Band power values for each band) for an individual channel. The values, thus obtained are stacked for all the 64 channels yielding a matrix of size 64 × 25. The matrix, thus obtained is converted into a heat map of 100 × 200 pixels. Figure 10.3 represents an AM generated in the proposed work. The AM represents the activity in a particular frequency band with respect to the time.

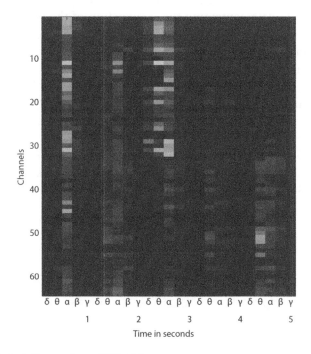

Figure 10.3 Activity map for an EEG trial.

10.4   Methodology

The proposed work is focused on the classification of the imagined Bengali vowels from EEG, and in this regard, a novel feature extraction methodology has been developed known as AM, which is subsequently converted into an image and classified with the help of a CNN.

The methodology of the proposed work is described in Figure 10.4. The different phases of the overall methodology are follows:

(a)   **Data collection:** Initially, the picture as well as the sound of the vowels are presented to the subject, after which the subject is instructed to imagine the sound of the vowel for 5 seconds in his mind. During the imagination of the vowel by the subject, the EEG of the individual is recorded. The EEG recording from an individual is conducted for five trials for each of the 5 Bengali vowels /আ/, /ই/, /উ/, /এ/, and /ও/ and the procedure has been described in Section 10.4.1.

(b)   **Data pre-processing:** The EEG data collected from different individuals are segmented to extract the part of the EEG data containing the imagination of the vowels. The EEG data is very sensitive and is often corrupted with artifacts. The EEG data is then processed to remove artifacts and noise. The removal of artifacts and noise from EEG is a complex procedure and requires the usage of different methods and has elaborated in Section 10.4.2. After the removal of artifacts, the EEG signal corresponding to the respective Bengali vowel is labeled.

(c)   **Generation of activity map:** The objective of the proposed work is concerned with the classification of the imagined Bengali vowels from the EEG of an individual. For the

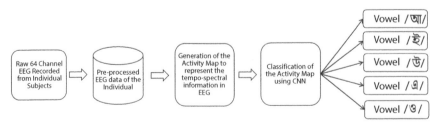

Figure 10.4 The methodology of the proposed work.

purpose of classification, activity map is generated from the processed EEG obtained after the pre-processing step. The activity map is generated according to the procedure described in Section 10.3.2. The activity map corresponding to the respective EEG is saved as an image file in .jpeg format and is then used for the purpose of classification.

(d) **Classification of the activity map using CNN:** The activity map generated in the previous step is saved as an image file. CNN has proved to be efficient for the purpose of image classification and is therefore adopted in the present task for the purpose of classification. The architecture of the CNN has been described in Section 10.4.4. The AM's corresponding to the different classes are then randomly split in 70:30 ratio for training and testing respectively and are fed to the CNN for the purpose of classification.

10.4.1   Data Collection

Data were collected at the National Institute of Technology, Silchar. A total of 22 subjects (16 Males, 6 Females) aged between 20–34 years took part in the experiment. The experiment was conducted after obtaining adequate permission from the authority and written consent from the subjects. The vowels considered for imagination were /আ/, /ই/, /উ/, /এ/, and /ও/. The reason for selecting the respective vowels is that the vowels resemble the pronunciation of the English language vowels /a/, /i/, /u/, /e/, /o/ respectively according to the International Phonetic Alphabet (IPA) which is a system of phonetic notation. 64 channel EEG was recorded using the standard 10–20 recording setup. The EEG data were sampled at 512Hz, and 5 trials were recorded for each vowel in the case of each individual reaching a total of 550 trials (22 Subjects × 5 Trials × 5 vowels). Figure 10.5 depicts the trial recording protocol followed in the present work for recording the EEG. Initially, the EEG recording cap is attached to the scalp of the subject after which, the subjects were asked to relax for 2 seconds, after which an audio-visual stimulus of the vowel to be imagined was presented to the subject for a duration of 4 seconds, the next phase was the fixation phase of 4 seconds where the subjects were instructed to focus on a fixed point at the center of the display screen, where the audio-visual stimulus was presented previously. After fixation, the vowel to be imagined was then displayed on the screen for 5 seconds, during which the subject was asked to imagine the vowel.

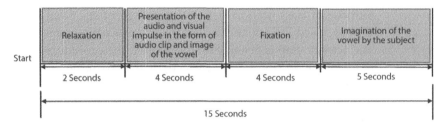

Figure 10.5 Trial recording protocol.

10.4.2   Pre-Processing

The pre-processing stage is primarily concerned with the removal of artifacts and noise from the EEG followed by the extraction of the segment of the EEG signal containing the imagination of vowels. Initially, it is observed that the data is corrupted by a 50 Hz power-line noise. Hence, a notch filter is applied to remove the same. After which the signals are filtered in the range of 0–60 Hz. After filtering the data, artifacts were removed from the EEG data using a hybrid method combining SVM and autoencoder which has been described in one of our previous works [6].

Figure 10.6 represents an EEG recording before the artifact removal. The artifacts are removed using a combination of autoencoder and SVM classifier. The SVM classifier has been used for the detection of artifacts

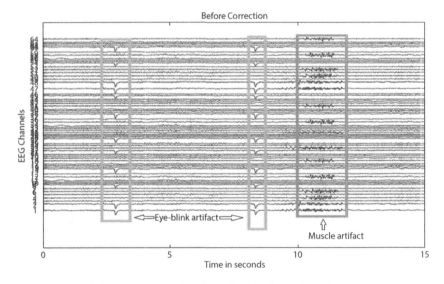

Figure 10.6 EEG data contaminated with eye blink and muscle artifacts.

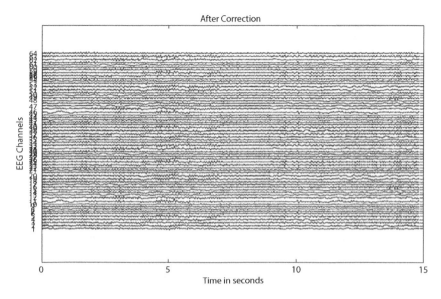

Figure 10.7 Channel EEG data corrected with SVM and autoencoder [6].

and the autoencoder has been used for correcting the identified artifacts. The artifact removal methodology has been described in [6]. The artifact removal methodology adopted in our previous work follows a windowed strategy, where a window size of 0.45 seconds is slid forward to traverse the entire signal. A pre-trained SVM classifier classifies the selected EEG window as corrupted or uncorrupted. If the window is identified as corrupted, it is forwarded to the autoencoder for correction. The autoencoder is trained to generate clean EEG segments from corrupted segments. On the other hand, if the window is not corrupted, the algorithm moves to the next window. Figure 10.7 represents the 64 channel EEG after the application of the artifact removal procedure. The final phase involves trimming the signal to keep the final 5 seconds of the data containing the imagination of the vowels by the subjects.

10.4.3   Feature Extraction

The proposed work focuses on the classification of imagined Bengali vowels from the EEG recordings of the subjects. The activity map is generated according to the procedure described in Section 10.3.2. The activity map provides a good time-frequency visualization of the EEG data. Moreover, it provides a visualization of the EEG activity only in the specific range of interest i.e., the delta, theta, alpha, beta, and gamma bands.

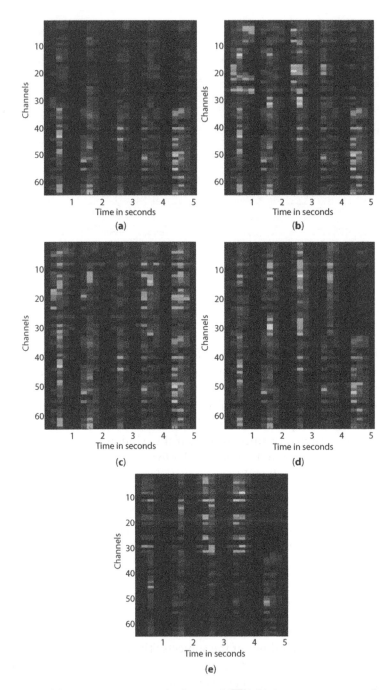

Figure 10.8 (a) Average activity map for the vowel /আ/. (b) Average activity map for the vowel /ই/. (c) Average activity map for the vowel /উ/. (d) Average activity map for the vowel/এ/. (e) Average activity map for the phoneme /ও/.

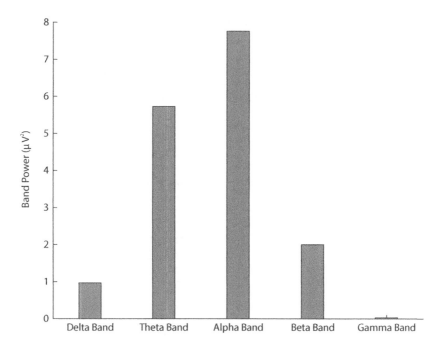

Figure 10.9 Average band power of the frequency bands.

Besides, the AM also creates a repetitive pattern which would be useful while classifying using CNN. The AM is generated from the trimmed EEG of all the 550 EEG trials. Figures 10.8(a), (b), (c), (d), and (e) represent the average activity maps of all 22 subjects for the imagined Bengali vowels /আ/, /ই/, /উ/, /এ/, and /ও/ respectively. From the average activity maps, it is clear that the activity maps provide a good differentiation among the EEG data representing the imagined Bengali vowels. Figure 10.9 depicts an average band power for the respective frequency bands obtained from all EEG segments. It can be inferred that the alpha band shows the maximum activity in comparison to other bands, thus confirming the wakeful-imaginative state of the subjects during recording.

10.4.4   Classification

The AM obtained during the process of feature extraction is classified with the help of a CNN. The architecture of the CNN used in the proposed work has been described in Table 10.1. The strategy adopted in design-ing the CNN is to subsequently reduce the dimension of the feature map. Table 10.1 describes the various layers used in the proposed work for the

Table 10.1 Description of the various layers of CNN used in the proposed work.

Layer number	Quantity	Property of the layer
1	Image input layer	Size of image: 100×200×3
2	Convolutional layer	No. of filters: 192; Size of the filter: 20×20; Stride: 2
3	ReLU layer	-------------
4	Max pooling layer	Size of filter: 20×20; Stride: 2
5	Convolutional layer	No. of filters: 128; Size of the filter: 10×10; Stride: 2
6	ReLU layer	-------------
7	Max pooling layer	Size of the filter: 10×10; Stride: 2
8	Convolutional layer	No. of filters: 64; Size of the filter: 3×3; Stride: 2
9	ReLU layer	-------------
10	Max pooling layer	Size of the filter: 3×3; Stride: 2
11	Convolutional layer	No. of filters: 32; Size of the filter: 1×1; Stride: 2
12	ReLU layer	-------------
13	Max pooling layer	Size of the filter: 3×3; Stride: 2
14	Flattening layer	----------------------
15	Fully Connected Layer	Size: 5
16	Softmax Layer	Size: 5
17	Classification Layer	Evaluates one out of the 5 class label depending on the probability obtained from the softmax layer

classification of the imagined vowel. The convolution layer uses the convolution operation to convert the image with a set of 192 filters to generate feature maps. The rectified linear unit (ReLU) serves as the activation function for the convolution layer. The advantage of ReLU lies in the fact that it is easier to compute and does not activate all the nodes at a time. The pooling layer combines the neighboring pixels into a single pixel, decreasing the dimension of the feature map generated. The normalization layer normalizes the gradients and activations in the network, thereby easing the training process of the network. The softmax layer normalizes the output of the fully connected layer, and the classification layer uses the probabilities of the softmax layer to assign labels to the individual input. The properties of the various layers are mentioned in Table 10.1. ReLU layer, followed by a max-pooling layer with the filter size of the preceding convolutional layer, was used after each convolutional layer. After four convolutional + ReLU + Max-pooling layers, a flattening layer was added, after which a fully connected layer with 5 nodes was added, followed by a softmax layer with 5 units and the final classification layer. In the proposed CNN, a stride of 2 has been selected in the convolutional and max-pooling layers.

10.5 Results

MATLAB R2019b has been used to develop the proposed methodology and run on an Intel i7 processor with 8GB RAM. The data was split randomly in the 70:30 ratio for training and testing, respectively. The AM was formed from the EEG segments representing the imagination of the vowels /আ/, /ই/, /উ/, /এ/, and /ও/, which was given to the proposed CNN for classification. The average classification accuracy of the CNN in identifying the individual vowels is represented in Table 10.2. It is observed from Table 10.2 that the CNN achieves an accuracy of 68.9% in classifying the imagined vowels. The precision obtained in classifying the imagined vowels /আ/, /ই/, /উ/, /এ/, and /ও/ are 73.9%, 66.6%, 69.5%, 68.1% and 59.1% respectively.

Besides, the CNN is also compared with different methodologies described in the literature for the identification of silent speech from EEG. It has been observed that the different methodologies described in the literature have used different combination of features and classifiers such as: autoregressive (AR) coefficients as feature and kNN as classifier [11], CSP as a feature, and SVM as classifier [9], spectrogram as a feature and LDA as classifier [14], DWT coefficients as features and MLPNN as classifier [13], and Riemannian distance (RD) evaluated from the correntropy spectral density (CSD) matrices as features and kNN as classifier [4]. F_1 scores have

Table 10.2 Performance metrics for the individual imagined Bengali phoneme.

Imagined vowel	Precision %	Recall %	F_1 score	Overall accuracy %
/আ/	73.9%	77.2%	75.5%	68.9%
/ই/	66.6%	60.8%	63.6%	
/উ/	69.5%	66.6%	68.1%	
/এ/	68.1%	65.2%	66.7%	
/ও/	59.1%	68.4%	63.4%	
Average:	67.5%	67.7%	67.5%	

been adopted for comparing the proposed CNN with the different methodologies. F_1 scores are an efficient measure to distinguish between two classifiers when multiple classes are present. F_1 scores balances between precision and recall and is therefore adopted for comparison with other classifiers. F_1 scores can be computed as:

$$F_1 = 2 \times \frac{Precision \times Recall}{Precision + Recall} \qquad (10.5)$$

Figure 10.10 presents the F1 score obtained using the proposed AM and CNN in comparison to the methodologies described in [4, 9, 11, 13, 14]. The F1 scores obtained by CNN are 75.5%, 63.6%, 68.1%, 66.7%, and 63.4% respectively for the imagined vowels /আ/, /ই/, /উ/, /এ/, and /ও/, which is higher in comparison to the methodologies described in [4, 9, 11, 13, 14].

However, the F_1 score obtained for the Bengali vowel /ই/ is lower in comparison to the methods described in [4, 9]. The F_1 score obtained using the Riemannian distance as features and kNN as a classifier [4] are: 69.54%, 65.12%, 63.2%, 64.32%, and 62.3% for the vowels /আ/, /ই/, /উ/, /এ/, and /ও/ respectively. The F_1 score obtained using the methodology described by Matsumoto *et al.* [9], which used CSP as a feature and SVM as classifier were: 62.48%, 65.23%, 67.2%, 61.5%, and 60.7% for the vowels /আ/, /ই/, /উ/, /এ/, and /ও/ respectively. Similarly, the F_1 score obtained using the methodology described by Brigham *et al.* [11], which used autoregressive coefficients as feature and kNN as classifier were: 55.23%, 59.3%, 58.4%, 54.2%, and 51.2% for the vowels /আ/, /ই/, /উ/, /এ/, and /ও/, respectively.

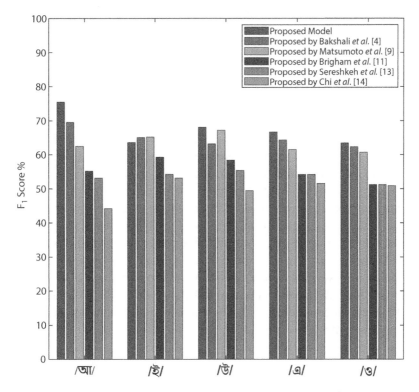

Figure 10.10 F_1 score comparison of the CNN w.r.t. the methodologies described in [4] which use Riemannian distance as features and kNN as the classifier, CSP as a feature and SVM as classifier [9], autoregressive coefficients as feature and kNN as classifier [11], DWT coefficients as features and MLPNN as classifier [13], and spectrogram as a feature and LDA as classifier [14].

The F_1 score obtained using the methodology described by Sereshkeh *et al.* [13], which used DWT coefficients as a feature and MLPNN as classifier were: 53.2%, 54.3%, 55.4%, 54.2%, and 51.2% for the vowels /আ/, /ই/, /উ/, /এ/, and /ও/ respectively. The F_1 score obtained using the methodology described by Chi *et al.* [14], which used spectrogram as a feature and LDA as classifier were: 44.3%, 53.2%, 49.5%, 51.6%, and 50.9% for the vowels /আ/, /ই/, /উ/, /এ/, and /ও/ respectively.

From Figure 10.10, it is clear that CNN outperforms the other methodologies described in [4, 9, 11, 13, 14] in the majority of the cases. The methods described in [4, 9, 11, 13, 14] use various feature extraction methodologies such as AR coefficients, CSP, DWT coefficients, and RD along with kNN, SVM, LDA, and MLPNN classifiers. F_1 scores obtained for the various methods establishes the suitability of the proposed AM and the CNN for the classification of the individual vowels.

10.6   Conclusion

The proposed work describes a novel feature extraction mechanism known as the activity map (AM) which captures the tempo-spectral information for the classification of the EEG related to the imagination of Bengali vowels আ/, /ই/, /উ/, /এ/, and /ও/. It is difficult to visualize the variation in the EEG data and hence, the AM provides a useful visualization of the spectral changes in EEG data w.r.t. time. The activity map is transformed into an image, which is subsequently classified with a CNN network with 4 convolutional layers. The average accuracy obtained in the overall classification is 68.9%. Moreover, it has also been observed that CNN outperforms other methods using various feature extraction methodologies such as AR coefficients, CSP, DWT coefficients, and RD along with kNN, SVM, LDA, and MLPNN classifiers. Hence, it can be concluded that the proposed AM in conjunction with CNN can classify the EEG data relating to the imagination of vowels effectively.

Acknowledgment

This work was supported by the Ministry of Communications & Information Technology No. 13(13)/2014-CC&BT, Government of India, for the project: 'Analysis of Brainwaves and development of intelligent model for silent speech recognition'.

References

1. Birbaumer, N. *et al.*, The thought translation device (TTD) for completely paralyzed patients. *IEEE Trans. Rehabil. Eng.*, 8, 2, 190–193, June 2000.
2. Wester, M., *Unspoken speech recognition based on electroencephalography*, Thesis, Carnegie Mellon University, Pittsburgh, PA, USA, 2006.
3. DaSalla, C., Kambara, H., Sato, M., Koike, Y., Single-trial classification of vowel speech imagery using common spatial patterns. *Neural Netw.*, 22, 1334– 1339, 2009.
4. Bakhshali, M.A., Khademi, M., Ebrahimi Moghadam, A., Moghimi, S., EEG signal classification of imagined speech based on Riemannian distance of

correntropy spectral density. *Biomed. Signal Process. Control*, 59, 1–11, May 2020.

5. Samanta, K., Chatterjee, S., Bose, R., Cross-subject motor imagery tasks EEG signal classification employing multiplex weighted visibility graph and deep feature extraction. *IEEE Sens. Lett.*, 4, 1, 1–4, Jan. 2020.

6. Ghosh, R., Sinha, N., Biswas, S.K., Automated eye blink artefact removal from EEG using support vector machine and autoencoder. *IET Signal Process.*, 13, 2, 141–148, 2019.

7. Fukushima, K., Neocognitron: A self-organizing neural network model for a mechanism of pattern recognition unaffected by shift in position. *Biol. Cybern.*, 36, 193–202, 1980.

8. Phang, C., Noman, F., Hussain, H., Ting, C., Ombao, H., A multi-domain connectome convolutional neural network for identifying Schizophrenia from EEG connectivity patterns. *IEEE J. Biomed. Health Inform.*, 24, 5, 1333–1343, May 2020.

9. Matsumoto, M. and Hori, J., Classification of silent speech using support vector machine and relevance vector machine. *Appl. Soft Comput.*, 20, 95–102, 2014.

10. Nguyen, C.H., Karavas, G.K., Artemiadis, P., Inferring imagined speech using EEG signals: A new approach using Riemannian manifold features. *J. Neural Eng.*, 15, 1–16, 2018.

11. Brigham, K. and Kumar, B.V.K.V., Imagined speech classification with EEG signals for silent communication: A preliminary investigation into synthetic telepathy. *2010 4th International Conference on Bioinformatics and Biomedical Engineering*, Chengdu, pp. 1–4, 2010.

12. Yamaguchi, H. *et al.*, Decoding silent speech in Japanese from single trial EEGS: Preliminary results. *J. Comput. Sci. Syst. Biol.*, 8, 5, 285–291, 2015.

13. Sereshkeh, A.R., Trott, R., Bricout, A., Chau, T., EEG classification of covert speech using regularized neural networks. *IEEE/ACM transactions on audio, speech, and language processing*, vol. 25, pp. 2292–2230, 2017.

14. Chi, X. *et al.*, EEG-based discrimination of Imagined speech phonemes. *Int. J. Bioelectromagn.*, 13, 4, 201–206, 2011.

15. Ghane, P., *Silent speech recognition in EEG-based brain computer interface*, Master's Thesis, Purdue University Graduate School, Indianapolis, Indiana, USA, 2015.

16. Wolpaw, J.R. *et al.*, Brain-computer interfaces for communication and control. *Clin. Neurophysiol.*, 113, 797–791, 2002.

17. Hassanien, A.E. and Azar, A.T., *Brain-Computer Interfaces Current trends and applications*, Springer, Switzerland, 2015.

18. Richards, T.L. and Berninger, V.W., Abnormal fMRI connectivity in children with dyslexia during a phoneme task: Before but not after treatment. *J. Neurolinguistics*, 21, 4, 294–304, 2008.

19. Mihajlovi, V., Garcia-Molina, G., Peuscher, J., Dry and water-based EEG electrodes in SSVEP-based BCI applications, in: *Biomedical engineering systems and technologies*, vol. 357, pp. 23–40, Springer, Berlin, 2013.

20. Freitas, J. *et al.*, *An Introduction to silent speech interfaces*, Springer, Switzerland, 2017.

21. Calliess, J., *Further investigations on unspoken speech. - findings in an attempt of developing EEG-based word recognition*, Bachelor work, Interactive Systems Laboratories Carnegie Mellon University, Pittsburgh, PA, USA and Institut fuer Theoretische Informatik Universitaet Karlsruhe (TH), Karlsruhe, Germany, 2006.

22. Mesgarani, N., David, D., Sharma, S., Representation of phonemes in primary auditory cortex: How the brain analyzes speech. *IEEE International Conference on Acoustics, Speech and Signal Processing*, Honolulu, HI, USA, pp. 765–768, 2007.

23. Galgano, J. and Froud, K., Evidence of the voice related cortical potential: An electroencephalographic study. *NeuroImage*, 41, 1313–1323, 2008.

24. D'Zmura, M. *et al.*, Toward EEG sensing of imagined speech, Human-Computer Interaction. *Part I, HCII 2009*, vol. LNCS 5610, pp. 40–48, 2009.

25. Santana, R., A detailed investigation of classification methods for vowel speech imagery recognition, in: *Technical report, department of computer science and artificial intelligence*, University of the Basque Country, San Sebastian, Spain, 2013.

26. Matsumoto, M., Silent speech decoder using adaptive collection. *Proceedings of the companion publication of the 19th international conference on Intelligent User Interfaces*, Haifa, Israel, pp. 73–76, 2014.

27. Kamalakkannan, R. *et al.*, Imagined speech classification using EEG. *Adv. Biomed. Sci. Eng.*, 1, 2, 20–32, 2014.

28. Salama, M. *et al.*, Recognition of unspoken words using electrode electroencephalographic signals. *6th International Conference on Advanced Cognitive Technologies and Applications, COGNITIVE 2014*, pp. 51–55, 2014.

29. Ghosh, R., Kumar, V., Sinha, N., Biswas, S.K., Motor imagery task classification using intelligent algorithm with prominent trial selection. *J. Intell. Fuzzy Syst.*, 35, 2, 1501–1510, 2018.

30. Wang, L. *et al.*, Analysis and classification of hybrid BCI based on motor imagery and speech imagery, *Measurements*, 147(20190), 106842, 1–12, 2019.

11

Optimized Feature Selection Techniques for Classifying Electrocorticography Signals

B. Paulchamy[1], R. Uma Maheshwari[1*], D. Sudarvizhi AP(Sr. G)[2],
R. Anandkumar AP(Sr. G)[2] and Ravi G.[3]

[1]Hindusthan Institute of Technology, Coimbatore, Tamil Nadu, India
[2]KPR Institute of Engineering and Technology, Coimbatore, Tamil Nadu, India
[3]Department of ECE, Sona College of Technology, Salem, Tamil Nadu, India

Abstract

The combination of hardware and software communication systems that consists of external devices or control computers that use cerebral activity is Brain-Computer Interface (BCI). BCI helps to communicate with severely impaired people who have been wholly paralyzed or "locked" by neurological neuromuscular conditions. A BCI system works to classify brain signals and carry out computer-controlled actions using machine learning algorithms. As a recording technique for BCI, electrocorticography (ECoG) is better suited for fundamental neuroscience. The signal acquisition stage in a generic BCI framework captures brain signals and reduces noise and process artifacts. The preprocessing phase prepares the signals for further processing in a suitable way. The extraction stage identifies discriminative information in the recorded brain signals. Once measured, the signal is mapped to a vector containing the signals observed with useful and discriminant characteristics. The function of the Auto-Regressive (AR) model and Wavelet Transform functions are extracted. The features extracted are merged. SVM uses a discriminative hyperplane to identify classes. The effect of ECoG signal function selection and SVM parameter optimization has been studied. Clonal Selection Algorithm is a particular class of Artificial Immune systems, which uses the Clonal Selection part's primary mechanism. The SVM and simultaneously optimizes the selection of the

*Corresponding author: umamaheshwari@hit.edu.in

M.G. Sumithra, Rajesh Kumar Dhanaraj, Mariofanna Milanova, Balamurugan Balusamy and Chandran Venkatesan (eds.) Brain-Computer Interface: Using Deep Learning Applications, (255–278) © 2023 Scrivener Publishing LLC

functionality. The test results show the SVM classification efficiency compared with the RBF classifier and the FUZZY classifier. At the final stage, a method is investigated for hybridizing CLONALG with a Genetic Algorithm (GA). In this method, an outer (GA) search circuit is used to check the current population for restriction and then divide them into practicable and unfeasible individuals. Introduced as an internal loop, CLONALG clones and mutates antibodies first and calculates the distances between antibodies and antigens. The most affinity individuals are selected, and the new antibodies are defined. Results demonstrate that in the classification of ECoG signals, the proposed method achieves a precision of 96.76%.

Moreover, the chapter provides better results for classifying fused features such as Autoregressive and SVM Classifier wavelet transformers. A particular class of artificial immune systems is also being studied, including the combination of GA and CLONALG to select the best SVM-RBFN kernel features and parameters simultaneously. Results show that GA and CLONALG are the most accurate in the ECoG signals classification.

Keywords: Brain interface, genetic algorithm, clonal selection, radial bias neural network, support vector machine, accuracy, precision, signal classification

11.1   Introduction

Change leads to change ALS, spinal cord injury, brain or muscle dystrophy stroke, cerebral and multiple cases of sclerosis are many of those degenerative conditions that affect the neurological pathways. The conditions are degenerative. These diseases affect more than five million people worldwide. The rate of involvement in syndrome is not international, however, roughly two people per 100,000 years in Europe and the US have ALS alone. Most affected people are unable to travel, move their arms and hands, speak and devour food. For physically challenged individuals, control and communication systems are available. In a BCI, user-unique features are eliminated and converted into device communication instructions.

11.1.1   Brain–Computer Interface

Brain–Computer Interfacing (BCI) technology enables the human being's capability to communicate or control (particularly impaired) equipment by thinking or expressing purposes to be increased through direct interaction with human brain systems and machines. BCI systems are becoming successful due to a better understanding of the brain oscillation dynamics. Neuronal nets create feedback loops in the brain that are recorded for electrical encephalography or oscillatory electrocorticography (ECoG) [1]. BCI is an authoritative communication and control option in interactions between people and systems and is an interaction beyond the keyboard by definition. The BCI communication and control system in the original definition is not dependent on the neuromuscular output channels of the brain. The BCIs have expectations with them. BCI provides direct connections between the brain and external devices. System – hardware/software enables persons without peripheral nerves/muscles to communicate with their surroundings and simply regulate messages from brain activity. The interface enhances communication chances for those with severe engine and neuromuscular difficulties. Different BCI applications include engines, environment, leisure, and multimedia. BCI makes it possible to transmit or regulate neural activity in the brain without direct physical motions through equipment, prosthetic limbs, and robots. Since computerized systems are a tool to develop life, ongoing BCI developments require both an understanding of brain waves and a study of EEG/ECoG data. BCI is recognized for its support in the provision of external communication to handicapped persons and a realistic tool for prosthesis control. Gadgets are also incorporated in BCI applications through the translation of concepts into video games and personal computers. BCI integrates medical, psychological, neurological, HCI, rehabilitative, signaling, and machine education. BCI offers a wide range of chances for research [2].

As Amyotrophic Lateral Sclerosis (ALS), BCI can circumvent corporeal mediation, enabling people to interact freely and spontaneously in a gaming setting, as acknowledged by patients who have already spoken with others and the environment despite full paralysis. However, a BCI that circumvents a physical encounter may seem unnatural in converting ideas into physical movements. The consequence is that you must be highly conscious of this activity, which develops new control levels when using the brain activity directly [3]. The initial step in developing an effective BCI system is to find the appropriate control signals from an ECoG or EEG [4]. The following is a suitable control signal: (i) Each person is accurately defined; (ii) easy for expressing intents to be modulated/transformed; and (iii) consistent tracking/detecting. The locked-in patients are completely aware and attentive, but cannot move their muscles to convey their wants, desires, and feelings. A healthy brain is closed to them in paralysis. The biggest reason for locking is unknown The motor neurons of the central and peripheral nervous systems eventually disappear during neurological diseases. Paralysis usually starts in the lower extremes and progresses to the arms and hands, paralyzing the respiratory and swallowing muscles. Patients can only live at this point if they decide to ventilate artificially. Brain-computer (BCI) interfaces are the sole way to interact and control the environment for confined patients.

11.2   Literature Study

To improve the accuracy of the BCI classification of MI-based ECoG with the hybrid algorithm Rathipriya *et al.* [5]. The classifier 32 SVM has been restored using the same features triggered by the classification cross-relation approach. The performance is tested using classification accuracy using a 10-fold cross-validation technique. The authors contrasted the behavior of the methodology proposed with the current one. Suggested that BCI use ECoG. The outcome of classification is based mostly on the extraction of features. Initially, discrete wavelet transformations are made using ECoG data from one patient. The individual was asked to move the left little finger or language imaginarily. In the following stage, the corresponding wavelet energy of the eight channels has been determined and a 40-dimensional vector has been built (PNN). ECoG signals have been used in BCI design and generated a novel method for the extraction of functionality and the classification of imagination movement in ECoGbased BCI research according to offline analysis. Suggested a wavelet analysis pattern recognition protocol and a generic ECoG BCI system FLDA protocol. Results demonstrated that 92% maximum precision was picked as an effective feature for ECoG for the test data, wavelet variance as well as wavelet packet variance. At the time of perception of the continuous discourse. Employed ECoG cortical signal to decode phonetic units. The scientists found ECoG electrodes with a discriminative response to a certain number of Chinese phonemes by investigating the wavelet time-frequency characteristics. Features relating to gamma and strong gamma power are linked to certain phoneme sets. The clustered assembly is closely synchronized with categories of phonology defined by place and expression. These findings were taken into account in 33 Chinese phonemes decoding models. We achieved a continuous level of accuracy that is larger than a chance for five patients who discriminate against certain phonetic clusters by using SVM classifiers. Kayikcioglu & Aydemir [8] The design proposal for classification of the ECoG signal captured by motor imaging in different time units. Using the k neighbors approach, extracted vectors were converted to wavelets and categorized. The proposed methodology was successfully implemented for DataSet I of the 2005 BCI contest and reached a 95% accuracy in classification in the test set. The preliminary research of the relations between EEG and Event-Related Potentials (ERPs) ECoG from one patient using a BCI speller was given. One test session and one identical session were carried out by the patient. In the experimental session, the spelling paradigm of BCI is applied and the EEG is scalp-registered, before the ECoG grid implantation and after grid implantation is monitored in the same ECoG session. The EEG and ECoG have attained almost perfect orthography correctness. Offline analysis was conducted to get the proper estimation of average EEG ERPs using ECoG data. Initial results showed that EEG ERPs may be predicted with proximal asynchronous accuracy. Data from ECoG that use simple linear spatial models. A BCI system and a comparison of feature selection methods were provided to increase classification efficiencies. The Wavelet Packet Tree was used to extract the properties after the ECoG signals were pre-processed. GA, Mutual Information (MI), and Info Gain Attributes are chosen to be used (IG). Dataset I BCI Competition III was used as an input dataset for experimenting with the proposed methodology in ECoG recording motor images. Results showed that the selection of features enhanced accuracy in categorization. Li *et al.* employed the power spectral density for the selection of features (2011). For the extraction of functions and the non-linear classification of engine imaging using SVMs, a common CSP protocol is used. The accuracy of the 83% classification rate is achieved on BCI III Dataset I. The new Protocol for classifying one-test ECoG in the motor scenario has been developed by Wei & Tu [11]. Initially, gas from multi-channel ECoGs is selected as an optimum channel subset, and power characteristics have been extracted by CSP, with FDA finally being used to classify. Dataset I of BCI Competition III has been used for the procedure and 90% classification precision is achieved with only seven channels. Zhang *et al.* introduced a 6.4 μ W ECoG/EEG Integrated Processing Circuit (EPIC) for increasing BCI applications with 0.46 μV rms noise flooring (2011). Results from the ECoG recording from the main engine cortex of an awake monkey have been observed *in vivo*.

Wang *et al.* developed improved extraction of features, a non-stationary approach of multi-variable adaptive auto-regressive (MVAAR) models using EEG data (2010). The BCI system has to be adapted in this case. Function extraction strategies have been compared between MVAAR and others. The outcome showed that the MVAAR system extraction was excellent. Recent research implies that ECoG signals may be utilized to successfully deduce the identification of engine, linguistic or intellectual functions. The BCI design requires a proper selection of mental functions and functional extraction methodologies. Studies reveal that the autoregressive model and wavelet transformation function extraction approach provides enhanced rating performance on the non-stationary biosignals, compared with current techniques. Wavelets give a temporal and frequency domain simultaneous localization and are calculated extremely rapidly. Even when data is non-monotonous and non-linearly separable input, SVMs may offer reliable and solid classification results on a good, theoretical basis. They can assist you to conveniently assess more relevant facts. Although numerous feature selection processes are examined based on optimization approaches, GA and CLONALG provide good classification precision and an ideal solution globally for selecting important classification feature groups. CLONALG makes it easy and universal to apply. It is comparable among various algorithms of evolution.

11.3   Proposed Methodology

A BCI system that pre-processes the ECoG signal and extracts features is provided. A feature fusion technology for improving the ECoG classification is tried in this chapter. Car regressive (AR) and Wavelet transform features are extracted. Auto-Regressive model benefits from the easy determination of the current output. An advantage of the modeling of AR is that variable estimating techniques are available. Utilitative AR Models for the EEG spectral parameter analysis (SPA), the advantage of the wavelet is that it has a great temporal resolution and a weaker frequency resolution at higher frequencies for the finer scale. The advantage of wavelets is that signals may be analyzed at several stages simultaneously.

For BCIs such as coiflets, bi-orthogonal, and so on, various wavelets are used. There are many decomposition strategies for wavelets, which are both wavelets and wavelets. The functionality extracted is fused. Features are picked with the Information Gain (IG) and selected features are categorized using the Support Vector Machine (SVM) (FC). This project experiments with the CLONALG technique to improve the parameters of C and Gamma on the RBF SVM kernel.

11.3.1 Dataset

For assessment of the suggested approaches, the ECoG recordings of the data set I for the BCI Competition III are utilized. The data set is made up of motor imaging signals that are produced when the participant performs short left-finger or tongue imagined motions in a BCI experiment. There was a sample rate of 1000 Hz for all ECoG signals. The recorded potentials have been enhanced and stored at microvolt levels to aid categorization. The sample recordings were captured for 3 seconds from either the imagined finger or tongue movement. Although the recording began 0.5 seconds after the visual cycle to avoid potentials induced visually.

11.3.2 Feature Extraction Using Auto-Regressive (AR) Model and Wavelet Transform

11.3.2.1 Auto-Regressive Features

An auto-regressive model (AR) depicts a random process in statistics and signal processing so that some time-varying processes are described. The AR models its output variable according to its historical values as linear. AR denotes an autoregressive order model p (p). The model AR(p) is defined as

$$X_t = c + \sum_{i=1}^{p} \varphi_I X_{t-I} + \varepsilon_t \tag{11.1}$$

where $\varphi_1, \ldots \varphi_p$ represents the parameters of the model, c is a constant, and εt is white noise. This can be equivalently written using the backshift operator B as

$$X_t = c + \sum_{i=1}^{p} \varphi_i X_{t-1} + \varepsilon_t \tag{11.2}$$

$$X_t = c + \sum_{i=1}^{p} \varphi_i B^i X_t + \varepsilon_t \tag{11.3}$$

so that, $\varphi(B)X_t = c + \varepsilon_t$

An AR model may therefore be regarded as the output of an infinite pulse response filter with white noise.

11.3.2.2   Wavelet Features

Orthogonal transformations are used in the identification of patterns because they provide a non-invertible transition from space to reduced dimensions. However, classification operations with fewer characteristics are completed with a little increase in classification error.

$$\Psi_{a,b}(x) = \frac{1}{\sqrt{a}} \Psi\left(\frac{x-b}{a}\right) \tag{11.4}$$

11.3.2.3   Feature Selection Methods

A promising area of research in the fields of engineering, data mining, statistics and pattern recognition, and so on was feature selection. A sub-set of input variables is to be obtained by removing characteristics that are either irrelevant or do not include any predictive information [6]. The choice of features proved to be quite successful in both theories and practice in minimizing the complexity of the findings, boosting learning efficiency, and enhancing predictive accuracy.

The main purpose is to discover a subset that delivers greater classification precision in supervised learning. When the size of a domain rises, N also increases the number of features. The identification of an optimum function subset is intractable and the issues with the selection of functions have proved NP-hard [7]. The selection of features prevents fit and enhances the model performance that delivers quicker and rentable models.

An extra complexity layer in modeling is included to identify optimal parameters for the whole range of functions. Optimal feature selection. It identifies the initial set of optimum subsets and optimizes model parameters. Selection techniques for attributes are classed as approaches to filters and wrappers [8]. Data mining algorithms are independent of the selected attributes and of the importance of the features solely by concentrating on the inherent characteristics of the filter technique.

The choice of characteristics is necessary since the number of unimportant features is excessive, loud, or deceptive. All listings of attribute subsets should be checked for attribute selection, which is in most instances inopportune since 2n subsets for n attributes are produced. Feature selection searches for an optimal d set [9]. A typical difficulty in global combinatorial optimization is the feature selection procedure.

11.3.2.4   Information Gain (IG)

The information gain (IG) approach for high-dimensional data is extensively utilized. IG is the anticipated entropy decrease (H). For a range of classes.

$C = \{c_1,..., c_k\}$, the information gain of a feature f, $IG(f)$ is given

$$IG(f) = H(C) - H(C\,|\,f) \qquad (11.5)$$

$$H(C) = -\sum_{i-1}^{k} P(c_i)\log P(c_i), \qquad (11.6)$$

$$H(C\,|\,f) = -P(f)\sum_{i=1}^{k} P(c_i\,|\,f)\log P(c_i\,|\,f) \qquad (11.7)$$

It is used to calculate entropy in all classrooms for all characteristics. The characteristics are according to their IG value based on their value. In comparison to others, the higher IG value would be more informative. Top N number of attributes to categorize the instance are picked and utilized.

11.3.2.5   Clonal Selection

Immune algorithms are based on immunological principles and are used effectively in many issues of optimization. CLONALG is the type of Artificial Immune System where the selected portion of the clonal is the principal method. CLONALG is a type of CLONALG system. Initially, this approach was presented to solve non-linear functions [10].

The notion of clonal selection is the basic premise of contemporary immunology and is therefore strongly linked to other immunological ideas. This is followed by such theories-inspired algorithms. For example, the issues of classification of negative selection algorithms in the additional area still depend on the notion of clonal selection to enhance the examples iteratively. Clustering and optimization network techniques leverage the excitation and suppression aspects of the network model, but also the clonal selection concept for repeated model refining [12].

CLONALG is a popular model, comparable to mutation-based evolutionary algorithms built upon the clonal selection and affinity maturation concept [13]. The clonal selection idea is inspired by the following factors:

- Maintenance of a specific memory set
- Selection and cloning of most stimulated antibodies
- Death of non-stimulated antibodies
- Affinity maturation (mutation)
- Re-selection of clones proportional to affinity with antigen
- Generation and maintenance of diversity.

The objective of this approach is to construct an antibody memory pool to solve an engineering challenge. An antimicrobial is a solution element or a single remedy to this problem in this example, while an antigen is a problem space element or an assessment. The method provides two search algorithms for the final memory neurons that you want to use. The first is a local search performed by cloned antibody affinity maturation. More clones for matching (chosen) colonies are created [14]. The second search method has a global dimension and includes the introduction into the population of randomly produced colonies to further enhance diverse populations and offers a technique of perhaps avoiding local optimism.

The artificial immune system approach is inspired by the CLONALG theory of clonal selection; (CLONal selection ALGorithm). Two populations are present in CLONALG: one of the antigens, Ag, an antibody. The string characteristics m = mL...m1, i.e. a point in L—dimensional forms space S, m = SL, indicate the individual antibody/antigen. The population of Ab is several current applicant solutions, Ag being recognizable in the environment. The method cycles for preset maximum generations after random initialization of the first population P(0). (Ngen).

11.3.2.6   An Overview of the Steps of the CLONALG

1. **Introduction** – The first stage in CLONALG is to start and divide an antibody pool size N into two parts: a memory anti-memory section m, which represents the solution of the algorithm, and an antibody pool r, used to introduce variation among solutions.
2. **Loop** – The solutions are iterated and all known antigens are exposed. Each repetition is called a generation, and either the user stipulates the number of generations G or a certain termination condition.
   a. Select Antigen – An antigen from the present generation is randomly picked.
   b. Exposure – The system is exposed to the chosen antigen, with all antibodies against the antigen calculated with Affinity values.

c. Selection of n clusters with the greatest antigen affinity.

d. Cloning – The clusters that are picked are cloned by their affinity.

e. Affinity Ripening (mutation) – The more closely relaxed the lower the mutation more affinity is exposed to the cloned antibody ripening.

f. Clone exposure – Antigen clones will be subsequently exposed and affinity calculated.

g. Candidacy – The most affinity antibodies are then selected as candidate memory antibodies that will be implanted in the population if their affinity is higher than that of the memory pool antigen m. h.

h. Replacement: in the last phase, new random antibodies are substituted in the existing r antigenic pool with the lowest affinity.

3. **Finish** – The memory part of the antigen pool is then considered an algorithm answer when the training round is completed.

11.3.3   Hybrid CLONALG

The hybrid CLONALG consists of an external (GA) search loop, which checks for limited violations of the present population and then divides it into viable (antigens) and ineffective persons (antibodies). If no viable person exists, the best unfeasible person (who is the lowest limit violation) is sent to the antigenic population. The AIS is presented here as an internal loop where clusters are copied first and subsequently mutated. Mutated. Next, antigens and antibodies are calculated for their distances (affinities). Those with higher affinity (smaller distances) are chosen so that novel antibodies are defined (closer to the feasible region). It is repeated several times during this cycle (CLONALG). The resultant population of the antibody is then transferred to the GA where restriction violations and fitness values for the viable individuals are calculated. The selection procedure is undertaken such that the selected parents produce a new population and terminate the external (GA) loop is applied to recombination and mutation operators. The GA selection technique is a binary technique. Tournaments in which each person is picked once and their opponent is drawn randomly from a population with replacement. The rules of the tournament are:

- every viable person is preferable over an unfeasible person,
- the one with a greater fitness value will be picked between two feasible people, and
- the other two with a minor restriction infringement between two infeasible persons. It must be mentioned that here affine is calculated by using a conventional Euclidean vector standard from the sum of phenotypical distances.

A pseudo-code for the proposed hybrid is given

```
Begin
for i = 0 to number Of Generations GA do compute
Violation();
dividePopulation();
antibodies <- infeasiblePop();
antigens <- TopFeasible();
for j = 0 to number Of Iterations CLONALG do
cloneAntibodies();
mutateAntibodies(); computeDistanceAntibodiesAntigens();
antibodies <- selectBetterAntibodies();
end - do;
computeViolationAntibodies();
computeFitnessFeasiblePop();
tournamentSelection(); crossover();
mutation();
end - do;
End
```

A serial algorithm scheme based on the artificial immune system is illustrated in Figure 11.1. This way, GA searches the globally optimal. The CLONALG assists the GA to attain an efficient area.

The performance is evaluated for:

ARC   -   Autoregressive feature selection using CLONALG

WAC   -   Wavelet features selection using CLONALG

ARWAC   -   Autoregressive–Wavelet fused features selection using CLONALG

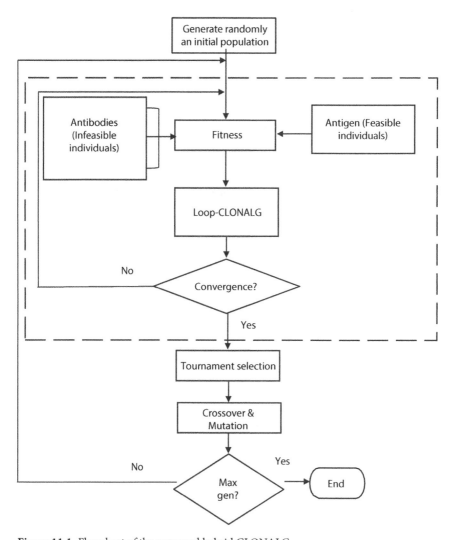

Figure 11.1 Flowchart of the proposed hybrid CLONALG.

ARWACSVM	-	Autoregressive–Wavelet fused features selection using CLONALG–Support Vector Machine Classifier
ARWAHCSVM	-	Autoregressive–Wavelet fused features selection using Hybrid CLONALG–Support Vector Machine Classifier

Autoregressive	-	Wavelet fused features selection using CLONALG Optimized Support Vector Machine Classifier
ARWAHCSVM-HOpt	-	Autoregressive–Wavelet fused features selection using Hybrid CLONALG–Support Vector Machine Classifier–Hybrid Optimization
ARSVM	-	Autoregressive Features, Support Vector Machine
WASVM	-	Wavelet features, Support Vector Machine
ARWASVM	-	Autoregressive–Wavelet fused features, Support Vector Machine

11.4   Experimental Results

The results of the SVM Classifier are presented in Table 11.1. The accuracy and precision of classification – recall for the SVM classifier are shown in Figures 11.2 and 11.3. The accuracy and reminder observed demonstrate that the ARWAIGSVM is 6.6 and 4.7 percent greater than those of ARIGSVM. The results demonstrate that the ARWAIGSVM is 6.6% over the ARIGSVM level, and 4.6% over the WAIGSVM standard.

The fused functional selection employing ARWAIG information gain results in a superior result as compared to the separate automobile regressive and wavelet functionalities due to little information loss.

The RBFN Classifier findings are presented in Table 11.2. Figures 11.4 and 11.5 illustrate the accuracy and accuracy of the classification, respectively the recall of the RBFN classifier. The accuracy of categorization and ARWAIGRBF reminder is 7.8% higher than ARIGRBF and 4.3%

Table 11.1 Performance metrics of SVM classifier.

SVM classifier	Accuracy	Precision	Recall
ARIG	73.74	0.7380	0.7374
WAIG	75.18	0.7525	0.7518
ARWAIG	78.78	0.7879	0.7878

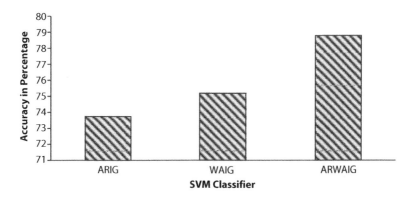

Figure 11.2 Classification accuracy of SVM classifier.

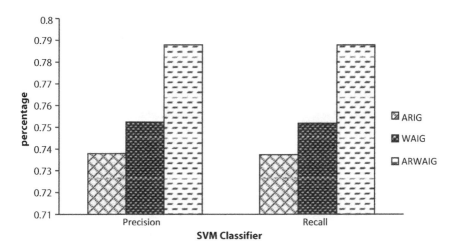

Figure 11.3 Precision and recall of SVM classifier.

Table 11.2 Performance metrics of RBFN classifier.

RBF classifier	Accuracy	Precision	Recall
ARIG	70.50	0.70505	0.7050
WAIG	73.02	0.73080	0.7302
ARWAIG	76.26	0.76305	0.7626

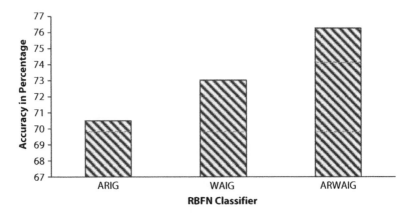

Figure 11.4 Classification accuracy of RBFN classifier.

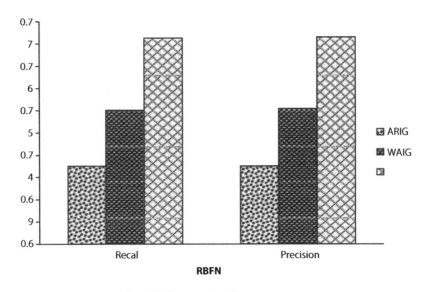

Figure 11.5 Precision and recall of RBFN classifier.

higher than WAIGRBF, 7.9% more than ARIGRBF, and 4.3% higher than WAIGRBF.

The fused selection with ARWAIG information gain results better than the individual car regression and wavelet features due to low loss of information.

Fuzzy Classifier findings are listed in Table 11.3. The classification accuracy and accuracy suggest Figures 11.6 and 11.7 are reminiscent of the Fuzzy Classifier. ARWAIGFC is 8.9% higher than ARIGFC and 5.7% higher than

Table 11.3 Performance metrics of fuzzy classifier.

Fuzzy classifier	Accuracy	Precision	Recall
ARIG	71.07	0.71155	0.7105
WAIG	73.38	0.73460	0.7338
ARWAIG	77.70	0.77750	0.777

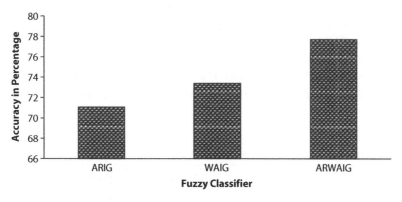

Figure 11.6 Classification accuracy of Fuzzy classifier.

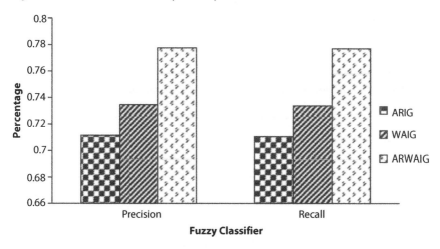

Figure 11.7 Precision and recall of Fuzzy classifier.

WAIGFC, as a result of its accuracy and recall. ARWAIGFC is 8.9 percent more accurate than ARIGFC and 5.7 percent more accurate than WAIGFC.

The fused selection with ARWAIG information gain results better than the individual car regression and wavelet features due to low loss of information.

11.4.1   Results of Feature Selection Using IG with Various Classifiers

The classification accuracy, accuracy, and reminder for features such as autoregressive, wavelet, and automatically regressive wavelet fuse utilizing data gain are shown in Tables 11.4 to 11.6 and in Figure 11.8 using classifier features such as SVM, RBF, and Fuzzy.

The classification accuracy of the SVM classifier is more effective than that of RBF and Fuzzy classification, as demonstrated in Table 11.4 and Figure 11.8. ARWAIGSVM is more successful than ARIGSVM 6.6% and 4.7% and then WAIGSVM 4.7%. Results demonstrate that ARWAIGRBF's accuracy is 7.8 percent greater than ARIGRBF for RBF classification, and 4.3 percent better than WAIGRBF. ARWAIGFC's precision is improved by 8.9% compared to ARIGFC in Fuzzy classifiers and by 5.7% compared to WAIGFC.

Table 11.4 Classification accuracy in percentage.

	SVM classifier	RBF classifier	Fuzzy classifier
ARIG	73.74	70.50	71.07
WAIG	75.18	73.02	73.38
ARWAIG	78.78	76.26	77.70

Table 11.5 Performance metrics – precision of various classifiers.

	SVM classifier	RBF classifier	Fuzzy classifier
ARIG	0.73800	0.70505	0.71155
WAIG	0.75245	0.73080	0.73460
ARWAIG	0.78790	0.76305	0.77750

Table 11.6 Performance metrics – recall of various classifiers.

	SVM classifier	RBF classifier	Fuzzy classifier
ARIG	0.7374	0.7050	0.7105
WAIG	0.7518	0.7302	0.7338
ARWAIG	0.7878	0.7626	0.7770

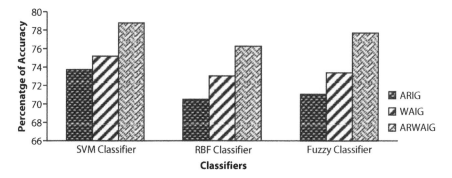

Figure 11.8 Classification accuracy in percentage.

The fused feature selection employing ARWAIG data in all three classifiers has been observed, since information is less lost, to better than the single-car regressive features and wavelet.

The accuracy of the SVM classification is seen better than that of the RBF and Fuzzy classification in Table 11.5 and Figure 11.9. The result demonstrates that ARWAIGSVM is better than ARIGSVM by 6.6 percent and better than WAIGSVM by 4.6 percent. ARWAIGRBF's accuracy is 7.9% greater than ARIGRBF for RBF classification and 4.3% more than WAIGRBF. The ARWAIGFC accuracy is 8.9% greater than ARIGFC and 5.7% better than the WAIGFC. For Fuzzy Classification. The fused feature selection employing ARWAIG data in all three classifiers has been observed, since information is less lost, to better than the single regressive features and wavelet.

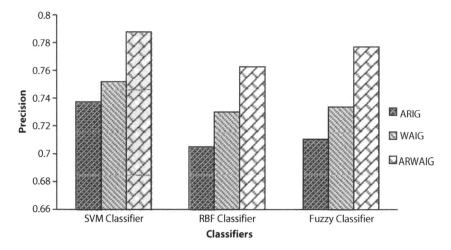

Figure 11.9 Precision of various classifiers.

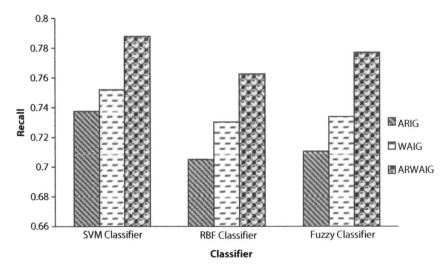

Figure 11.10 Recall of various classifiers.

The recording of the SVM classification is shown from Table 11.6 and Figure 11.10 to be better than that of the ratings of RBF and Fuzzy. Results demonstrate that ARWAIGSVM is 6.6% better than ARIGSVM and 4.7% better than WAIGSVM. This result ARWAIGRBF recall is 7.8% better than ARIGRBF and 4.3% more than WAIGRBF for RBF classification. For the classification Fuzzy, ARWAIGFC is more effective than ARIGFC by 8.9% and WAIGFC by 5.7%. It is also noticed that the fused feature selection employing ARWAIG information is superior to the separate auto regression system in all three classifiers.

11.4.2   Results of Optimizing Support Vector Machine Using CLONALG Selection

Root Middle Square Error and Accuracy (RMSE) SVM results with different RBF parameter values Optimized Gamma, C, and SVM The RBF characteristics in Table 11.7 and Precision and Call are compared and presented. SVM results with different RBF parameter values Compared and presented in Table 11.8 are Gamma and C and Optified SVM RBF parameters. The accuracy of classification, RMSE, Precision and Recall for the classification of the functions with the RBF kernel optimized using CLONALG selection are shown in Figure 11.11.

Table 11.7 Classification accuracy and RMSE for various Gamma and C values.

SVM RBF parameters		Classification accuracy %	RMSE
Gamma	**C**		
0.125	0.125	77.3381	0.4760
0.125	1.000	77.3381	0.4760
0.250	0.125	71.9424	0.5297
1.000	0.125	62.9496	0.6087
CLONALG optimized SVM with RBF kernel		91.3700	0.1621

It is observed from Table 11.7 that varying the parameter C does not affect the classification accuracy or the RMSE. Also, a higher value of Gamma leads to inefficient performance of the SVM.

The accuracy of the categorization and RMSE are shown in Figures 11.11 and 11.12. The optimized kernel SVM is observed as achieving better results than other SVM values. Gamma rose by 36.8% over Gamma value 1 and RMSE dropped by 115.9% over Gamma value 1. This is because the SVM parameter with the RBF kernel is regularized, hence there is no overfit. SVM employs the kernel function to include the kernel knowledge of the issue. By improving the regulated parameters C and Gamma using CLONALG, the RBF kernel performance is enhanced.

Table 11.8 Precision and recall for various Gamma and C values.

SVM RBF parameters		Precision	Recall
Gamma	**C**		
0.125	0.125	0.773	0.773
0.125	1.000	0.773	0.773
0.250	0.125	0.720	0.719
1.000	0.125	0.635	0.629
CLONALG optimized SVM with RBFkernel		0.9158	0.91365

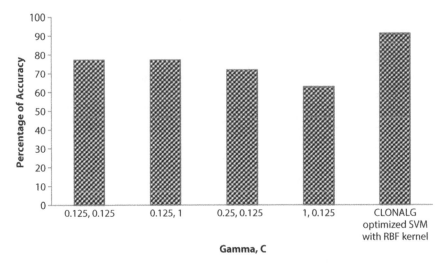

Figure 11.11 Classification accuracy for various Gamma and C values.

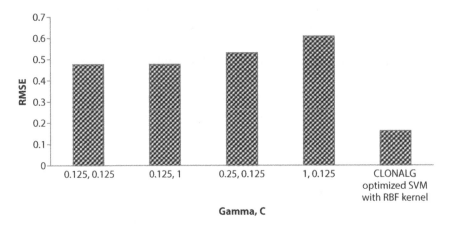

Figure 11.12 Root mean squared error of SVM.

11.5 Conclusion

The preceding findings show that Autoregressive feature fusion technology with wavelet increases the accuracy of the categorization. The selection of hybrid optimism has a critical influence that decrypt user's intents, also in RBF kernel SVM classification for regularization Parameter C checks the balance between the hyper huge margin Classification aircraft and minimal error rate. It is seen that Hybrid optimization performance metrics for the selection of functions and Better than the other findings is the SVM classifier. Use of signal grading RBF kernel SVM.

References

1. Pour, P.A., Gulrez, T., AlZoubi, O., Gargiulo, G., Calvo, R.A., Brain-computer interface: Next generation thought controlled distributed video game development platform, in: *2008 IEEE Symposium On Computational Intelligence and Games*, IEEE, pp. 251–257, 2008, December.
2. Alomari, M.H., AbuBaker, A., Turani, A., Baniyounes, A.M., Manasreh, A., EEG mouse: A machine learning-based brain computer interface. *Int. J. Adv. Comput. Sci. Appl.*, 5, 4, 193–198, 2014.
3. Bos, D.P.O., Reuderink, B., van de Laar, B., Gürkök, H., Mühl, C., Poel, M., Heylen, D., Brain-computer interfacing and games, in: *Brain-computer interfaces*, pp. 149–178, Springer, London, 2010.
4. Wolpaw, J.R., McFarland, D.J., Vaughan, T.M., Brain-computer interface research at the Wadsworth Center. *IEEE Trans. Rehabil. Eng.*, 8, 2, 222–226, 2000.
5. Rathipriya, N., Deepajothi, S., Rajendran, T., Classification of motor imagery ECoG signals using support vector machine for brain computer interface, in: *2013 Fifth International Conference on Advanced Computing (ICoAC)*, IEEE, pp. 63–66, 2013, December.
6. Abiri, R., Borhani, S., Sellers, E.W., Jiang, Y., Zhao, X., A comprehensive review of EEG-based brain–computer interface paradigms. *J. Neural Eng.*, 16, 1, 011001, 2019.
7. Young, B.M., Nigogosyan, Z., Walton, L.M., Song, J., Nair, V.A., Grogan, S.W., Prabhakaran, V., Changes in functional brain organization and behavioral correlations after rehabilitative therapy using a brain-computer interface. *Front. Neuroeng.*, 7, 26, 2014.
8. Kayikcioglu, T. and Aydemir, O., A polynomial fitting and k-NN based approach for improving classification of motor imagery BCI data. *Patt. Recognit. Lett.*, 31, 11, 1207– 1215, 2010.
9. Wu, C.H., Chang, H.C., Lee, P.L., Li, K.S., Sie, J.J., Sun, C.W., Shyu, K.K., Frequency recognition in an SSVEP-based brain computer interface using empirical mode decomposition and refined generalized zero-crossing. *J. Neurosci. Methods*, 196, 1, 170–181, 2011.
10. Rao, R. P., Stocco, A., Bryan, M., Sarma, D., Youngquist, T. M., Wu, J., Prat, C. S., A direct brain-to-brain interface in humans. *PloS One*, 9, 11, e111332, 2014.
11. Wei, Q. and Tu, W., Channel selection by genetic algorithms for classifying single-trial ECoG during motor imagery, in: *2008 30th Annual International Conference of the IEEE Engineering in Medicine and Biology Society*, IEEE, pp. 624–627, 2008, August.

12. Hwang, H.J., Kim, S., Choi, S., Im, C.H., EEG-based brain-computer inter-faces: A thorough literature survey. *Int. J. Hum.-Comput. Interact.*, *29*, 12, 814– 826, 2013.

13. Lin, C.T., Chang, C.J., Lin, B.S., Hung, S.H., Chao, C.F., Wang, I.J., A real-time wireless brain–computer interface system for drowsiness detection. *IEEE Trans. Biomed. Circuits Syst.*, *4*, 4, 214–222, 2010.

14. Sokhal, J., Aggarwal, S., Garg, B., Classification of EEG signals using novel algorithm for channel selection and feature extraction. *Int. J. Appl. Eng. Res.*, *12*, 12, 3491–3499, 2017.

12

BCI – Challenges, Applications, and Advancements

R. Remya[1*] and Sumithra, M.G.[2]

[1]*Department of BME, Dr. N.G.P. Institute of Technology, Coimbatore, India*
[2]*R&D, Dr. N.G.P. Institute of Technology, Coimbatore, Tamil Nadu, India*

Abstract

Brain–Computer Interface (BCI) has regarded as a multidisciplinary active domain in the research field. This study focuses on the survey of BCI applications developed yet and their significance. Also, it explains the available data sets, feature extraction method, previously available BCI algorithms, and classifiers used. Furthermore, the hardware utilization in BCI had explained. Lastly, it examines the technologies used nowadays and the challenges encountered by BCI not proved with a suitable solution.

Keywords: BCI, hardware, brain waves

12.1 Introduction

Direct communication between computers and the brain has been an interesting topic for researchers and experts. The BCI system has connected between the computer and brain. It is with the support of hardware and external parameters, instead of sharing the information from the brain through the finger on a mouse. It makes users work on external devices not possessed by the peripheral nerves.

Currently, research made on non-invasive BCI; since in an invasive (traditional) BCI, a mechanical device is embed in the brain to control the operation. Usually BCI does not read the brain as it is; instead, it reads

Corresponding author: remiamernath@gmail.com

M.G. Sumithra, Rajesh Kumar Dhanaraj, Mariofanna Milanova, Balamurugan Balusamy and Chandran Venkatesan (eds.) Brain-Computer Interface: Using Deep Learning Applications, (279–302) © 2023 Scrivener Publishing LLC

any slight changes in the energy emitted by the brain. Depend upon the imaging techniques incorporates Magnetic Resonance Imaging (MRI), Electroencephalography, BCI aims for any real-time activity.

Recently, BCI has been interpreted as a new domain and has a direct communication exists among the brain and technology. It has been one of the fastest-growing fields. Many types of research tried and utilized variegated communication methodologies among humans and computers and translated them into a required outcome.

BCI is also known as Brain-Machine Interfaces (BMI). Every application utilizes variegated approaches and methodologies. Furthermore, each one has its shortfalls and advantages. Most BCI methodologies have their structure and system.

12.1.1   BCI Structure

The basic structure of BCI includes various operations; image acquisition, pre-processing, feature extraction, image classification, and control over the entire devices. It is depicted in Figure 12.1. The control operation plays a key role; it performs the primary operation.

Signal acquisition: It measures the signal from the brain and converts them into commands to control the real-world application. To collect the signal from the brain, a commercial device has been utilized, which belongs to a Neurosky's company. Such a commercial device is cheap, portable, and easy to handle. The brainwave collection kit has been given in Figure 12.2.
Pre-processing: The signals captured during the signal acquisition have been usually corrupt with noise. It will get replaced first to enhance the quality of the signal.

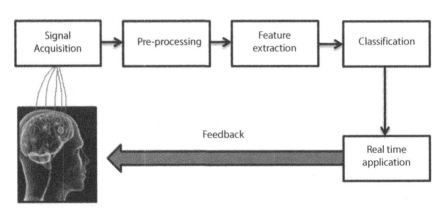

Figure 12.1 BCI structure.

Figure 12.2 Brainwave collection kit from Neurosky's company.

Feature extraction: It analyses the signal and extracts the data from the noise-free signal. If the signal liveliness of the brain gets risky, then it is regarded as difficult to extract the information. So a suitable technique has to be constructed to extract the features of the brain.

Classification: It determines the category of the mental task, which incorporates whether the task is the persons' command or the person is performing.

Control devices: The classifier passes the command to the feedback device. For instance, the implementation may be to move the robotic arm to the right, move the cursor, and so on.

12.2   Related Works

Hans Berger [1] is the first person; who records the Electroencephalogram (EEG), which shows the brain's electrical activity and has calculated via the scalp of the brain. Furthermore, the experimentation on the brain disorder boy records the brain disorder information more promptly. In another work [2], cochlear implants for the deaf and deep brain stimulation are to be carried out for Parkinson's disease. Furthermore, detection of lie, monitoring the alertness, education, art, and so on, are the BCI uses.

Tiwari *et al.* [3] stated a basic concept of extracting the signal from the brain. But there exist challenges that the human brains' thinking has regarded as non-linear. To develop a system to keep track of deep thoughts of the human brain, Bablani *et al.* [4] utilize an invasive and non-invasive signal acquisition system, which includes Magnetoencephalography (MEG), Electroencephalography (EEG), Electrocorticography (ECoG), and Magnetic Resonance Imaging (MRI). The signal captured from this will get examined with any deep learning approaches. Zhang *et al.* [5] discussed the classification of non-invasive signals of the brain and the deep learning approach. The appropriate deep learning selection algorithm and cutting-edge models explained concerning brain signals. Gu *et al.* [6] stated the recent research in the EEG signals; its collection and cleaning. Also, variegated techniques such as fuzzy, deep learning, transfer learning, and a combination of monitoring, maintaining, tracking the human activities and the application explained.

Nijholt [7] explained that one person raises a command, in contrast with the fact that the other can listen to the command. It has to be calibrated by the electrodes based on brain impulses to behave appropriately. Bousseta *et al.* [8] pointed out in their work that an experimental technology to control the movement of a robotic arm with the captured brain image, so that the robotic arm can move towards right, left, up, and down.

Peralas *et al.* [9] explained their work that examined youngsters during playing time with the help of cerebral play. Also, Shim *et al.* [10] stated in their research work about the capture of EEG signals to detect brain tumor [11], analyses breast cancer [12], Parkinson's disease [13], etc., and furthermore, diagnosis of various diseases such as neurodegenerative diseases, inattentiveness, epilepsy, and so on. Birbaumer *et al.* [14] proposed that EEG signal creates a poor resolution relating to space signal compared to the fMRI (functional Magnetic Resonance Imaging); due to non-invasive scalp recordings. So constructing EEG with high-intensity mapping enhances the spatial resolution leads to high computational cost and a reasonable SNR across all channels [15]. Because EEG captures electric field with Blood Oxygen Level Descriptor (BOLD), the cognitive process may increase BCI performance.

12.3   Applications

BCIs had utilized in variegated applications. It has two variegated usability: One can command; while the other can listen. The application receives brain waves using electrodes to do any activity. Few applications have to explain below:

Applications	Images
Robotic Arm: The arm of the robot has to be controlled by a brainwave sensor. Such a brainwave sensor has to utilize in various applications by capturing the brainwave signals via eye blink, meditation, etc.	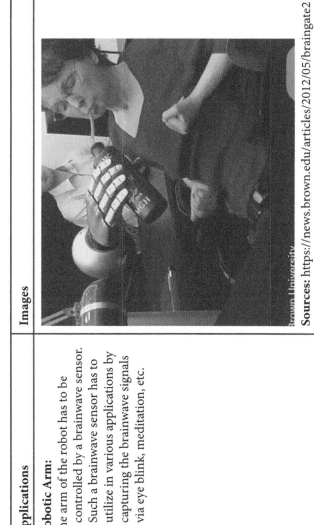 Brown University **Sources:** https://news.brown.edu/articles/2012/05/braingate2

(Continued)

(Continued)

Application	Images
Drowsy Driver Detection: The accident may happen due to the tiredness of the Driver. To reduce this, BCI has to detect the brain waves continuously. By utilizing the brain waves, a setup has to create to monitor the vehicle; when drowsiness creates for the driver.	**Sources:** https://doi.org/10.1007/s13177-019-00199-w

(Continued)

(Continued)

Application	Images
Emotion Identification: By using EEG sensors, the brainwaves have to be detected. Afterward, process the collected data and segregate the emotions felt in every reaction.	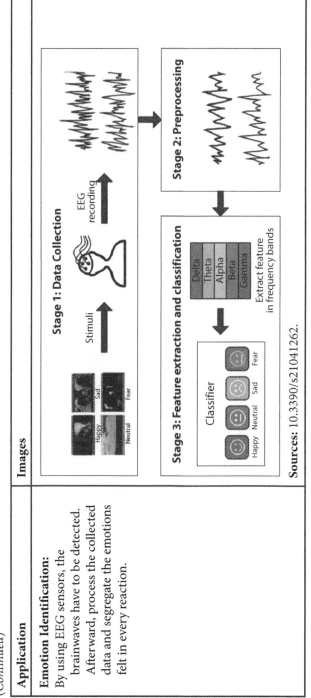 **Sources:** 10.3390/s21041262.

(Continued)

(Continued)

Application	Images
Fly The Helicopter With Brain Waves: The helicopters will flies based on the concentration. It flies up when one concentrates, if he/she in relaxed condition, it will be back.	

Sources: https://mikeshouts.com/you-can-make-your-own-brain-controlled-rc-helicopter/

(Continued)

(Continued)

Application	Images
Password Authentication: EEG has been utilized biometric identification; since brain wave is unique for every individual. It provides greater protection from highly reserved areas to ones' home.	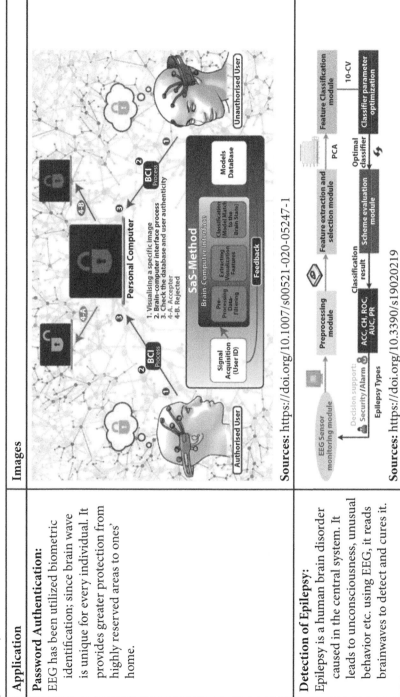 **Sources:** https://doi.org/10.1007/s00521-020-05247-1
Detection of Epilepsy: Epilepsy is a human brain disorder caused in the central system. It leads to unconsciousness, unusual behavior etc. using EEG, it reads brainwaves to detect and cures it.	**Sources:** https://doi.org/10.3390/s19020219

(Continued)

(Continued)

Application	Images
Neuromarketing: This kind of technology helps to monitor the emotion of buyer; while purchasing the product with the support of EEG sensors and MRI (Magnetic Resonance Imaging); it monitors several parameters from the brain; which supports the manufacturer to select the apt product and advertisement to increase the sales.	

Sources: https://www.bitbrain.com/blog/neuromarketing-research-techniques-tools

(Continued)

(Continued)

Application	Images
Robotic Car Race: The car has been controlled with the help of variegated parameters like eye blink, attention level etc.	

Sources: https://nextnature.net/story/2014/braindriver-the-mind-controlled-car

(Continued)

(Continued)

Application	Images
Optimizing Learning Habits: EEG learns users' learning capacity. After a few learning sessions, the software can able to: tell at what time, the learner is having better learning performance to plan the learning session accordingly; also, it tells at what time the learner should stop learning and to take rest.	**Sources:** https://www.scmp.com/tech/start-ups/article/3005448/ brainwave-tracking-start-china-schoolchildren-controversy-working

(Continued)

(Continued)

Application	Images
Brain Controlled Wheel Chair: The design involves receive, process and classify the input EEG signals and based on that input signal, it control over the wheel chair. So based on the brain waves, the command it passed to control the wheelchair.	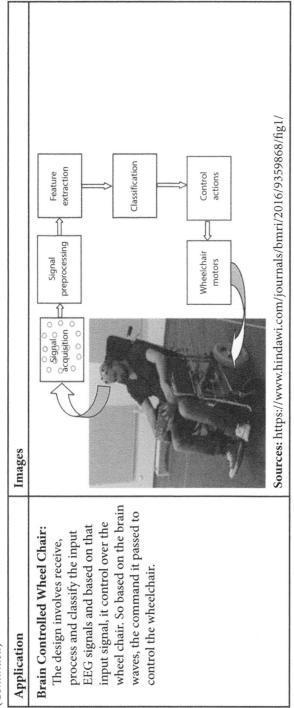 **Sources:** https://www.hindawi.com/journals/bmri/2016/939868/fig1/

(Continued)

(Continued)

Application	Images
Home Automation System: It is mainly used for the person, who suffered from motion and speech related activities, as well as for an elder person. EEG waves are utilized to control the activities of the disabled people with the support of Arduino boards, speakers, personal computers and so on.	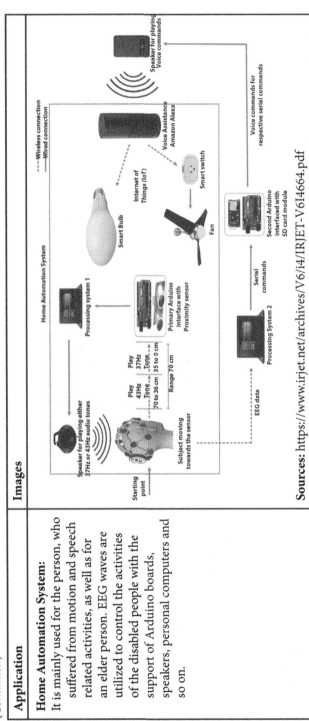 **Sources:** https://www.irjet.net/archives/V6/i4/IRJET-V6I4664.pdf

(Continued)

(Continued)

Application	Images
Eye Blink Detection: It interfaces the brain wave with an Arduino board. LED is available to control the eye blink; also the blink level is displayed in a serial monitor.	 **Sources:** https://www.pantechsolutions.net/blink-led-with-your-eye-blink-data-using-brainwave-starter-kit-and-arduino

(Continued)

(Continued)

Application	Images
Automatic Braking System: EEG signals have been utilized to control over the brake pedal. Initially it records the bioelectrical signals, when the person starts to drive. It avoids collisions during the emergency braking period.	

Sources: https://www.frontiersin.org/files/Articles/316225/fninf-12-00029-HTML/
image_m/fninf-12-00029-g001.jpg

(Continued)

(Continued)

Application	Images
Neurofeedback: It is nothing but the mirror of the brain, which sends the feedback of how it is working as well or not. The feedback signal has been shared with the support of video.	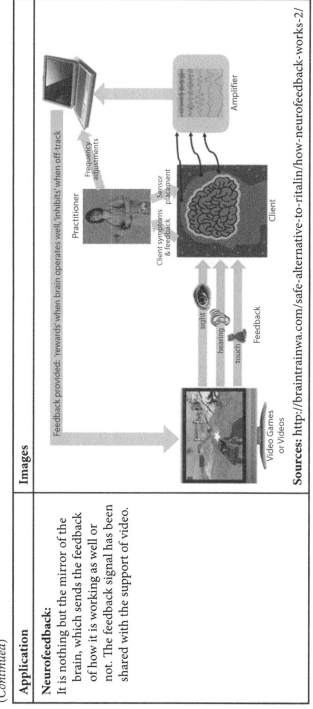

Sources: http://braintrainwa.com/safe-alternative-to-ritalin/how-neurofeedback-works-2/

(Continued)

(Continued)

Application	Images
Neuro-telepathic communication: The connection among the individuals exists without any sensory understanding. Numerous information transfers may happen. Multi-channel electrodes has been utilized to communicate with the brain.	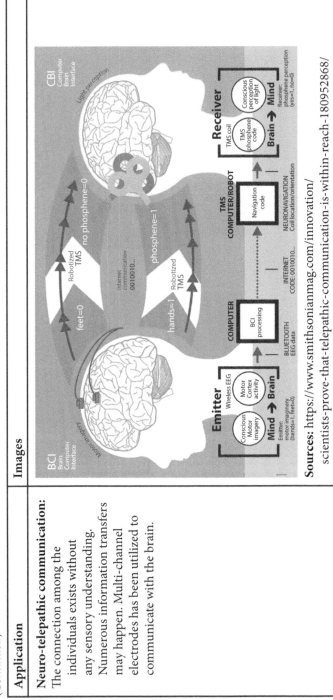 **Sources:** https://www.smithsonianmag.com/innovation/scientists-prove-that-telepathic-communication-is-within-reach-180952868/

12.4   Challenges and Advancements

Most of the current BCIs utilize one or more sensors to collect the data from hundreds of neurons. Nowadays, researchers introduced a future BCI system; they utilized wireless micro-scale sensor neurons with a fine grain size to supervise brain activity. Such a sensor shares the electrical pulses collected from the neurons to the central hub wirelessly.

One of the challenges in BCI faced till now, most of the BCI utilizes several beds of needles of monolithic devices. The Experts from Baylor University California found that tiny neurograins chips have been utilize to transmit the signal.

Another challenge raised in developing a communication hub is to receive the signal from tiny chips. The tiny chip gets placed in the scalp. It acts like a cellular phone tower to coordinate the signal. It transmits the signal wirelessly to neurograins, which utilize a limited current. The challenge that arises here is; during integrating electromagnetics, wireless communication, circuit design, and neuroscience to operate the neurograins system. Based on the new study conducted on the animals, it has stated that the team placed 48 neurograins on animals' brains and monitored the characteristics of neural signals. Also, the team tested the device's ability during simulation and recording. In the animals' study, they limited the count of neurograins to 48. But in the current configuration, it experiments with the support of 770 neurograins. It may extend to several thousands of neurograins to receive the brain's activity in an unattainable picture.

Another challenge is developing networking at a rate of megabits per second and simultaneous wireless power transfer. Researchers pointed out that so much work needs to do to make it into a real one.

Furthermore, many technologies have to develop for old aged people to live their comfortable lives healthily. Non-invasive BCI technology also supports this. The brain functionality starts to reduce from the middle-aged people in their adulthood; it leads to loss of memory, depression, anxiety, mental sharpness [16], reduced blood flow in the brain, and mood swings [17]. Moreover, brain disorder including Alzheimer's, Dementia, heart attack, and obesity reduces the functionality of the brain [18]. Over the '60s; they faced Parkinson's disease, which results in instability in their posture and lack of stiffness. To improve the life quality of an elder one, BCI will assist the motor control finely.

In addition to this, the old aged person facing various issues such as depression, epilepsy, and HIV (Human Immunodeficiency Virus) sickness; has been identified with suitable invasive and non-invasive technologies to identify and prevent such disorders. One of the major challenges of BCI is that while developing less invasive or non-invasive technologies needed for disabled individuals. Utilizing non-invasive technology; reduces the total investment in surgery and physical injury. Even though; it undergoes a low Signal to Noise Ratio (SNR) and low spatial content. It overcomes by utilizing a deep learning approach in BCI technology [19].

The BCI-controlled wheelchair has to regard as a wonderful advancement in technology [20]. BCI with EEG and Event-Related Potentials (ERP) signals to utilize to control the wheelchair. Also, smart home technologies have to introduce to old-aged people [21]. Using EMG and SSVEP, three emergency numbers have to be a dial to control the activities for older ones. Another major challenge in the clinical field in BCI is that the elder has any swallowing issues or spinal disorders. Current wheelchair and exoskeleton technologies have been developed to assist the elderly and allow them to go about their daily lives while also providing rehabilitation for degraded muscle and motor function. Smart home environments can help the elderly live independently and safely in their own houses.

In addition to this, the neural control interface serves the medical field more efficiently. It supports the patient who got affected with brain disorders, especially coma. It utilizes an artificial limb to transfer the electrical impulses from the brain to the machine via a jugular vein without any open brain surgery.

Furthermore, BCI is not limited to the medical field, it extends towards entertainment and education, and it solves any mental-related issues. Improvement in neuroinformatics might improve BCI in-home utilization. By keeping this in mind, Researchers develop a method of using reduced channels in EEG channels. Moreover, in the home-based utilization for an elder one, improved hardware, and software components has to be used. Also, the existing components are available in the market include recoveriX, mindBEAGLE, and Unicorn Speller.

Huge developments have to carry out in this field by 2050. It is not so far, where man guides an application by their thoughts during both natural and complex emotions in their everyday life. We hope to develop a new system that creates perception into the brain and new methodologies in the medical field that could support people who got infected with any incurable diseases. Also, it could monitor the activity of human beings' health continuously. If any crisis arises, it should be reported earlier and save one's life well in advance.

12.5 Conclusion

The BCI technology utilized for communication that connects the wired brain and external devices. The BCI performs all the activities in connection with brain waves. Here it aimed to learn about the variegated applications utilizing nowadays. The basic structure of BCI techniques are explained elaborately. It gives an outline of the current methods in creating variegated BCI systems. Also, it explains the challenges faced in BCI frameworks, plus suitable solutions. Finally, it presents the future advancement. The technologies discussed in this article will help to promote the development of new BCI-based technologies and BCI technology has already demonstrated promising results in cognitive and physical support and rehabilitation, and we look forward to future advancement in this essential area of research that will eventually affect all of us. Now, most of the BCI approaches are in real time usage includes pre-clinical and clinical usages. The combination of both researchers and industry technicians need to earn the benefit to all communities through proper communication.

References

1. Ubber Das, B.H., Elektroencephalogram des menschen. *Archiv. Psychiatry*, 87, 527–570, 1929, Doi: 10.1007/BF01797193.
2. Zeng, F.G., Rebscher., S., Harrison., W., Sun., X., Feng., H., Cochlear implants: System design, integration and evaluation. *IEEE Rev. Biomed. Eng.*, 1, 115–142, 2008.
3. Tiwari., N., Elda., D.R., Dodia., S., Bablani., A., Brain computer interface: A comprehensive survey. *Biol. Inspired Cogn. Arch.*, 26, 118–126, 2018.
4. Bablani, A., Edla, D.R., Tripathi, D., Cheruku, R., Survey on brain computer interface, an emerging computational intelligence paradigm. *ACM Comput. Surv. (CSUR)*, 52, 20, 1–32, 2019, doi: 10.1145/32977/3.
5. Zhang, X., Yao, L., Wang, X., Monaghan, J.J., Mcalpine, D., Zhang, Y., A survey on deep learning based non-invasive brain signals: Recent advances and new frontiers. *J. Neural Eng.*, 18, 031002, 2021, doi: 10.1088/1741-2552/abc902.
6. Gu, X., Cao, Z., Jolfaei, A., Xu, P., Wu, D., Jung, T.P., Lin, C.T., EEG based brain computer interfaces (BCIS). A survey of recent studies on signal sensing technologies and computational intelligence approaches and their applications. *IEEE/ACM Tran. Comput. Biol. Bioinform.*, 18, 5, 1645–1666, 2021, doi: 10.1109/TCBB.2021.3052811.

7. Nijholt., A., The future of brain computer interfacing, proceedings of the 2016. *5th intl. conference on informatics, electronics and vision (ICIEV)*, pp. 156–161, 2016.

8. Bousseta., R., Ouakouak.I, E.I., Gharbi., M., Regrarui., F., EEG based brain computer interface for controlling a robot arm movement through thought. *IRBM*, 39, 129–135, 2018.

9. Peralas, F.J., Riera, L., Ramis, S., Guerrero, A., Evaluation of a VR system for pain management using binaural acoustic simulation. *Multimed. Tools Appl.*, 78, 32869–32890, 2019.

10. Ramasamy, M.D., Periasamy, K., Krishnasamy, L., Dhanaraj, R.K., Kadry, S., Nam, Y., Multi-disease classification model using strassen's half of Threshold (SHoT) training algorithm in healthcare sector. *IEEE Access*, 9, 112624–112636, 2021.

11. Irfan, S. and Dhanaraj, R.K., BeeRank: A heuristic ranking model to optimize the retrieval process. *Int. J. Swarm Intell. Res. (IJSIR)*, 12, 2, 39–56, 2021.

12. Prasanth, T., Gunasekaran, M., Kumar, D.R., Big data applications on healthcare. *2018 4th International Conference on Computing Communication and Automation (ICCCA)*, 2018, December.

13. Christensen., J.A., Koch., H., Frandsen., R., Kempfner., J., Arvastson., L., Christensen., S.R., Sorensen., H.B., Jennum., P., Classification of iRBD and Parkinson's disease patients based on eye movements during sleep, in: *Proceedings of the 2013 35th annual international conference of the IEEE engineering in medicine and biology society (EMNC)*, Osaka, Japan, pp. 441–44, 2013.

14. Birbaumer., N., Brain computer interface research: Coming of age. *Clin. Neurophysiol.*, 177, 479–483, 2006.

15. Chen, X., Wang, Y., Nakanishi, M., Gao, X., Jung, T.P., Gao, S., High speed spelling with non-invasive brain computer interface. *Proceedings of the national academy of sciences*, vol. 112, pp. E6058–E6067, 2015.

16. Hertzog, C., Park, D.C., Morrell, R.W., Martin, M., Ask and ye shall receive: Behavioural specificity in the accuracy of subjective memory complaints. *Appl. Cogn. Psychol.*, 14, 257–275, 2000. doi: 10.1002/(sici)1099-0720(200005/06)14:3<257::aid-acp651>3.0.co;2000.

17. Kumar, D.R., Krishna, T.A., Wahi, A., Health monitoring framework for in time recognition of pulmonary embolism using Internet of Things. *J. Comput. Theor. Nanosci.*, 15, 5, 1598–1602, 2018.

18. Kumar, R.N., Chandran, V., Valarmathi, R.S., Kumar, D.R., Bitstream compression for high speed embedded systems using separated split Look Up Tables (LUTs). *J. Computat. Theor. Nanosci.*, 15, 5, 1719–1727, 2018.

19. Nagel, S. and Spüler, M., World's fastest brain-computer interface: Combining EEG2Code with deep learning. *PloS One*, 14, e0221909, 2019, doi: 10.1371/journal.pone.0221909.

20. Kaufmann, T., Herweg, A., Kübler, A., Toward brain-computer interface based wheelchair control utilizing tactually-evoked event-related potentials. *J. Neuroengin. Rehabil.*, 11, 7, 1–17, 2014, doi: 10.1186/1743-0003-11-7.

21. Jafri, S.R.A., Hamid, T., Mahmood, R., Alam, M.A., Rafi, T., Haque, M.Z.U. *et al.*, Wireless brain computer interface for smart home and medical system. *Wirel. Pers. Commun.*, 106, 2163–2177, 2019, doi: 10.1007/s11277-018-5932-x.

Index

Printed and bound by CPI Group (UK) Ltd, Croydon, CR0 4YY

27/10/2024

14580173-0002